HISTORY OF ART CRITICISM

LIONELLO VENTURI

History of Art Criticism

Translated from the Italian
by CHARLES MARRIOTT

New, revised edition

A Dutton  Paperback

New York
E. P. DUTTON & CO., INC.

PREFACE

PREFACE

IF YOU wish to know how difficult it is to judge a work of art, please read three or four critics' judgments of one work of art: you will find three or four different standards of appraisal. Because there is only one true judgment, the others are merely partially true, and therefore false. How is one to understand which one is true and why it is true?

About twenty-five years ago, I started on a long journey in order to answer this very simple question, and because I was not satisfied with a purely theoretical solution, I tried to solve it through historical experience. By historical experience I mean re-living both the historical facts of art and aesthetic ideas at the same time, as if the historical facts and aesthetic ideas were one and the same thing.

In this book I have tried to expound as clearly as I could the historical experience of which I speak.

I am aware that some of my affirmations may be hard to understand, for they are founded on the idealistic thought, which, while it is familiar in Italy, is unusual in America. May I ask you not to renounce reading this book if the first chapter should prove quite difficult to interpret? Please read the chapters that follow, for you will find that the historical information

PREFACE

contained therein will justify the theoretical ideas to which the first chapter is the key, and perhaps you will be tempted to re-read it, in which event you may even admit that this book contributes to the understanding of art.

Here I wish to express my gratitude to Mrs. Stephanie Dabo, to the late unforgettable Professor Kingsley Porter, to Professor John Shapley and to Professor Philip McMahon, who assisted me in the publication of this book.

LIONELLO VENTURI

New York, March 20, 1936.

CONTENTS

ix

TABLE OF CONTENTS

THE MIDDLE AGES

THE RENAISSANCE

TABLE OF CONTENTS

TABLE OF CONTENTS

TABLE OF CONTENTS

CRITICISM OF CONTEMPORARY ART IN THE NINETEENTH CENTURY

TABLE OF CONTENTS

TABLE OF CONTENTS

HISTORY OF ART CRITICISM

HISTORY OF ART GREECE

INTRODUCTION

IN 1931, WHILE Professor of Art History at the University of Turin, Lionello Venturi refused to sign the oath of loyalty to the Fascist regime demanded by Mussolini; soon afterward he became the first of Italy's leading intellectuals to leave the country for political reasons. In 1940, he was appointed visiting professor at Johns Hopkins University; his lectures there were published as *Art Criticism Now*.[1] In that book, he repeated his belief, also expressed in the *History of Art Criticism*, that "Art criticism is our only means of understanding a work of art as art. And because the history of art aims at the understanding of a work of art as art, the final step in the history of art must be and is art criticism." He spent the year 1942 teaching at the University of Mexico and returned to the United States in 1943. For two years he was associated with Dr. Alvin Johnson's *École Libre des Hautes Études*, which had been organized expressly for the purpose of providing facilities for important European intellectuals who sought refuge in the United States. During this period he participated in the anti-Fascist activities of *Guistizia e Libertà* and the Mazzini Society. In 1945, he returned to Italy and until 1955 held the chair of Art History at the University of Rome. Professor Venturi delivered the Bampton Lectures at Columbia University in 1955; they were published as *Four Steps Toward Modern Art*.[2] He died in 1961 at the age of 76.

II

Professor Venturi was responsible for a fundamental change in the purpose and attitude of contemporary art criticism. He

[1] Lionello Venturi, *Art Criticism Now*, Baltimore, Johns Hopkins University Press, 1941.

[2] Lionello Venturi, *Four Steps Toward Modern Art*, New York, Columbia University Press, 1956.

3

insisted on the importance of exact interpretation of style and penetration to the form behind illustrative content. In other words, he emphasized a visual approach without regarding visual elements as ultimate aesthetic values. For him, they symbolized attitudes of mind and indicated historical changes in taste. He considered the history of criticism to be an essential part of the historiographic method; the *History of Art Criticism*, his best known work, is the most comprehensive of his numerous studies in the field. Since its first publication (in New York) in 1936, nearly all Western art critics have to a greater or lesser extent come under the influence of Venturi's ideas. There have been few other scholarly contributions of equal significance to the study of art criticism.

The *History of Art Criticism*—probably the first such work —remains the boldest, and is an essential foundation of this discipline. Venturi was a specialist in Italian Renaissance painting, and he was also deeply interested in the art of the nineteenth and early twentieth centuries; in 1906 he published one of the first serious studies of Cézanne. (The first, by Bernard, had appeared in *Les Hommes d'Aujour d'Hui*, in 1889.) His ideas on the theory of criticism developed early during his career at the University of Turin where he taught between 1915 and 1931. He modeled the teaching of art history in his department after his guiding principle: "The critical experience of present-day art is a necessary condition for the understanding of the history of art." In Venturi's view, the study of art is inextricably involved with the history of thinking about art. A work of art is not a spontaneous occurrence, but an object produced by a thinking, feeling, and responding individual who is part of a larger social environment. It is the total situation that is responsible for the meaning inherent in the art object. The method, style, or form of any given art work indicates the

4

ideas current in the time and place in which it was made. Without considering the original environment of the work, the observer cannot fully experience its meaning and purpose, and will very often entirely miss its point. During an interview with Dore Ashton for *The New York Times* in 1958, Venturi said: "When I look at a Raphael, I don't want to see Raphael with the eyes of Leo X. If I look at a Raphael with the eyes of his time I don't see what Raphael gave us of his personal way of feeling. When I like an artist of the past what I like is his way of creation."

He was among the first to recognize that positivism in art criticism had outlived its usefulness, and he abhorred the treatment of criticism as a natural science. Croce, too, had attacked positivism in aesthetics, and his notions of criticism originally seemed revolutionary and liberating to Venturi. On applying Croce's theory of aesthetics to art criticism, however, he discovered its limitations—in particular, that it gave no encouragement to formal or cultural interpretation of a work of art. He therefore attempted to correlate Croce's aesthetic ideas with those of such leading German art historians as Riegl and Wölfflin. He was largely responsible for making these writers known in critical circles in Italy and elsewhere. Nonetheless, he remained Croce's disciple to the extent that he laid great emphasis on the importance of intuition in art, without defining intuition with any great exactitude. Croce says, for instance:

> Now, the first point to be firmly fixed in mind is that intuitive knowledge has no need of a master, nor to lean upon any one; she does not need to borrow the eyes of others, for she has excellent eyes of her own.[3]

. . .

---

[3] Benedetto Croce, *Aesthetic*, New York, Noonday Press, 1953, p. 2.

The total effect of the work of art is an intuition; and notwithstanding all those intuitions, the total effect of the philosophical dissertation is a concept. The *Promessi Sposi* contains copious ethical observations and distinctions, but does not for that reason lose as a whole its character of a simple story or intuition. The difference between a scientific work and a work of art, that is, between an intellectual fact and an intuitive fact, lies in the difference of the total effect aimed at by their respective authors. This it is that determines and rules over the several parts of each, not these parts separated and considered abstractly in themselves.[4]

He goes on to emphasize that intuitive knowledge is free from any suggestion of intellectualism and indeed of any external additions of any kind. Similarly, Venturi, in explaining Wackenroder's theory of intuition, remarks:

They, the divine inspiration, the spontaneity of creation and its non-rational character, the intuition of the artist who does not know the secret he possesses, the abandonment of the artist to the inspiring motive, the absolute value, outside all hierarchies, of the artistic personality ... all these motives are certainly affirmed but not demonstrated, yet everybody feels that they are just and true, and therefore belong not to the abstract but to the concrete human reason. Nobody before the very young Wackenroder had felt them in their entirety nor had expressed them; his mode of feeling, his "love" has brought them all well within rational reach.[5]

III

Such are the ideas fundamental to the *History of Art Criticism*. Venturi makes it clear that he feels a work of art must

[4] *Ibid*, p. 3.

[5] Lionello Venturi, *History of Art Criticism*, p. 177.

be judged from the position of the artist, and therein lies the importance of the book. It should, however, be pointed out that despite its title, it is not a completely comprehensive critical survey of the subject. Some important material has been omitted, other material has been over-emphasized, and there are some unusual—and dubious—judgments made. (For example, there is no mention of Horatio Greenough, an omission that may surprise American readers. Greenough's reputation is, however, largely confined to this country, and as Venturi remarks in the first chapter, writers on art who are considered of the first importance in one country may be almost unknown in another: "All, or almost all the writers on art on the continent have read the books of Berenson, or Hill, but who has read the *Speculations* of Hulme?")

Venturi accepted the inevitability of personal bias in judging works of art. Each work of art has its own aesthetic approach, or, in Venturi's terminology, taste. To study every aspect of the artist's taste with equal thoroughness must lead to pedantry; yet to choose some aspects for emphasis rather than others is to lose objectivity. The only way out of this dilemma is to do as Venturi did, and explicitly recognize the personal, and to some extent subjective, nature of one's own artistic judgments. It was precisely this appreciation of the personal and social nature of judgment that enabled Venturi to approach the art criticism of the past with a fresh understanding. He insisted that his students familiarize themselves with the earliest critical statements by or about any artist with whom they were concerned. As Creighton Gilbert says:

> All historians read sources, but usually to determine dates and attributions, or at the best cultural history. Venturi's *History of Art Criticism*, abused because it is full of judgments of good and bad . . . is surrounded by the special

contributions of his [Venturi's] pupils. If Woelfflin goes a step beyond feeling to the analysis of past forms, Venturi goes a step further again to the analysis of past feelings about their own forms.[6]

Writers on art in various periods of history quoted in the book prove that much modern thinking about art is less strikingly new and original than is generally believed. (This, of course, is equally true of art itself.) For example, the following statement by the late Franz Kline is a characteristic description of the art process by a major modern artist:

> When I work directly, I work fast. I suppose I work fast most of the time, but what goes into a painting isn't just done while you're painting. There are certain canvases here in my studio—the little one over there—that I've worked on for a good six months—painting it over and over again. I think I've got it now.[7]

Yet Venturi quotes Wackenroder, who published his *Effusions from the Heart of a Friar Enamoured of Art* in 1797, as saying:

> If for a long time the artist cannot fix the imagination which a celestial ray of sun puts in his mind, there comes the moment in which without perceiving it he has achieved the work, and a clear splendour warns him of the miracle which has happened.[8]

The *History of Art Criticism* is not intended solely for the professional art historian and critic; it also offers the art public

[6] Creighton Gilbert, "Lionello Venturi," *Arts Magazine*, Vol. 36, No. 5, February 1962, p. 59.

[7] Katherine Kuh, *The Artist's Voice*, New York, Harper and Row, 1962, p. 145.

[8] Lionello Venturi, *History of Art Criticism*, p. 175.

a substantially supported approach to modern art and modern art thought. For, of course, the artist does not produce his work for the critics and historians alone; he also appreciates a wider audience. Stuart Davis once said, "I paint for myself, but I'm pleased to know that my own interests correspond to those of many other people." Or, as Venturi quotes Lucian and Kallistratos, writing many centuries ago:

> A work of art requires an intelligent spectator who must go beyond the pleasure of the eyes to express a judgment and argue the reason for what he sees.
>
> . . .
>
> A connoisseur is one of those men who with a delicate artistic sense, know how to discover in works of art the various qualities they contain and mix reasoning with such an appreciation.[9]

IV

The most detailed chapter of Venturi's book is that on the Renaissance; but perhaps of greatest interest to the contemporary reader is the one entitled "Introduction to the History of Art Criticism." There Venturi defines his concept of "taste" and the place and meaning of artistic judgment, and also introduces the factors of judgment. In that chapter, and throughout the work, the author combines narrative history with personal theories of judgment and of the elements that go into the formation of judgment. Indeed, his own theory of artistic judgment is based upon a "re-living" of judgments made in the past by other writers. This, too, is one of Venturi's major contributions to art thought.

[9] *Ibid*, pp. 50-51.

The changing and at the same time immutable character of art criticism is nowhere more sharply illustrated than in the chapter on "The Middle Ages." In the latter part of that period Dante was discussing Giotto and Cimabue, and in Tuscany, Boccaccio, Sacchetti, Cennino Cennini, and Filippo Villani were forming standards for artistic judgment, recording the names and, in a primitive fashion, cataloguing the works of the artists. Venturi notes that in medieval writings on art ". . . contemporary artists are compared with the artists of antiquity as a standard; and from the comparison arises a first sketch of history, not of artists only, but of art-historical epochs." [10] In 1962, Harold Rosenberg reminded us that "Consciousness of art history is the outstanding phenomenon in the painting and sculpture of our time . . ." [11] and that

> As tradition was an inescapable ingredient of the art of earlier centuries, proposing both what to paint and how to paint it, the consciousness of history in a modern painting or sculpture is as palpable as its form or motif; often, as in "over-all" abstractions, it is the only content. [12]

The "consciousness" that Rosenberg refers to will soon be felt by critics as it is now by painters, and criticism cannot fail to become more aware of its past than it is at present.

Venturi concludes his discussion of the Middle Ages with a survey of the writings of the remarkable fourteenth-century critic, Cennino Cennini. The alert reader is bound to note a certain similarity between Cennini's critical ideas and approach and that of several of the popular journalist-critics writing in

[10] *Ibid.*, p. 75.

[11] Harold Rosenberg, "The Art Galleries," *The New Yorker*, October 27, 1962, p. 152.

[12] *Ibid.*

the United States today. What is admirable in a medieval writer is not, however, necessarily so in one of the twentieth century. Venturi points out that the laws of painting and criticism laid down by Cennini defined "not art in general, but the art of which he speaks; the art of Giotto." Just as there are contemporary painters who paint from the notions and environment of some other period, so there are critics content to criticize the art of the present with the tools of the past. Venturi's work brings home the fact that, as the stages and problems of art criticism become more familiar, its practitioners will be forced to adopt a more honest and meaningful position than some of them do at present.

V

This edition of the *History of Art Criticism* includes material never before published in English. When a new Italian edition was issued in 1948, Venturi took the opportunity to make a number of revisions in the text and to supply some additional material. He extensively revised and reorganized Chapter XI, "Art Criticism and Pure Visibility," making it more readable in the process. He enlarged the book with an entirely new chapter on modern art and replaced the old final section, entitled "The Critical History of Art," with a new, briefer "Conclusion." In the present edition both "The Critical History of Art" and the "Conclusion" are retained, giving the reader an opportunity to compare the two.

In Chapter XII, "Modern Art," Venturi established licence for a new criticism for modern art. Of particular interest is his detailed discussion of Cubism and his analysis of Georges Lemaître's contribution to the Cubist perspective. Venturi applies Lemaître's division of Cubism into four branches (a division that was primarily intended to refer to literature) to the visual arts. In this chapter, too, Venturi surveys twentieth-century art criticism, outlining the views of such writers and artists as André Lhote, W. R. Valentiner, and Stephen C. Pepper—the reader's attention is especially directed to the account of Pepper's four hypotheses on the nature of art. Venturi also attempts to explain why the critical writings of Herbert Read seem so strangely inadequate to many students today.

The reader may be momentarily startled by the omission of some of the best known names in modern American art criticism, but will soon realize that most of the more significant writings of such figures as, for example, Suzanne Langer and Clement Greenberg appeared after the earlier editions of this book. The only modern American critics and aestheticians of any stature to be discussed are John Dewey and Alfred H. Barr, Jr. Less easily explicable is the omission of Clive Bell, J. P. Hodin, and Ortega y Gasset, but the sustained brilliance of the argument more than makes up for a few omissions.

The new chapter on modern art also contains a most valuable discussion of architectural aesthetics and criticism. It includes comments on such relatively unknown but important documents as Sant'Elia's *Manifesto of Futurist Architecture* as well as, more predictably, an evaluation of the work and ideas of Gropius, Le Corbusier, and Frank Lloyd Wright.

The section entitled "The Critical History of Art" which formed the conclusion of the earlier editions presents a summary review of the critical intuitions expounded in the preceding chapters. In the "Conclusion" that replaced it in the Italian edition of 1948, Venturi reiterates his belief in the experience of contemporary art and its importance in teaching us to see the art of the past. In these few pages Venturi's contribution to the critical study of the history of art is summed up, and its importance can be immediately appreciated. He has defined the respective roles of art historian and critic and has recognized, perhaps more clearly than any writer who preceded him, the hopelessness of attempting to find an art definition for all time. He has shown us that we can look at the art of the past only with the eyes of the present and define it only in the terms of our own time.

VI

Some of Venturi's profoundest remarks on the totality of art, the meaning of artistic experience, and the difficulties of the critic are to be found in the chapter entitled "Criticism of Contemporary Art in the 19th Century," which reveals his deep interest in and understanding of Impressionism and subsequent art movements in France. His appreciation of these movements is still relevant in the context of the art of our own day. For example, he remarks: "Through not being able to justify impressionism with regard to the universal idea of art, criticism was not even able to understand the new artistic tendencies in art at the end of the nineteenth century." [13] In the view of some modern critics, including Clement Greenberg, a similar situation faces those involved with the art of today:

> It may be that we cannot yet see far enough around the art of our own day; that the real and fundamental source of the dissatisfaction we may feel with abstract painting lies in the not uncommon problems offered by a new "language." [14]

[13] Lionello Venturi, *History of Art Criticism*, p. 270.

[14] Clement Greenberg, *Art and Culture*, Boston, Beacon Press, 1961, p. 136.

HISTORY OF ART CRITICISM

Art criticism, like art itself, is not necessarily the worse for being ephemeral, or for restating the problems that had pre-occupied one age in the vocabulary of another. There is a criticism appropriate for each period. As E. C. Goosen says of Stuart Davis:

> When Davis set out to be a "modern artist" and to find out how to "paint the pictures" he "wanted to paint," he was seeking an *order*, not necessarily absolute and for all time, but one that might serve him as he went along.[15]

All any artist, or any critic, can do is to find such an order. Rightly read, therefore, the *History of Art Criticism* is not, as some might think, a record of the fallibilities and inadequacies of human judgment; rather, it is a reminder that in art criticism, as in every other field, man can use only what his environment makes available. There can be no such thing as an absolute judgment, valid for all ages; no critic can afford to lose contact with the art situation of his time.

GREGORY BATTCOCK*

*New York City
1964*

---

[15] E. C. Goosen, *Stuart Davis*, New York, George Braziller, 1959, p. 30.

* Gregory Battcock is a New York painter, and lectures on art history at Hunter College and Queens College.

CHAPTER I
Introduction to the History
of Art Criticism

IF ONE considers the progress of art history during the last fifty years one cannot fail to be astonished and delighted, for the results have been prodigious. The number of monographs on artists and monuments, the general histories of art, or special histories for nations, epochs or single arts, the essays on iconography and technique, the publications of documents, the catalogues of museums and collections, the technical reviews for connoisseurs or cultural reviews for the public, and finally and above all the reproductions of works of art of all times and places — all these constitute a monumental mass of material for study. Some libraries of art history have assumed a special importance: for example, at Rome the Italian Institute of Archaeology and Art History and the library of the Hertz Foundation; at Florence the Germanic Institute; at Paris the Institute of Art and Archaeology, which includes the splendid Doucet Library; at London the Courtauld Institute, with the Witt Library and the Warburg Library; and finally the Fogg Art Museum of Cambridge, Massachusetts, which is the laboratory of art history of Harvard University, a laboratory in which are to be found not only the photographs and books necessary to research, but also authentic pictures of Blessed Angelico and Botticelli.

Anyone who has had opportunity of frequenting any of these great institutes knows that there have been reproduced all the principal works of art and even many secondary works of little or very little importance, relative to all the arts of all places and epochs, so that the knowledge of graphic documents, even if naturally incomplete, is accessible not only to specialists but also to the man in the street. As much, if not more, has been done to discover and publish historical data relative to works of art and artists, so that of this field also the greater and more important part has been conquered. The number of the documents, and the chaotic nature of their publication, make complete knowledge of them very difficult for the isolated scholar; and it happens that several scholars announce the same "find" because they are unaware of what each is doing. These are inevitable inconveniences and in themselves not too serious. A well-made index, kept up to date, of all that has been published in the art reviews, such as those which are being organized by the Frick Art Reference Library of New York and the Hertz Library at Rome, will certainly allow inconveniences to be remedied. Moreover, a proof that a certain unity has already been reached for what concerns the publication of graphic and documentary materials is furnished to us by the *catalogues raisonnés* of the works of a single artist. Almost everywhere in Europe, as in America, the author of a monograph composes the *catalogue raisonné* of an artist in the same way. It is already an important result which deserves to be emphasized.

It is evident, however, that the history of art, though it includes the *catalogue raisonné*, is not composed of it only. Museography has made such progress, and artistic publications have treated it to so great advantage, that these may be regarded as a species of universal museum. For the diffusion of the facts acquired, for the explanation of the documents which serve as a basis for researches, the hard labour of art historians has been necessary, and it is notable and praiseworthy. It can be understood that art historians, warned of the necessity to gather, enrich and perfect the material collected, have been absorbed in that basic task and have not thought of any other.

The fact is that if, after having admired the work of publication of artistic and documentary materials, we wish to inform ourselves of the directive ideas of the existing history of art, of the spiritual values which it represents, of the relations which it institutes with philosophy, history and literature, we are immediately aware that unity is lacking and anarchy reigns. In the various nations the history of art assumes different characters. An Englishman who occupies himself with Giorgione reads all the documents which have been discovered on this artist, all the arguments which induce him to favour the attribution of this or that work of art, even if they have been published in Italian, German or French. But if an Italian has expounded certain critical theories which may serve to formulate an appreciation of Giorgione and many other artists, one can be sure that the Englishman in question will never read them. It is understood that the reverse is true. All, or almost all, the writers on art on the Continent have read the books of Berenson or Hill, but who has read the "Speculations" of Hulme (1924)? Moreover, a similar phenomenon may be observed within separate countries. The way in which art history is taught in two universities might give the impression that they deal with two different disciplines. Whence comes, then, this total absence of unity, this methodological chaos, evident in art history, except for the work of museography? The answer is easy: the progress achieved in the publication of documents and their philological commentary, disappears when it is a case of expressing a *judgment* upon a work of art or an artist. What is worse is that there is often lacking the consciousness that this judgment is necessary. The true cause of the lack of progress is precisely this defect of consciousness, because the first condition to obtain an advance is to wish for it.

If you say to a professor of art history that his lessons are entirely without judgment he will be offended. But if you ask him what are the standards of his judgments, he will reply that he sticks to the facts, that art is felt or not felt; or he will improvise some scheme used as a standard of appreciation — for example, the perfection of classical art, respect for reality, decorative value, technical perfection, the predominance of form, and so forth. If you go on to compare the solidity of these ideas with the precision of the facts which he expounds, you will perceive that his culture, unquestioned in all that concerns the documentation of the facts, shows some ignorance of all that refers to the ideas.

It is well understood that such a condition does not exist without its reasons. It is necessary, in fact, to go back to the beginning of the nineteenth century to find a special flourishing of all the historical disciplines, promoted by the idealistic philosophy. Those who, on the base of the idealistic concept of development, dedicated themselves to discover and fathom the historical facts, ended, on one hand, by interesting themselves so exclusively in the authentication of the facts that they forgot on the way the ideas from which they started, with the view of interpreting them; and on the other hand they perceived that the philosophers of idealism had reported facts inexactly, and were induced to attribute that inexactness, not to the real defect of precision, but to the ideas themselves. Therefore the new historians were philological historians, and rejected and disparaged the philosophical historians. Thus, little by little, was lost the ideal nexus between the facts and the ideas, above all when, in the positivistic period, which is not completely over, they renounced thinking and reduced every scientific activity to classifications of the natural history type. The historical facts, placed in series, even if most exact, lost their significance to the human mind, except to erudite curiosity, because interpretation of their aesthetic value was neglected. History was reduced to chronicle; and since this way of making history, without judgments, for the history of art, appeared an absurdity even to the most elementary minds, judgment was improvised. Rather than meditate, discuss and perfect it through the knowledge of the development of judgments, the new historians drew it either from the academic tradition of art, which is the most inartistic of traditions, or from elements extraneous to art, like scientific truth, moral law, or the history of manners. Taine carried this deviation to extreme conclusions with the law of the ambient, considering the work of art as a product of the social conditions of peoples and epochs: his was a determinism in which art lost all autonomy and all freedom.

After having thus touched the lowest depth, aesthetics rose again at the beginning of our century, and in spite of the dissensions and contradictions surrounding it, a new sense of the autonomy of art pervades it and has done away with an endless series of prejudices and errors.

The moment has come, then, to complete a revision of the directive standards of the history of art and to reflect upon the relations between art history, art criticism and aesthetics. Recently an authoritative voice in France has insisted upon the differentiation of the three disciplines. The history of art should present works of art — all the works of art — without judging them, without commenting upon them, with the richest possible documentation of the facts. Art criticism should judge works of art in conformity with the aesthetic feeling of the critic. Aesthetics should formulate the definition of art in its universal meaning.

But it is evident that to distinguish thus the three disciplines succeeds in nothing but to empty them of all sense. In fact, as political history cannot be conceived without the control of a theory which serves to choose and interpret the facts which it needs to expound, and to neglect the infinity of facts of no importance, and so speaks of Bismarck and not of his porter; as the history of philosophy has need also of a theory of philosophy which serves as a standard to reject all the fantastic ideas which it has pleased humanity to invent; so art history has need of a theory which will allow it to distinguish whether a picture or a statue is a work of art — an artistic creation — or a rational, economical or moral fact. Similarly, if the critic is to obey only his own feeling it is preferable that he should hold his tongue; because, if he has renounced all theory, he cannot know whether his aesthetic feeling has more value than that of the man in the street. Finally, an aesthetics which ignored all the concrete artistic creations could be nothing but an intellectual game, not a science and not a philosophy. Besides, in order to grasp the absurdity of such distinctions, it is only necessary to recall the principle of Kant, according to which every concept without intuition is empty and every intuition without concept is blind.

Since the distinctions, pushed to extremes, arrive at the ridiculous, let us turn to unity. The gravest error which placed art history in the condition outlined above, was the distinction between art history and art criticism. If a fact referred to is not considered as a function of judgment, it is perfectly useless; if a judgment does not rest upon a knowledge of the historical facts, it is completely false.

The double exigency was thus analyzed in an exemplary manner by Benedetto Croce:

"Art criticism appears to be entangled in antinomies similar to those which Immanuel Kant had formulated. On one side the thesis: A work of art cannot be understood and judged except by taking it back to the elements from which it results; followed by the pretty demonstration: if this be not done, a work of art would become something taken away from the historical complex to which it belongs and would lose its true significance. To which thesis is counterposed, with equal energy, the antithesis: A work of art cannot be understood and judged except by itself; and here also follows the demonstration: that, if this cannot be done, the work of art would not be a work of art, since the scattered elements of it are also present in the minds of non-artists, and the artist is he only who finds the new form, that is to say, the new content, which is then the whole soul of the new work of art.

"The solution of the antinomy expounded above is: that a work of art has, certainly, value in itself; but this self is not something simple, abstract, an arithmetical unity; it is, rather, something complex, concrete, living, an organism, a whole composed of parts. To understand a work of art is to understand the whole in the parts and the parts in the whole. Now, if the whole is not known except through the parts (here is the truth of the first proposition), the parts are not really known except through the whole (and this is the truth of the second proposition). The antinomy is of the Kantian type; the solution is of Hegelian type.

"This solution establishes the importance of the historical interpretation for aesthetic criticism; or, better, it establishes that the true historical interpretation and the true aesthetic criticism coincide.

"However, the necessity of the historical interpretation by the aesthetic criticism reaffirmed, one puts the question: What are the historical facts of which the art critic must take account? The country in which the artist is born and formed, the geographical, climatic and racial conditions among which he lives? The political and social conditions of his historical moment? His private life? His physiological and pathological constitution? The relations which he had with the other artists? His religious and moral ideas? Which of these categories of facts? Or all together?

"The answer must not consist in saying, as is customary, that all these categories are indispensable; nor that some are indispensable and others not. The correct answer is, instead: that all the categories may be indispensable, and none of them is so of necessity.

"But as soon as from the generic thought of the totality one passes to the consideration of the single work of art (and the critic can only consider single works of art, and series and groups of them that figure as series and groups only after the single example has been considered), the elements of fact, which the critic must hold present, are only those that have entered effectively to constitute the work of art which he examines, and which are indispensable for the solution of the critical problem which he propounds to himself. What these may be, nobody can say, in general: the problem, determined case by case, is only resolved case by case."

The identity of art history and art criticism thus established, a perceptibly more delicate problem remains — that of the relations between critical history of art and aesthetics. It is necessary to discard, as we have said, the hypothesis of a judgment founded only on feeling. On the other hand, Kant defined that aesthetic judgment, though it pretends to universal validity, cannot be demonstrated as one demonstrates a logical judgment. This depends upon the fact that the idea of art is not concrete in aesthetic judgment, without the right intuition of the work of art to be judged. The judgment is therefore a relation between a universal idea and an individual intuition.

Now, we already know that this intuition is not simple, but

rather contains in itself all the constituent elements of the work of art, which are the historical elements. Croce has told us that the systematisation of those elements is not possible, that the use of them changes from case to case. There does not exist a philosophy of history; there exists only history. Both the intuitive knowledge of the artistic synthesis in a work of art and the knowledge of the historical elements inherent in the work of art and participating in the intuition of it, are historical knowledge.

Knowledge of the artistic intuitions is the history of art. But the knowledge of the historical elements participating in the intuition — what is that? Not art history, because in the examination of those elements one abstracts from intuition. Not the history of aesthetics, because among those elements are included practical, rational and moral factors, distinct from the aesthetic factors.

Let us analyse for a moment how these elements present themselves to the mind of the artist. He creates them by drawing inspiration from the universe. In nature he may turn for inspiration to this human figure, or to that tree, and he will pay attention now to this line or that colour, or more to this line and less to that colour, or the other way about, and he will choose from among the means of reproduction marble or bronze, or oil or tempera colour, according to preference, and he will choose a light now bright and diurnal, now contracted and nocturnal, and he will put into relationship his vision with his way of feeling religion (Christian or pagan), with his scientific knowledge (perspective, anatomy and so on), with the social class to which he belongs, with the aesthetic discussion which he will have had with friends or masters. All this is not science, or religion, or aesthetics, inserted in the work of art, but it is a way of feeling science or religion or aesthetics, it is an individual preference, which is not justified by reasoning, but certainly by the work of art. A preference in art is always a principle of art criticism. But it is criticism without a universal idea, judgment without a universal pretension; it is a tendency towards criticism, a desire for criticism, a judgment of the senses. It is not yet either art or criticism, it is a process and not a result; it is individual and may belong to a group of individuals. It is not criticism, it is *taste*.

In the critical tradition of the figurative arts the use of the word "taste" is frequent and ancient. As far back as 1681 Baldinucci adopted the word "taste" in a double sense: 1 — faculty which recognises the best; 2 — mode of working of each artist. In 1708 De Piles wrote: "Taste is an idea which follows the inclination of the painter, in which he is formed by education. Each school has its taste in design." In 1762 Anthony Raphael Mengs tried to overcome the double meaning of Baldinucci, to identify the faculty proper to each painter of choosing what *appears* the best to him with his mode of working. A genial idea, which takes the concept of absolute perfection out of reality, and allows to be admitted the existence of a relative perfection within the concrete work of art, relative, it is understood, to the preferences manifested by each author. "Taste is that which produces and determines in the painter a principal aim and makes him choose or reject what suits or is contrary to him; hence it is that, whenever one sees a work in which everything is expressed without distinction or variety, one says that the author is in fact without taste, since there is to be observed in it nothing in particular, and such work remains, so to speak, without significance. The work of every painter succeeds according to his choice; what he understands of colouring, chiaroscuro, drapery and any other thing relative to painting... It is well, however, to reflect that, painting being composed of many parts, there has not been a master who has had a taste equally good in everything; but often in one part he has known how to choose very well, in another very badly, and in some not at all."

In a form which seems too material in the distinctions, according to eighteenth century use, there appears in the prose of Mengs the clear knowledge of taste, as of that moment in the activity of the artist which is not art and not even criticism, which is not intuition and not even reason, but which is the preference between the elements of art in accordance with, not an aesthetic idea, but art itself.

It is obvious, then, that a critical history of art should benefit from aesthetics as well as from historical facts.

However, to assume a book of aesthetics to be the vessel of all information, to accept its principles blindly, profess them ostentatiously and impose them mechanically upon historical knowledge, would be the worst way to obtain aesthetic experience. To understand an aesthetic principle means to verify it by personal experience, and in some way to criticise it. On the other hand, it is necessary that the historical experience should be illuminated by the aesthetic principle assumed, and so transformed. There is, therefore, only one way to know an aesthetic principle: that of understanding in it the theoretical value by the light of the history of aesthetics.

On the other hand, as is evident, there is no other way of understanding art except that of compiling a critical history of it.

But the relation between aesthetics and art, between the idea of art and artistic intuition, is art criticism. If the art historian must know the history of aesthetics, with even more reason must he know the way in which aesthetic principles have been applied to works of art; he must know, that is to say, the history of art criticism. Now, however strange it may appear, there does not yet exist a history of art criticism.

There exist monographs, indeed there are many of them; but of works which embrace the field of art criticism in its entirety there is not even one, and of those that deal with large periods there are very few. And this without taking into consideration the fact that what different writers look for in this field varies considerably, and often conflicts.

For classical antiquity there exist two histories of aesthetics which deal superficially enough with the history of art criticism: that of Edward Müller (1834 and 1837), and that of Julius Walter (1893). More useful and better adapted to the aim that we propose here is the "Essay on Painting and the Criticism of Art in Antiquity," by Ed. Bertrand (1893).

Mr. Albert Dresdner had the intention of writing a complete history of criticism, but only the first volume (1915), which goes as far as Diderot, has come out. And what has been published seems to concede too much importance to the practical and social side of criticism, too little to judgments on works of art.

The work of Mr. Julius Schlosser, "The Literature of Art" (1924), has obtained a merited success. As a reasoned bibliography of writers on art history from the Middle Ages to the end of the eighteenth century, nothing better could be desired. In it are found noteworthy items of information and judgments on art criticism, but they are fragmentary, precisely because the author is more interested in historical data than in critical values.

Similarly, the two volumes by Mr. William Waetzoldt, "German Art Historians" (1921 and 1924), expound the development of art history in Germany from Sandrart to Karl

Justi, taking into account the critical values of the art historians, but excluding from the treatment almost all those critical values which have not assumed the explicit and complex form of histories of art.

In France the best work remains always that of Mr. André Fontaine – "The Doctrines of Art in France" (1909). It is an excellent picture of the artistic tendencies and critical reactions from Poussin up to but excluding Diderot, so that this book has an essential value for the comprehension of French criticism of the seventeenth and eighteenth centuries.

In Italy must be noted the excellent study by Miss Mary Pittaluga, "Eugene Fromentin and the Origins of Modern Criticism" (1917-1918), which is an outline of art criticism from the Renaissance to Romanticism. And the author of the present work has already attempted to write a history of art criticism from Plato to Ruskin, limiting it to a single problem, that of judgment of value on primitive artists ("The Taste of the Primitives," 1926).

Recently two important contributions have been brought by English writers, that of Mr. Kenneth Clark on "The Gothic Revival" (1928) and that of Mr. C. Hussey on "The Picturesque" (1927). Even Chinese criticism has already found its illustrator, *O. Sirén,* "The Chinese on the Art of Painting," Peiping, 1936.

It is necessary, then, to profit by the monographic work of others in tracing in a general line the development of art criticism, and to indicate the principal results.

In the following chapters we shall expound some of the principal judgments brought to bear upon the figurative arts through the centuries, and we shall comment upon them according to the aesthetic ideas and artistic creations which have conditioned them: art criticism among the ancient Greeks and

Romans, that of the mediaeval men, and above all, of the Italians at the end of the Middle Ages; that of the Italian Renaissance; and that of the baroque period in which Italians and French hold the field. Arrived thus at the eighteenth century, we shall be present at the origin of neo-classical criticism, a work accomplished chiefly in Rome by two German writers; and of romantic criticism, in which Germans and English predominate. We shall see how at the beginning of the nineteenth century German idealistic philosophy tried to create a criticism which should synthetise neo-classicism and romanticism. Through the nineteenth century and the beginning of the twentieth, we shall follow the contributions, sporadic and fragmentary, but not on that account less important, which philologists, archaeologists and connoisseurs, above all the German and Italian ones, have brought to criticism. We shall be present at the exceptional critical blossoming which took place in France towards the middle of the nineteenth century, with regard to modern painting. Finally we shall study how some German critics of the second half of the nineteenth century, have tried to give themselves a rule of judgment outside idealistic or positivistic aesthetics, creating the theory of pure visibility. After that we shall seek to draw from our rapid survey a corollary, to realise the verity, or the partial verity, of the judgments of all epochs, controlling them by their own historical development, not without suggesting to the reader the ambition to derive from the historical experience of criticism a solid foundation for the comprehension of art.

In order to treat the subject homogeneously it is necessary to define its object with exactness. The object of our treatment is art criticism. But we know how complex this is, because we have had to identify the history of art with art criticism. Now in this complex subject the elements are numerous, and they cannot all be put on the same plane without risk of making the treatment fragmentary and scattered. The *catalogue raisonné* of the works of an artist, and the philological criticism of an historico-artistic source, are important and sometimes essential contributions to the critical history of art, but they are not identical with it. The theory of art as sensible appearance of the idea, which is Hegel's, and the theory of pure visibility, which is Fiedler's, are not themselves art criticism. On the other hand, the painting of Giotto was, above everything, a work of art, but it was also a critical event, an act of taste, in as much as not only many artists have profited by his taste in creating their works of art, but some writers also have judged art according to the models of Giotto.

Neither a philological work nor an aesthetic theory nor an act of taste fully realises art criticism. In order that it should be realised, it is necessary that it be centralised in judgment. Let us think, for example, of the judgment of Baudelaire on Delacroix: there is the principle of the spirituality of art; there is the historical determination of the taste of Delacroix, distinct as romantic taste not only from neo-classicism, but also within romantic taste defined in its new sense of form; there is the intuition of the individuality of the painter and of his creativity. And all this is realised in a judgment, in the appreciation of the greatness of Delacroix. The centre of Baudelaire's activity is precisely there, in *judgment*; and he is a critic in the full sense because he centres himself in judgment.

Judgment of the artist or of the work of art must be the centre of our treatment.

If then we examine the principal factors of judgment we perceive them to be:

1 — the pragmatic factor, which is given by the work of art on which the judgment is brought to bear;

2 — the ideal factor, which is given by the aesthetic ideas of the critic and in general by his philosophical ideas and moral needs — in short, by the civilisation to which he adheres and which he helps to form;

3 — the psychological factor, which depends upon the personality of the critic.

The psychological factor is more important for a monograph on a critic than for a general history of art criticism. In so far as some critical personalities are important, and have influenced the general course of criticism even with their desires and passions, these contribute to the essential aim of criticism but never identify themselves with it. In fact, as we are accustomed to say popularly, criticism is worth more than critics.

The ideal factor is essential to the historical importance of judgment. Without the theory of art as a spiritual activity, without the refusal of the idea of art as imitation of nature, Baudelaire would never have been able to understand that the drawing of Delacroix, instead of being incorrect as compared with that of Ingres, has its own perfection. Nevertheless the history of criticism is not the history of the genetic process of critical ideas. The perfectioning of critical ideas, that is to say criticism of preceding ideas, is an essential condition. But it is necessary to bear in mind that critics create their ideas not only by criticising preceding ideas, but above all by the intuitive experience of works of art — that is, by its pragmatic factor. Without this continual return to the origin, to the intuitive impulse, to contact with the work of art, contact of man to man, of mind to mind, outside the limits imposed by the critical tradition, the creation of a new criticism would not be possible. In other words, progress does not come like a turning of a wheel, according to a regular order; it takes place by leaps and bounds, and the springboard for the critic is the inspiring work of art.

It is necessary, however, to avoid the dualism which would exist if the origin of artistic judgment were indicated as, on the one hand, in aesthetic ideas and, on the other, in works of art. They are abstractions, these, and useful for direction; but in reality aesthetic ideas and works of art are fused in one impulse of judgment, in a tendency, in a mode of feeling that we know already under the name of taste. Judgment on art obeys the same antinomy that art obeys: it is analysable into the elements of the critic's taste, and those elements are illuminated precisely in the synthesis of the judgment.

The essential condition of the artistic judgment is to have a universal idea of art, and at the same time to recognize it in the personality of the artist to be judged. In other words, the artistic judgment must consider the personality of the artist as an expression of universal art. No concrete personality has to be sacrificed to any abstract idea of art. On the other hand, everyone wants a universal principle of judgment; otherwise any personal preference whatever would be justified in the presence of history, without any discrimination of true or false judgment, or even of good or bad taste. In that case, the history of art itself would be no longer history, but mere historicism, pure erudition.

The solution of this new antinomy is to be sought in the coïncidence between artistic personality and artistic perfection. It is generally considered that the contingent and ephemeral character of a work of art consists in its belonging to an individuality, and that its eternal value depends upon "rules of art." But art history and the history of criticism convince us of the contrary: that it is precisely the "rules of art" which have a contingent and ephemeral character, which are valid only for a period or a school, and never for all times and all places. They are elements of taste which, under the dazzling light of the artistic personality adopting them, create the illusion of being rules. It is necessary, therefore, to reverse the relation between personality and rules. It is the personality of the artist which impresses eternal character upon the elements of taste, the so-called "rules of art." That a personality is truly artistic only the intuition of its works can make manifest to us. We know how complex is that intuition, full of experiences of every dominion of the mind. But if the intuition of art is there, the judgment of the work of art is not to be limited by any law extraneous to the personality.

Personality is a law to itself. Some applications of this principle are accepted by all. For example, if I think that Delacroix is an artist, I must not seek the merits and defects of his paintings. There are neither merits nor defects in the painting of Delacroix, there is only the style of Delacroix. Therefore Baudelaire could say that Delacroix did not draw less well than Ingres, but drew in a different manner. To believe that Delacroix drew less well than Ingres signifies abstracting the drawing from the work of art in which it is realised, and so emptying it of all artistic value. On the other hand, it has been noted that the abstract perfection of the drawing of Ingres is more evident in his allegorical figures than in his portraits, because in the portraits even Ingres was constrained to deform his abstractly perfect drawing, and he was constrained there precisely by his artistic impulse, in the best moments of his creativity. What, then, is that abstract drawing which is lacking in Delacroix and found in Ingres in his worst moments? It is academic drawing; that is to say, a scheme of drawing, which Ingres considered useful for pedagogy but which remained outside his art. To-day all this is commonly known, and it is therefore not necessary to insist upon it here.

But if to-day lack of academic drawing is no longer considered as a defect, other schemes, equally abstract, have an undue influence on artistic judgment — for example, the proportions. We know how much has been said from Polycleitos onward about the proportions of the human body. The fact is that for lack of accord, only some proportions of the human body were chosen as models. The same is true in architecture: an Egyptian temple has different proportions from a Greek, but even in Greek temples Doric proportion is different from the Corinthian. Who, then, can say which one of those proportions is perfection? The truth is that if art is the expression of the personality of the artist, then proportions — any proportions — participate in art only so far as the artist desires. If an artist adores the proportion called the "golden section," he can very well make a work of art in which this proportion occurs. But what will be artistic in that work will be the expression of that desire, the idolising of the golden section and not the golden section itself. However, if a painting presents a human figure with extraneous or unusual proportions, with reference to our common experience, it is difficult of appreciation even by connoisseurs of art; indeed they are led easily to decide that any difference from normal human proportions is an artistic error. Elongation of the proportions by artists like Greco or Modigliani is accepted neither by the public nor even by many good critics. In this connection one might ask here why criticism does not control with equal severity the proportions of trees as it controls those of men; and this question suggests that the root of the traditional severity of judgment on human proportions is a certain pride in the human form as compared with the other forms of nature, a pride that carries with it an unwillingness to have our infinite and absolute beauty touched. However it may be, if we believe that art is the expression of the feeling of the artist, the human proportions have positive value in art only if the artist who uses them has the faith and pride of human beauty. Greco and Modigliani had another faith; they were not so optimistic about human nature and its wonders: the first through the mystical vision of the divine, the second through tenderness towards the fallen angels. Why, then, should their mode of feeling avoid an adequate and coherent expression? Possibly in homage to the theory of proportions? It is enough to put the problem in such a way to understand that if the love of proportions can lead to art, the theory of proportions is and has been an obstacle to the judgment of art.

It is understood that abnormality of proportions may be either an expressive necessity, or a technical ignorance. But when a painter who has given proof of perfect technical knowledge, having become master of his style, renounces proportions and realises proportions not normal according to tradition, then he is entitled to claim that, rather than deride him, one should seek to understand the intimate reason of his disproportions.

The problem is still more delicate when, instead of the particular case of proportions, one has to deal with the general problem of the imitation of nature. The immense popularity that the definition of art as the imitation of nature has had through the centuries explains the delicacy of the problem. To-day we know that a painter who reproduces a tree is an artist, not in so far as he reproduces that tree, but in so far as he expresses his own way of feeling that tree, large or little, flowering or dying, strong or graceful, and so on. However, even in the best talents of idealism, though they have well understood the creative character of art, there is a residue of naturalism. Hegel, for example, wrote that painting is more incomplete than poetry, because to express feeling and passion, it has at its disposal only the face and the attitudes of the body. Now, anybody who has experience of the art of painting knows that the face and the attitudes of the body give an incidental contribution to artistic expression. The painter expresses himself through forms and colours, not through bits of nature imitated as the face can be. The work of some of the greatest artists indeed, has constituted precisely a contrast between the image of the face and the artistic expression. The case of Leonardo is typical. In his paintings the faces are smiling; and for a long time writers believed in the happy soul of Leonardo. Up to Stendhal nobody was aware that Leonardo expressed a melancholy mind in his paintings: he expressed his melancholy precisely in his shading, with a continuous gradation in half tone, and the smile on his faces is nothing but an accent on his melancholy.

It is necessary, then, not to think of nature, not to relate to nature the work of art if it is to be understood. However, the abstract painting and sculpture which have been raging for about thirty years do not result in a work of art which convinces and exalts us. The reason is that such painting and sculpture are intellectual games, coldly composed. When Hegel thought of the face and the attitudes of the body become painting, he thought, in effect, of the eyes turned to the heavens by Guido Reni, "painter of the soul," an expressionistic rhetorical picture of Jesuitical origin. This also was an abstraction, a scheme to make feeling as hateful, as false and immoral; coldly composed like a cubistic construction. The intellectualistic or moralistic scheme has displaced a mode of feeling in the craftsman; and the work of art is not born.

But when Leonardo expresses his mode of feeling through gradations of half tone, he does not adopt abstract schemes; he feels. His feeling is nature, true nature in art. He has no need to have recourse to schemes of external nature. His work is artistic because it is according to nature, not because it is imitation of nature.

Innumerable similar problems are faced in a work of art, and they can all be resolved when one bears in mind the character of the work of art — intuitive and not logical, concrete and not abstract, individual and not universal.

Thus is clarified the character, both absolute and relative, of artistic judgment. Its absolute aspect depends upon the eternal value of art, and its relative aspect depends upon the fact that that eternal value is not found except in the single personalities of artists. Between the universal and the individual there is nothing that has the value of a rule of judgment. Not drawing nor colour, not the classic nor the romantic, not the true nor the false, not the good nor the bad. Every truly artistic personality comprehends in itself all the schemes, and creates them in a special way, which constitutes, precisely, the personality. To comprehend if that personality be truly artistic or not, there is only one way: to have intuition of art, to feel its spiritual value, and reflect upon the character of art distinct from that of other human activities, rational or religious, moral or utilitarian.

It has been necessary to let this explanation of the nature of the artistic judgment precede the historical exposition of many judgments expounded through the centuries, in order that the reader may understand why and when I shall agree or disagree with these judgments.

CHAPTER II
The Greeks and Romans

THE criticism of sculpture and painting, which arose in Greece about the third century before Christ, reached us incidentally through Pliny the elder in his "Natural History." The critical judgments on Greek artists to which he refers, are taken — it is true, indirectly — from the treatises on painting and sculpture of Xenocrates of Sikyon (a sculptor of the school of Lysippos) and of Antigonos of Karystos, both of whom lived in the first half of the third century B.C. It is difficult to know to which of them to attribute the judgments referred to, and therefore scholars have the habit of grouping them under the name of Xenocrates, who seems to be the more important of the two. So we say Xenocrates wrote a treatise dedicated to painters and sculptors in order to give advice and principles. But it was not a purely abstract treatise, as, for instance, the Canon of Polycleitos, who occupied himself solely with the proportion of the human figure; Xenocrates tried to fix a relationship between his own artistic principles, as categories of artistic judgment, and some concrete artistic personalities. What is criticism if not a relationship between a principle of judgment and the intuition of a work of art or of an artistic personality? Xenocrates therefore, as far as we know, reached for the first time a high intellectual standard of art criticism. Two factors, the pragmatic and the cultural, enabled Xenocrates to reach such a standard:

1 —The artistic grandeur of Greece, during two centuries, the fifth and fourth centuries B.C., gave the impression to contemporaries and to posterity of an exceptional civilisation and of a continuity of ideals, so as to make of sculpture and painting two complete disciplines, with fixed doctrines. It was natural

that an artist who lived a little after that miraculous epoch should establish a record of the steps by which the completion of the discipline, considered as the perfection of art, was reached, and that he should identify those steps with the contribution made to the discipline by each artistic personality. Both the theoretical purpose and the historical experience helped Xenocrates to refer his artistic views to concrete artists.

2 — The cultural factor was equally important. Of course, the first mythical artist, after having made the first work of art, judging it, passed the first artistic criticism. But that judgment assumed a particular value of thought only when the thought on art, as the historical experience of art, reached a certain maturity. Now, Xenocrates had before him as an example of artistic thought none less than Plato and Aristotle, and he found in the latter and in the first Peripatetics a great deal of historical interest on art. In Aristotle's book on Poetry there were many effective references to the history of poetry, to its origins and to the contributions to it by the different poets. The Peripatetics liked to make use of genealogical tables in order to show the development of the artistic schools, similar to those they made for the philosophical schools, and they liked to recount anecdotes and sayings of the artists. Duris of Samos, a pupil of Theophrastos, who lived in the second half of the fourth century, recounted the lives of the artists without discussing their works, but even he expressed sometimes an artistic judgment: for example, when he explained the idealistic character of the art of Zeuxis by the legend about his choice of the best parts of several women's bodies, because he believed that human bodies are never perfect; and so criticism by Duris arises from the lives of the artists when the anecdotes relate to an idea; just as criticism by Xenocrates arises from the art treatise when an artistic law is applied to an artist or to a work of art. This

was the double origin of art criticism, as it began at the end of the fourth and the beginning of the third centuries B.C.; and so it continued, with rare exceptions, until the eighteenth century, when people wrote the history of art instead of the lives of the artists, and began to create reviews of art exhibitions.

The limits of the criticism of Xenocrates lay in his being bounded by the experience of Greek art in the fifth and fourth centuries B.C. (though that offered a wide enough field), and by the degree of development reached by Greek aesthetical and historical thought.

Regarding the historical thought, it is necessary to observe that the ancient Greeks did not try to represent the development of human values, either in art or in science, but they tried to determine the facts that occurred, to explain them by their immediate and mundane causes, and to use them as standards. In the same way, those who wrote on art occupied themselves, beyond the determination of the facts that occurred (that is to say, of the artistic personalities and their works), only to draw from those facts the way to perfect artistic discipline. The sketch of the history of Greek philosophy with which Aristotle preceded his "Metaphysics" ought to be the model for the artistic accounts of the art treatises; and the recognition paid by Aristotle to Socrates for having found the definition and the idea of the universal, corresponds to the recognition paid by the art treatises to Lysippos and to Apelles for having attained the perfection of sculpture and painting.

Regarding the aesthetic thought, it is necessary to remember that Plato and Aristotle vacillated between the theory of beauty and the theory of art, without letting the two theories coincide. Nor is there reason to be unduly astonished when we think that even to-day the consideration of beauty as the perfection of art is quite rare. The fact is that for the Greeks, art was *mimesis*,

which is imitation or representation of nature; and that for
them beauty had a moral character identified with the good,
or a mathematical character identified with geometrical proportions. The relationship between the two problems of art and
beauty which was not determined by philosophy, was suggested by compromises. They said that it was necessary to
imitate nature, but that it was necessary also to idealise nature,
following the concept of physical and moral beauty; that is
to say, following mathematical proportions and nobility of
sentiment. All this was not very rigorous, but it had the advantage of allowing people to look at works of art from different
points of view: that of the technical ability for imitation, that
of the abstract form, and that of the moral contents.

The concept of imitation suggested to Xenocrates to omit
all sculptors previous to Polycleitos, to praise him for having
made "his statues rest their weight on one leg," and to blame
him for having represented too monotonous figures. He believed that Myron had surpassed Polycleitos in variety, but that
he was not yet able to represent the hair of the head. Pythagoras
improved the hair, and knew how to portray the sinews and
veins. Lysippos, finally, could represent hair perfectly, and his
execution of even the smallest details is accurate and delicate.
And so the standards of judgment professed by Xenocrates in
order to obey the mimetic necessity of art, are: the natural balance of a statue, the variety of bodies, the difficulty of representing in marble or in bronze the softness of the hair, and delicacy in the execution of details. On the other hand Xenocrates
observed that Polycleitos used too heavy proportions, that Myron improved them, and that Pythagoras was the first to find a
relation between symmetry and rhythm that is, to find right
proportions even in a figure in action; and that finally Lysippos

modified the canon of proportions, making the human figure more slender and elegant, so as to represent man not as he is but as he appears. Observe that from this last judgment arises the consciousness of a way of art parallel to that of nature, but not identical with it. It is no longer a question of abstract geometrical form, but of an artistic effect. In fact, the change from heavy to slender proportions corresponds with a change of opinion on beauty which has *nothing* to do with art; truly we know that an artist, in order to express his feelings, may want heavy proportions and realise through them the perfection of his art. But the idea of representing man not as he is, but as he appears, has *much* to do with art, because it is a kind of deliverance from imitation of nature, in a naturalistic sense, and an effort to reach an artistic level in sculpture. This effort was made perhaps under the influence of the scepticism of Pyrrho, and its value goes beyond the particular historical judgment on Lysippos.

On painting, the judgments by Xenocrates were more numerous and important from a critical point of view, than were those on sculpture. The criticism of primitive artists continued to be limited, or almost so, to the conquest of the ability in imitation. The development of painting is conceived as parallel to the teaching in the schools contemporary to Xenocrates: first the drawing, then the use of only one colour, then chiaroscuro, then various colours with their reflections, and finally tone as unity and harmonisation of colouring. To Kimon of Kleonai was attributed the merit of having invented foreshortening, of having known anatomy and having treated drapery under the rule of chiaroscuro. Polygnotos represented clothes on female bodies as transparent, with their ornaments multicoloured; the mouth open, showing the teeth, and the faces of various types. The scientific basis of painting was the work of Pamphilos:

"the first painter who was thoroughly trained in every branch of learning, more particularly in arithmetic and geometry; without which, so he held, art could not be perfect."

Speaking of more modern painters, Xenocrates gave less importance to the problem of imitation, and occupied himself with the problems of form, not only in the abstract sense. He said that, if Zeuxis painted heads and limbs too big, Parrhasios gave them their right proportion, and that no one surpassed him in contours, even if "he failed in modelling." At this point the definition of the contour by Parrhasios was so sensitive and delicate that it became no longer of abstract form, but of real art. "The contour seems to withdraw, and so enclose the object as to give assurance of the parts behind, thus clearly suggesting even what it conceals." Because of his vanishing contour Parrhasios was led to the effects of full relief, in which Nikias distinguished himself: "he was painstaking in his treatment of light and shade, and took special care that his figures should be relieved against the background." The relief of Nikias showed high lights on a dark background, and his was the principle of plastic form; but critics saw that Pausias followed a different principle.

"The most striking instance is that, wishing to display an ox's length of body, he painted a front and not a side view of the animal, and yet contrived to show its size. Again, while all others put in the high lights in white and painted the less salient parts in dark colour, he painted the whole ox black, and gave substance to the shadow out of the shadow itself, showing great art in giving all his figures full relief upon the flat surface, and in indicating their form when foreshortened."

But it is not clear whether Xenocrates had an absolutely sure consciousness that the chromatic character of Pausias' style was opposed to the traditional type of plastic form. In fact, allusion to chromatic values were rare in Xenocrates: sometimes he complained that certain colouring was too hard, and praised Apelles for having given, after finishing his pictures, a black "glazing to prevent the brilliance of colours from offending the eyes." But this appears to us to be nothing more than a trick and an evidence of academic taste. Apelles, and in a lesser degree his contemporaries, represented for Xenocrates the perfection of art; and he tried to indicate the perfection of each one: "Melanthios was perfect in his distribution of figures, Asclepiodoros in perspective arrangement – that is, in giving the accurate distance between different objects. Apelles excelled all painters who came before or after him. He admired the works of his contemporaries, praising every beauty and yet observing that they failed in the grace, called *Xáris* in Greek, which was distinctively his own; everything else they had attained, but in this alone none equalled him. He laid claim to another merit," with respect to Protogenes, "namely, in knowing when to take his hand from a picture; a memorable saying, showing that too much care may often be harmful." In conclusion, grace and natural facility of creation were the unsurpassable qualities of Apelles and these were also the extreme achievements of the Xenocrates criticism. They were free from abstract form and from imitation; they were capable of reaching the focus of aesthetic values; they revealed the art of a painter, whom we, alas! do not know but whom we believe we are meeting when we look at a masterpiece by Raphael. And so the criticism of Xenocrates on painting was so far superior to that on sculpture, that we doubt whether he would have been able to reach such a level without the influence of Apelles' treatise on his own art.

The moral contents, as a principle of artistic judgment, were considered by Aristotle. To explain the phenomenon in poetry he alluded to painters: Polygnotos represented human beings superior to us, Pauson inferior, and Dionysios similar. Socrates had already said: "It belongs to the sculptor to represent the working of the soul in a visible form," and Aristotle noted the necessity of the moral expression in painting: Polygnotos is a clever painter of character, but this does not interest Zeuxis. Young people must not contemplate the pictures by Pauson, but those by Polygnotos and of other painters and sculptors who portray moral expression. We know of only two references by Xenocrates to this problem: "Euphranor first gave to heroes their full dignity," and "Aristeides of Thebes was the first among all painters to paint the soul and gave expression to the affections of man and also the emotions." Polygnotos, whose moral value was emphasised by Aristotle, is on the contrary considered by Xenocrates only as one of the contributors to the imitating ability. That is because the perfection of Apelles, veils his understanding, as the perfection of Lysippos prevents him from seeing the grandeur of Phidias. The consideration of moral expression in art could correct the conception of a perfect physical imitation and of an absolutely abstract form, attributed to the technically more evolved art, as a symbol of the perfection of art; because one could not reduce to a uniform type of perfection the moral expression, on account of it depending upon the different temperaments of artists. But a moral judgment of art is right when it conceives the process of artistic creation and not the subjects represented. For example, a painter may show his moral finesse when he represents a still life, and another may reveal his base nature when he represents a hero. But the Greeks did not understand this; they looked at the motive, and became proud of their choice of subjects, and therefore even the moral aspect of art did not free their criticism either from the abstract consideration of nature, which was to be imitated, or from the science of imitation. The happy intuitions of Xenocrates on the appearance of reality in the art of Lysippos and on the grace and natural facility of Apelles, remained isolated and limited to his conviction of the technical perfection of Lysippos and Apelles; and did not extend to other artists, such as Polygnotos, whose grandeur had already been understood by Aristotle. Art criticism was not able to recognise the absolute perfection of a primitive artist, in the way that Aristotle understood Homer as the poet par excellence; that is, art criticism was lacking in determining, not the general perfection of art, but the particular perfection of each artist.

The exclusive admiration for Lysippos and Apelles, began to disappear at Pergamos, where arose the custom of formulating the canons of great artists, in imitation of the canons of ten orators chronologically arranged with a fixed scale of appreciation. This tradition influenced Cicero, Dionysios of Halicarnassos and Quintilian. The universal idea of art and the different artistic styles were considered by Cicero in opposition. "There is only one art of sculpture: Myron, Polycleitos, Lysippos excelled in it; but they are different one from another and, in spite of that, you could not wish them to be different from what they are. The same is true of painting: Zeuxis, Aglaophon and Apelles resemble each other very little, but it seems that nothing is lacking in the perfection of each one." Such an observation would be an improvement on the criticism of Xenocrates, as it would renounce the prejudice of artistic progress. In fact, if every artistic personality should reach its own perfection, there would not exist beyond any one personality an abstract artistic perfection, towards which one could aspire, which one could attain, and from which one could decline. Technique may progress, but not art.

But it must be noted that Cicero, who had a great deal of finesse and sensibility, lacked coherence of thought. Therefore he wondered why people preferred old to modern masters, who showed so many improvements. And so the canons of painters and sculptors which were transmitted by Cicero and Quintilian were wanting in true critical interest, because of their lack of concentration and competence. They collected contradictory opinions without a dialectic investigation. As an example we may cite the following judgment of Quintilian: "It is said that Lysippos and Praxiteles were the best reproducers of reality, because Demetrios abandoned himself too much to reality and preferred resemblance to beauty." So the value of Lysippos and Praxiteles did not consist in the reproduction of reality, but in an ideal creation, such as was lacking in Demetrius. This shows that Quintilian was unable to base his judgment on one principle only: he allowed himself to be carried away by opinions, by fragmentary observations, which, although right in themselves, had no reciprocal relation. He looked at critical problems from the outside; he noted them without penetrating further, thus falling below the criticism of Xenocrates. And so Cicero's and Quintilian's judgments are interesting to us more as testimonies of the opinions of their contemporary connoisseurs, than of their own.

In the first centuries of the Christian era sprang up the fashion of art collecting, connected with the new Roman luxury, and a reaction from the contemporary art, which was felt to be decaying from the standard of the great Greek art of the fifth and fourth centuries. On account of this many connoisseurs arose, whose task was thus defined by Lucian and Kallistratos: "A work of art requires an intelligent spectator who must go beyond the pleasure of the eyes to express a judgment and to argue the reasons for what he sees." "A connoisseur is one of those men who, with a delicate artistic sense, know how to discover in works of art the various qualities they contain, and mix reasoning with such an appreciation." Such connoisseurs did not allow themselves to be guided in their appreciation only by the perfection of execution, and began to appreciate even the faculty of invention. A statement by Pliny is important in this case: "Timanthes is the only artist whose works always suggest more than what is painted, and great as is his dexterity, his faculty of invention exceeds it." The effect of this new orientation of mind was the discovery of the absolute value of the artists prior to the fourth century, and the liberation from the illusion of the absolute perfection of Lysippos and Apelles. Quintilian noted such preferences without understanding them, and therefore he became malicious: he believed that it was due to the mania to prove themselves connoisseurs. But in any case nobody in the time of Quintilian dared resist the critical truth of the absolute and eternal value of Phidias. The opinion was that Phidias represented gods better than men, that he had a sumptuosity and a grandeur unknown to others; for example, to Polycleitos, who idealised human form, but did not reach such a high level of divine majesty. Through these and similar indications which were always referred to the motive and not to the kind of representation, we feel that the connoisseurs were aware that Phidias reached his own perfection by his own sense of the divine; and this is another purely critical result, which surpassed every limit of the imitation of reality, of mathematical form, and of moral contents. The poetical form of this intuition is found in the Anthology: "Either Jupiter descended on earth to show you his features, oh Phidias! or else you ascended into heaven to see the God himself." In order to explain the same statue of Jupiter, Cicero's critical point of view was the traditional idea of a type of beauty which inspired the sculptor and Dio Chrysostom, wrote: "No sculptor or painter could reproduce wisdom and intelligence in themselves, because they never could embody in form pure wisdom and pure intelligence, and because such forms would be outside human experience, and would be unreal. Therefore people had recourse to a body where we may recognise the presence of a spiritual value. Because of the lack of a model, God is represented in a human form likened to a vase of wisdom and reason; by a visible and sensible material we try through a symbol to express an invisible and unattainable being. This symbol is higher than that through which some barbaric people identify the divine nature with the form of animals, in accordance with absurd and debased cults." In this passage is dimly seen the principle of art, as a sensible form of idea, which is the basis of the Hegelian aesthetic, and the distinction is affirmed between the intuitive symbol of the artist and the arbitrary symbol of religion. The motive of Dio Chrysostom was repeated by Philostratos (third century): "Who guided Phidias in his representation of a God he had never seen? Something else guided him — a thing full of wisdom. What was that? You cannot mention any such thing except imitation. It was *imagination* that wrought these forms, a more cunning artist than imitation. Imitation will make what it has seen, but imagination will make what it has not seen." Of course the "imagination" of Philostratos does not distinguish between the imagination of things not seen and the creative imagination of the artist. The same must be said of Quintilian, when he speaks of *visions*, which the Greeks called *fantasias*, through which the images of far distant things are represented by the soul in such a way that we think to see them with eyes and to have them present. In another aspect Dio Chrysostom did not limit his idea to the relation between the invisible and the visible, between the spiritual and the material, but he also conceived the distinction between the different arts: "We sculptors have to make each likeness in a single attitude, which must be stable and permanent, and comprise in it the whole nature and quality of the god. But the poets may include many forms in their poetry, and ascribe movement and rest and actions and words to their personages." In this passage is presumed that distinction which made famous the Laocoön of Lessing. Of course no conclusions were drawn from these happy ideas, which were exceptional fruits, rather than seeds of new plants, and did not fertilise thought before the eighteenth century when an absolutely different type of thought matured.

Until now we have spoken about criticism of sculpture and painting. The ideas on architecture in antiquity are known to us through the treatise by Vitruvius. But it is necessary to add that those ideas are much more elementary and rude than those on painting and sculpture, as is the case even to-day with the ideas on architecture. The two exigencies of architecture are the training in construction, and the science of mathematical proportions. The judgment of architecture, following Vitruvius, has six categories, where the practical aspect — that is, the economical one — is juxtaposed to the pseudo-aesthetical one, in such manner that even literal interpretation is rather uncertain. It seems at any rate that by the Latin word *ordinatio* Vitruvius considered the convenience of the building to its scope; by the word *dispositio*, he understood the aspect of the building following the plan and the elevation; by the word *distributio*, he regarded its economic convenience; but he gave an aesthetic content to the following categories: *eurythmia*, which is the value of the repetition of certain elements; *symmetria*, which is the proportion between the various elements and the whole;

decor, which is the perfection of the execution. Notwithstanding, it was necessary, for an aesthetic exigency and on the example of painting and sculpture, to refer the categories of architecture to the idea of imitation of nature and link them to the other works of art. But architects did not become popular heroes as did painters and sculptors, and so their historical interest has not been so vital; in addition, buildings were of various types, and bowed to practical necessities, so that it was necessary to bring out the artistic element in them. The column, and the parts dependent on it, were considered as this artistic element; and they let Vitruvius classify the three orders: Doric, Ionic and Corinthian. The choice of the column depended on the fact that it had proportions similar to those of the human body. That is to say, the human proportions justified the imitative character of architecture and allowed it to be considered as a work of art. The history of architecture consisted then in the history of those three orders, and it is unnecessary to add that such a history was a pure legend.

Another type of art criticism was that of literary description. It had as model Homer's famous description of the shield of Achilles, it was cherished by the poets of the Anthology, and became fashionable as it gave the pleasure of competing by words with forms and colours. Statius, Martial, Apuleios, Pliny the younger and the two Philostratos followed this fashion. Because the critic is a philosopher added to an artist, and not an artist added to an artist, description may be a work of art, but not an important critical achievement. But what was perhaps the most beautiful description, that of Lucian on the Centauress by Zeuxis, was the occasion for acute and new observations. Lucian was aware of the ideas of the artists; he had been on the point of becoming a sculptor, and knew that his descriptions had no relation to the figurative aspect of art. He said: "I am not sufficiently a connoisseur to be able to judge the visual beauties of this picture. It is the task of painters and of those who are professional connoisseurs to praise the different parts which constitute a perfect painting: for example, the correctness of drawing, the truth of colour, the effect of light and shade, the exactitude of proportions, and the general harmony. My task is to explain how Zeuxis showed all the richness of genius, in giving to the Centaur a terrible and savage expression, ... to the Centauress ... an aspect similar to the famous mares of Thessaly." Also Lucian occupied himself with the pyschology of the figures represented and with the naturalness of the physical representation, leaving to the technicians the task of explaining the afore-mentioned schemes, which were not related to the individual vision of the artist. The proportions of Zeuxis belonged, of course, to his own art, but they were appreciated, not according to the individuality of Zeuxis, but to a general canon of proportions. This is why neither artists nor connoisseurs, as Lucian defined them, treated effectively the art of Zeuxis. Lucian refers to the legend of the anger of Zeuxis, when one of his paintings was highly praised for the novelty of its theme, instead of for the ability of its execution. And so certain people were interested in the pictorial romance, and others in the ability: both remained outside art criticism. In any case, the consciousness of the two ways of looking at a picture was quite new, and it was an approach to art criticism. Sometimes even Lucian bordered on criticism, as when he appreciated the fusion of the two bodies of woman and mare in the Centauress, and explained how those two bodies were merged with a great art, so that the elements of a fusion pleasant and easy, vanished before the eyes of the spectator, who was not aware of the transformation. Even the ancient artistic guide books, such as that by Pausanias the traveller, never went beyond the description of works of art.

Some antinomies of art and art criticism did not escape the Greeks and Romans, who discussed them in a manner that was maintained by later criticism. One of them was the rationality and the irrationality of the representation. Everyone knows that Horace invited his friends to have a good laugh in looking at a picture representing a beautiful woman whose body terminated in the form of an ugly fish, as a mermaid. In spite of that, we can admire a siren. The popularity of the grotesque, which formed fantastic combinations instead of imitations from reality, brought forth the following protest from Vitruvius: "How can you admit that reeds are able to support a roof, or that the candelabra could bear the dome of a temple with all its decorations, or that a tender and trembling stem could carry the weight of a seated figurine? Even if men knew such imagination to be false, not only did they not criticise it, but they condoned it, and this because they considered neither the true reality of things, nor the authority of the motive, not the rule of convenience. Therefore one should avoid praising those paintings, which did not imitate truth, even though they were painted with the greatest ability, and avoid judging unless one has well founded and clear reasons." Consequently, as Vitruvius, who considered the rational clarity as the only measure of art, so his adversaries, who appreciated the ability and not the art of the grotesque, proved themselves to be outside of a true critical judgment. The defect of the grotesque was really in the lack of moral seriousness and not in its irrationality.

The second antinomy was that of beauty and ugliness. According to Plato, beauty in itself is not found in the living creatures or their representations, but in geometrical figures. These are beautiful in themselves, by their own nature; and their beauty goes beyond sensual pleasure. And Aristotle confirmed the mathematical origin of the beautiful. Both, searching for beauty outside nature and art, found the principle of art not in beauty but in imitation. Because of his logical severity, Aristotle concluded from such an idea that art may represent ugliness as well as beauty: "Those things, which in nature we can not look at without disgust, give us pleasure when reproduced by art, above all when represented with the greatest realism; as, for example, the most hideous animals or dead bodies." But the reason for praising is, in the opinion of Aristotle, the pleasure of the spectator in discovering and recognising the content of the figures, and not in the aesthetic contemplation. Plutarch repeated the idea of Aristotle and added. "If a painting represents a hideous being in a lovely form it errs against its own nature and ceases to have verisimilitude." And this is said for realistic truth rather than for the liberty of art against the idea of beauty. Nevertheless Plutarch and the Stoics in general alluded to the solution of the problem by taking away from the body and reserving for the soul all reason of beauty; the ugly becomes a means of setting off the beauty of the soul. Vergil had said that virtue has a better grace in a fine body, and Seneca denied it: "Virtue has no need of ornament; it is its own beauty. It is not necessary to damage the soul with the deformities of the body, but to adorn the body by the beauty of the soul." Plutarch affirmed that physical ugliness is beautiful in itself when moral beauty is added. Therefore the idea of ugliness is sometimes denied, and sometimes it is cherished for polemical reasons.

But even this approach to a truth, which was a truth of the

romantic criticism, did not go farther. The principles of rationality and of geometrical beauty required of the artist an accurate execution. Zeuxis said that easy and rapid execution could not give to a work of art a very long life, nor that perfect beauty which is the result only of diligent care. But when the technical perfection became technical facility, then Xenocrates said that Apelles understood the necessity of taking the hand from a picture at the right time, and Cicero said that Apelles realised the meaning of the word *enough*. This was the source of a new conception of the finishing of pictures. And the ancient connoisseurs probably felt the value of a sketchy picture, because it revealed the mind of the artist in a more direct manner, more spontaneous, and more intimate, without considering the necessities of a public expression. Pliny gave us, though in an incidental and distracted manner, the example of such a state of mind: "What is quite curious and noteworthy is that people admire less the finished productions of an artist than his last works, left incomplete, as, for instance, the Venus of Apelles. In fact, people appreciate the interrupted sketch and the first idea of the artist; while sorrow for the hand that perished at his work beguiles us into the bestowal of the prize."

The antinomies of rationality and irrationality, of beauty and ugliness, of works finished and unfinished, involve the antinomy of form and colour. We will not affirm that form and colour constitute always and necessarily an antinomy, bound up with the other already suggested antinomies; the fact is that the ancient artists of Greece and Rome and the modern artists of the Renaissance and of Neo-classicism understood form and colour in this way, but the artists of the Middle Ages did not. History cannot fix the cause of events, but only their conditions. And the conditions of the above-mentioned antinomies are the following: the rationalisation of beauty is founded on the mathematical proportions of form. Of course, even colour may be rationalised, and Aristotle himself wrote a treatise on colour, in which he distinguished three elements: 1 — light, 2 — the matter through which light passes, 3 — the local colour of the object from which the light is reflected. These were scientific observations, but nobody thought of assuming one light or one colour as a standard of perfection to be imposed on every picture or work of architecture, as human proportions were imposed on the form of figures and columns. That is to say, there was invented a canon of the proportions of the human form, and not a canon of the harmonies of colours. Proportions were considered as laws, even by artists who wished to elude them, but harmonies of colour were treated only by sensibility. The rationalised form, and not the sensitive colours, could exhaust beauty, beauty being considered as rational. The antithesis of beauty is ugliness, but colours were beautiful in themselves, according to the opinion of Plato and others. But their beauty should be subordinate to that of form, which was not only beautiful, but of rational, absolute beauty. On the contrary, when colours dominate form, the result is a barbaric taste and ugliness.

In his "Poetics," Aristotle, in order to explain how the basis of tragedy is myth, and characters take only second place, builds up a comparison: "Something similar happens in painting. If someone smears a surface, even with the most beautiful colours, but without a preconceived drawing, he would not be able to charm so much as another who draws only the contours of a figure in simple white." Philostratos wished to demonstrate the exactitude of this idea by an example: "Even if we use only white to paint an Indian, he still appears black: his broad flat nose, the curly hair, the prominent cheek bones, and a peculiar expression of the eyes, all show the lineaments as being black, even if we see them white, and they represent an Indian to every practised eye." From this we can understand of what kind was the pleasure the ancient people called aesthetic or the imagination they called phantasy: the pleasure depended on recognition and only the artist's skill suggested imagination. Instead of a true aesthetic pleasure, they spoke of an intellectual knowledge. Therefore in antiquity there is a relationship between the rationalised aesthetic, and the preference of form to colour.

The development of art tended towards a constant growth of interest in colouring. And in the first century A. D. Dionysios of Halikarnassos objectively observed: "In ancient paintings the scheme of colouring was simple and presented no variety in the tones; but the line was rendered with exquisite perfection, thus lending to these early works a singular grace. This purity of draughtsmanship was gradually lost; its place was taken by a learned technique, by the differentiation of light and shade, and by the full resources of the rich colouring to which the works of the later artists owe their strength."

But this objectivity of judgment did not always receive assent. Greek art prevailed over Oriental art in general, and Persian in particular, for its sense of proportions, but not for creative capacity of colouring; and it was difficult to distinguish the art of colouring from the richness of material, because of the luxurious character of the Oriental productions. Besides, the development of colouring, as Dionysios pointed out, coinciding with the decay of art, was considered by the Roman critics as responsible for this decadence.

How general was the opinion identifying colouring with a barbaric luxury was indicated by Lucian in the following description of a hall: "Its magnificence was the only reason for surprise. Neither art, nor beauty, nor right proportions, nor the elegance of form, gave value to the distribution of splendid metals. That was a spectacle made for the eyes of a barbarian. Barbarians cannot appreciate beauty, they display the magnificence of their treasures in order to astonish spectators and not to charm them, because to barbarians what is gorgeous is considered beautiful."

Both Pliny and Vitruvius made colouring responsible for the decay of art: "Four colours only were used by Apelles and others in their immortal works... While now that purple clothes our walls, and India contributes the ooze of her rivers and the blood of dragons and of elephants, there are no more masterpieces; and so everything was better when instrumentalities were fewer. That is really so, because people attach greater value to material than to genius." And Vitruvius: "While in ancient times people appreciated only the talent of the artist and the perfection of his work, today they praise only one thing: the splendour of colours. The science of the painter no longer counts."

Against these condemnations arose later the voice of Plutarch: "Colouring is superior to drawing, and produces a more living impression on the mind, because it is the source of a greater illusion." This was a presentiment of a new era which was arising, but not a critical confutation.

Finally even the antinomy of the finished and unfinished works responded to that of form and colour, because the effect of colour needs an uneven surface, whose touches give an unfinished impression. Such an effect was noted in a quotation from the Anthology relating to the picture by Parrhasios, representing Philottetes: "The picture had an uneven aspect, due no doubt to the effect of the brush, and the tone had a certain asperity."

These are the most important testimonies, very fragmentary and sporadic, of critical activity on the figurative arts, preserved from classical antiquity. The principles which antiquity followed are true even now, but now they are understood in a more profound conception of the nature of art. Antiquity launched the critical problems of art without solving them, but used acute and unbiased observations and a very fine sensibility. Therefore it is wise, not only to avoid the mistakes of the critics of antiquity, but also to develop their truths, and to meditate upon their schemes: of imitation, proportion, moral content, relation between mind and matter, between vision and myth, between the analysis of the technique and the description of the subject, rationality and irrationality, beauty and ugliness, completion and incompletion, form and colour.

CHAPTER III
The Middle Ages

UP TO the fourteenth century, a characterisation of artists or of works of art, such as classical antiquity was able to produce, is lacking in the Middle Ages. For nearly ten centuries it seems that art criticism was silent: only seems, it is true, because testimonies remain of discussions upon art and with reference to works of art; but the desire for transcendency induced the men of the Middle Ages to seek God, the supreme beauty, in a work of art and to speak only of God, while it hindered them from interesting themselves enough in the things of the earth, among which are works of art and the personality of the artist. At the end of the antique era a loftier aesthetic theory than those preceding was formed by Plotinus, because in it nature was spiritualised by way of mysticism, and the concept of imitation was in some sort overcome. St. Augustine realised that spiritualisation in some principles of figurative art. Later, Duns Scotus and St. Thomas realised it in the determination of some faculties, in which art could be included. By virtue of such thought, art was in effect liberated from nature, naturalistically understood as by the Greeks. The destruction of the contact between art and nature facilitated for artists the creation of masterpieces in Romanesque and Gothic architecture, in Romanesque and Gothic sculpture, in Byzantine and Romanesque mosaics, in stained glass, in textiles, and so on. But in the fervour of those creations nobody was able to render count of them critically. To render count of them it was necessary to fuse the consciousness of the logical process of criticism, as the ancients were able, with the consciousness of the a-logical and mystical process of art. The men of the Middle Ages had this last, not the first. Therefore, and also following the weakened culture, they limited themselves to giving empirical receipts. During the Middle Ages art criticism divides itself into three modes, none of which, naturally, could exhaust the subject. These are: the mystical aesthetic, the iconographical repertory, and the body of receipts. All these three modes interest us only in what they can suggest to us of contemporary artistic knowledge, or as they may have come true in subsequent criticism.

Historically for the naturalistic conception of man proper to antiquity, was substituted in the Middle Ages the conception of his spiritual value; and for the concepts of fate and fortune was substituted the concept of Providence. In art also a spiritual value was recognised, but in a transcendental manner and without distinction of spiritual categories, so that the idea of art was completely absorbed in the idea of God. Through love of universality the individual became indifferent, and was reduced to an anonymous instrument of religious exaltation. It was a happy condition for the creation of art — but at the same time it was the most desperate condition for making a critical history of art.

The principle that allowed Plotinus to progress beyond the concept of *imitation* was that of *emanation* — of Oriental origin. He says: "Imagine to have before you two pieces of marble and one may be without form, unworked, and the other may be instead already a carved statue, which represents a figure divine or human, and if divine, the statue may be of some grace or muse, and if human it may be not the portrait of an individual man, but of something in which the beauties of various models have been assembled. The marble, then, which by means of art has assumed beauty of form, will immediately appear as beautiful, not by the fact that it is marble, because otherwise the other marble would be equally beautiful, but precisely because it has a form produced by art. The material did not in fact possess this form which was in the mind of the author before it had passed into the marble, and it was in the artificer, not because he had eyes and hands, but because he was furnished with art. There was, indeed, in art a much greater beauty than this," since in its passage from art itself and from the author to the material, a part of the beauty is lost. It is not true that artists imitate simply that which they see with their eyes, "but they have recourse to those same reasons of which nature consists and with which she works, besides creating many figures by their imagination and correcting others, where perfection was wanting, so that the figures receive beauty." Therefore the artist transforms the material, which is ugly, into a rational form. The bodies become beautiful because they participate in the reason which is God. Everything that symbolises in sensible form the eternal reasons of the world has the right to be called beautiful. As Chrysippus had said already: beauty is of the universe and not only of man. Even Plotinus opposes the idea of the identity of beauty and proportions, because these proportions are of man, or rather of the human body, and beauty is spiritual. Beauty is complex. There is a simple beauty, that of colour, because it consists in the victory of light over darkness.

Detaching itself from the material the soul reaches out to the supreme beauty, which is also the supreme good, God, by a mystical process which, says Plotinus, is *intuition*. This is the process of contemplation, which is opposed to reasoning, in which subject and object are identified. The vision is no longer external but internal. The eye does not see the sun if it has not first grasped its form. The soul does not see beauty if it has not become beautiful itself. The mystical process ends in the vision, which unites and simplifies everything: in *ecstasy*. That is to say, the artistic activity remains rational in its aim of attaining the reason of God, but its process is intuitive, imaginative. For the finite world of the classical era is substituted the infinite world of the modern age, and if it is still somewhat chaotic, it is impressed with the new knowledge of the spirituality of art.

St. Augustine, who through his whole life is passionately devoted to aesthetics, follows the ideas of Plotinus, and defines some of them. For example: ugliness is not only a lack of form but also a minor degree of beauty — a concept which, as does also the preceding concept of sublimity, leads back to the reality of the work of art, apart from the transcendence of absolute beauty. Equally, besides unity, gradation, variety and distinction, he judges contrast to be among the qualities of beauty. If the colour black is put in its right place in a picture, the picture is beautiful, even though the colour black is not beautiful; as the universe is beautiful even though it contains sinners, who are ugly in themselves. Not only that, but beauty itself has a certain relativity: compared with man the ape is ugly. But the ape also has a rhythm of its own, the unity of its members, the agreement of its parts, and so forth. The beauty of the ape would be diminished if its body were altered. Beauty exists as long as things are natural. Here, then, is an infinite enlargement of the world of artistic inspiration, and at the same time a transcending of nature, even of that of an ape, by the sense of the divine.

Such transcendency found its rationalistic form in the concept of allegory. This arises if one thing sounds in the word and another thing is designated in the mind: the lamb and Christ, for example. Here St. Augustine does not ask himself if the artistic character of the lamb consists in the reference to Christ or in the manner of representation. St. Augustine has arrived at a particularly genial intuition when he speaks of the judgment of the work of art. Direct judgment is judgment of senses; there is also the superior judgment of reason, which judges according to the laws of beauty (number, relationship, balance, unity) which come from God. But he cannot demonstrate that these laws have reason. In which is outlined the antinomy between non-demonstrability and the pretension of universality in the judgment of taste, which Kant will be able to settle.

Finally, St. Augustine does not love painting and sculpture among the arts, but certainly music and architecture. Among the figurative arts architecture is the furthest abstracted from natural imitation: his preference was therefore consequential, and permeated the mediaeval taste; to this is due the great flourishing of Romanesque and Gothic architecture. St. Augustine prefers a rigorous correspondence among the parts, a balance of windows, a rational architectonic measure; that is to say, he did not yet feel the need of liberation from the mathematical reason, a liberation which was the glory of the mediaeval architects. There is, however, a detachment from the classical taste in the consideration of the window as an artistic value in architecture (Aristotle occupied himself instead with the column); and in the consideration of space as an element self-emancipated (of the intervals rhythmically connected, rather than of the closed and finite elements, preferred by the classical taste).

The continuity of neo-Platonic thought relative to art is proved by the passages that St. Thomas, in the thirteenth century, dedicates to aesthetics. He recognises the rational value of the two superior senses – sight and hearing: these are a means to formal knowledge, by way of assimilation. The contemplative life is an act of reason: therefore reason is intuitive knowledge. Thomas exalts the value of the senses. The senses delight in proportions, because these are similar to those that the senses contain in themselves. That is to say, we feel objective relationships as if they were in us. Here St. Thomas anticipates the modern theory of empathy, *Einfühlung*. Finally, the good as much as the beautiful is lovable. The good pleases desire directly; the beautiful pleases it by its theoretical interest. Passion is pacified in the beautiful through the possession of the discernible image. The beautiful is therefore objective, but its power depends upon the subject, upon the discernible image created by the subject.

In short, from Plotinus to St. Thomas, from the third to the thirteenth century, there is a continuous process of aesthetic thinking, in spite of aversion of a theological order, rich in anticipation of the modern aesthetics: a process consisting of the consideration of the spiritual value of form, of the universal and infinite value of beauty, of art as intuition and as ecstasy, of the relativity of the ugly, of the judgment of the senses, not demonstrable yet pretending to universality, of the exaltation of architecture among the figurative arts. It arrives at valuing the artistic senses as a theoretical activity, and at recognising the subjective character of art.

If these and other happy intuitions did not realise themselves in an aesthetic discipline, as came to pass in the eighteenth century, it was due to the lack of relationship between the consideration of art on the one hand and the beautiful on the other; that is to say, the psychological observations, sometimes very subtle, and the metaphysical intuitions, often marvellous, were not applied to works of art. Architecture, painting and sculpture were considered under their practical aspect as handicrafts. Naturally, when one spoke of the aesthetic function of the colour black in a picture, or of the spatial rhythm in an edifice, painting and architecture were not considered as handicrafts; but from such truths no conclusions were drawn, and so they continued to consider painting as a craft like that of building boats. The defect being aggravated by the decline in general culture, the treatise on art which had been raised by Xenocrates to a standard of criticism, was reduced to the level of a book of receipts.

Among the more remote mediaeval writers of treatises appears Heraclius, perhaps a Roman, an exalter of Rome, desirous of discovering the secret of Roman art. But in what does that secret consist? In the manner in which the Romans were successful in including gold within the glass of some phials in order to make them splendid. He who offers the most encyclopedic treatise of technical information, and includes in his survey the production of Greece and Italy, France and Germany, and even Arabia, is Theophilus, in the twelfth century. The programme of his book is the following: "One learns art little by little, and part by part. Fundamental to the art of painting is the composition of colours, then giving attention to their blending. Preoccupy yourself with that, and be exact to extreme limits, so that what you paint may be freely ornamented and spontaneously created. In following the practice of art you will be helped by the experience of many craftsmen of talent." Here is a picture, vague enough, but capable of representing the painter of the Romanesque period. His preoccupation is the composition and blending of colours. Theophilus does not speak of drawing. That is not a difficulty, because it is not a torment. One learns drawing from the experience of the craftsmen of talent, that is to say, by copying their examples. Nor does Theophilus speak of the imitation of nature. What matters is to blend the colours well within the contours, so that the effect may be ornamental, free, as if it had flowered. One could not touch the central point of Romanesque art with greater ingenuity; everything seems a convention, but the execution is so passionate, fervent and full of faith, that an infinite creative freedom is released from the convention itself.

Theophilus does not speak of painters, but only of the House of God. Nor does he concern himself with the history of painting: he limits himself to recording that art is born in craftsmanship, to which Adam has been constrained since the banishment from Eden. Between pure craftsmanship — the blending of colours — and the image of God, the artist, according to Theophilus, does not pass a single step: he does not know nature, nor proportions, nor the schemes of the human reason. The individuality of the artist is annulled in the House of God through the mystical process. Theophilus thus imagines the work fulfilled: "Adorning the ceilings and walls with varied work and diverse colours you have in some way exposed to the eyes of the faithful the Paradise of God, decorated with innumerable flowers. You have succeeded in letting the Creator be praised in creation and in showing God to be admirable in his work. At first the human eye does not know upon what to rest: if it looks at the ceilings they are flowery, like shining tissues; if it considers the walls, there is a kind of delightful garden; if it is dazzled by the flakes of light that come through the windows, it admires the priceless beauty of the glass and the varieties of most precious workmanship. If the faithful soul observes the spectacle of the Passion of the Saviour represented in drawing, it is filled with compassion." Observe that drawing (*liniamenta*) appears here to inspire compassion, through psychological expression. But when it is a matter of praising the Creator in creation, when the contemplation of Paradise is concerned, colours and lights are enough. That is to say, ingenuously, without clear knowledge, Theophilus assigned to formal representation a moral task; and a value of mystical contemplation to colour and light.

Painting also, then, when it has not an aim of religious oratory, when it is beauty of colour and light, is placed in the conditions of architecture, to be an object of contemplation, without being a representation. It is not necessary to insist: it is clear, indeed, that this is a critical discovery which links itself to mediaeval art but has an eternal value, particularly vivid in the consciousness of modern art.

If to the treatise of Theophilus be compared the "Guide to Painting" of the monk Dionysius, a work of uncertain date, perhaps of the sixteenth century but reflecting an older tradition, there is no critical intuition to be discovered in the body of receipts. It is true that the author says that he wishes to explain the measurements and characters of the figures, but he does not maintain the project, and limits himself to offering receipts for colours and an iconographical repertory. Given the aim of moral teaching assigned to paintings in churches, it was natural that it should obey not only the general dogma of the Church, but, in order to avoid mistakes, also a special iconographical dogma. For example, the guide to painting wishes that the creation of Adam be represented thus: "Adam, young, beardless, upright, naked. In front of him the Eternal Father, surrounded by brilliant light, supports him with the left hand. All around, trees and different animals. Above, the sky with sun and moon." The iconographical dogma had, then, a practical and cultural aim, without any relationship to art. The artist could obey it because his artistic freedom was elsewhere, in "free ornament," as Theophilus said. It is only with the Renaissance that the traditional iconography will be modified, with a freedom advantageous to art and disadvantageous to the Church, so that the Counter Reformation will have to recur to remedy and reconstitute an iconographical dogma. In the guide of Mount Athos there is even a hint of the quarrel of iconoclasm, with the allegorical justification of images. "We do not say that this or that pictorial representation is Christ or the Virgin; but when we make homage of veneration to an image we refer this homage to the prototype which the image represents to us." Nothing of the kind is found in Theophilus, because the West had been little touched by iconoclasm, and any diffidence towards the image, for fear of idolatry, even in the West — for example, in St. Augustine — found its solution in contemplation of the abstract image of the representation; it was, therefore, an artistic solution.

From the books of rhetoric and poetry there passed to writings on the figurative arts the theory of ornamentation, that is to say of style regarded for itself, distinct from its symbolical content. This had great importance for the criticism of the Middle Ages. Today we know that the work of art is neither a thing of nature nor an artificial thing, but is created, as nature creates, without imitating that which nature has created. But the Middle Ages, when freed from the concept of imitation of nature, fell into that of human artifice. A Polish philosopher, a friend of St. Thomas, Witelo, writes a treatise on perspective in which he is not content to profit by the antique and Arabian science, but preoccupies himself with placing it in relation with art. He comes out with an unexpected affirmation: "Artificial things appear more beautiful than the natural," which reveals at a stroke that a new world is born, in opposition to the ancient naturalism, with the confidence of man in human artifice. This affirmation is connected with another: "Almond-shaped eyes are more beautiful than round," in which one surprises an ideal of taste, originating in love of the East, deduced from Gothic art, imposed by Gothic art upon the character of the eye. It is a phenomenon typical of the art which creates nature, a climax of artistic spiritualism. Witelo also adores light, according to the neo-Platonic tradition, but notes also that the beauty of colour is of sparkling colours, because they diffuse a light of their own, and darkness is beautiful only because it gives relief to light. Concerning the relation between distance and beauty he affirms that "distance is beauty, because it takes away the sharpness. But if there are small and delicate accents in the form, lines dignified by the arrangement of the parts, nearness is beauty. And if from a distance you observe a very small painting, the merit of which is only in the finish, it will seem to you ugly." Here he seems to present himself with a problem (that of the proper distance for looking at a picture), which will have its development only in the nineteenth century. To Witelo's treatise, one may add the treatise on proportions, illustrated with drawings, the work of the thirteenth century French architect, Villard De Honnecourt: a fundamental graphic treatise for the studious "learned" in the craftsmanship of the period.

Isidorus of Seville (6th – 7th centuries), copied by Vincent of Beauvais (13th century), had affirmed that "beauty is something that one adds to buildings for ornament and richness, as occurs in gilded roofs, in precious marble incrustations, in coloured paintings." The greater part of the historical records and descriptions of monuments dwell on their sumptuousness, on their shining colours, on the light that is released from them. The typical example is the description of St. Sophia at Constantinople, by Paul Silentiarius, in 563: "The shell of the apse is like a peacock with plumes of a hundred eyes. From the golden immensity of the vault is diffused such a light that it dazzles vision: it is a barbaric and a Latin pomp in one. The altar is of gold, supported on columns and bases of gold, and the gold is broken only by splendid jewels. At evening such a light is reflected upon things from the temple that you would say that a midnight sun was there. The splendid night smiles like day and yet appears to come with feet of rose. The sailor needs no other beacon, it is enough for him to look at the light of the temple."

From the records of the seventh to the ninth centuries on the gifts from popes or bishops of Ravenna, and the inscriptions on mosaics, down to the memorandum of Suger on the work accomplished at St. Denis, light, gold, silver and jewels are the symbols of artistic value. But in the twelfth century St. Bernard rises up against the luxury of churches, against gold, against the ornaments of the sculptors and their fantastic treatment of animals and monsters. "Everywhere there appears such a strange variety of forms that one prefers to read in the marbles rather than in the liturgies, and to occupy the whole day in admiring one or other of these things rather than in meditation upon the commandments of God." This expresses the pleasure of the monks before Romanesque sculpture and at the same time the wish to avoid that pleasure for religious reasons. Dante was moved to oppose the excess in mediaeval decoration, but with an artistic rather than a moral demand: "and it is a fine rhetorical mode when things appear unadorned externally and within are truly embellished." This is the announcement of a new era of artistic severity, of spiritual concentration.

In what character of painting consists that apparent lack of adornment which was a deepening of beauty, is indicated by Boccaccio with reference to Giotto, in a passage in which is recovered from classical antiquity the concept of the imitation of nature and that of judges of art, who, according to Quintilian, understand the reason of art, while the unlearned feel only the voluptuousness. He says that Giotto has "brought again to light that art which had been buried for many centuries, because of the mistake of those painters who delighted the eyes of the ignorant rather than pleased the intellect of the wise." In accordance with the painting of Giotto, containing mind within limited and solid bodies, inciting to reflections upon human nature those who are capable of it, Boccaccio opposed himself to Byzantine mosaics, all jewelled lights and fascinating gold, which ask nothing of man's reason.

Hardly twenty years have passed since the death of Giotto, and Boccaccio has a clear knowledge of a new artistic era that Giotto had initiated. Such a judgment, critical and historical at the same time, had not been given for ten centuries. The division into aesthetic tradition, iconographical repertory and technical receipts is ended by that Italian civilisation which had to close the Middle Ages and open the door to the modern era. Dante speaks of Cimabue and Giotto. After him Petrarch, Boccaccio, Sacchetti, Filippo Villani and Cennini write on the Tuscan art of their time: from it they derive the incentive to form for themselves a criterion of artistic judgment: now they venerate it, now they fear for its fortune; now they seek to form its laws, now they wish to transmit to posterity the names of the artists who were the glories of their city. In such a way a bridge is flung between figurative art and literary culture, classical, erudite and critical. The principles learned from ancient writers are put into relation with the everyday experience of art: the theoretical principle is applied to the living reality of art, to be solidified in judgment. On the other hand, contemporary artists are compared with the artists of antiquity as a standard; and from the comparison arises a first sketch of history, not of artists only, but of art — historical epochs.

The first who set himself to compile a treatise on the figurative arts, that was not merely a mass of receipts, was Petrarch, but from the few fragments that remain, it is clear that to the information and ideas gathered from Pliny he wished to add only a new moral sensibility. In the "letter to posterity" Petrarch affects to be a despiser of his own age and a praiser exclusively of antiquity, thus initiating the question which was to become the "quarrel between the ancients and the moderns." The painters who were his contemporaries believed themselves superior to the ancients, but the sculptors were not so daring. Petrarch believes that sculpture is an art more lively and closer to nature than painting. Here is a notion that will be developed more fully later: the material and naturalistic superiority of sculpture against the artificial and spiritual superiority of painting. But he is enamoured of the painting of his friend Simone Martini; he compares him to Vergil, believes him superior to Zeuxis, and imagines an elevation of the painter to Paradise for having been able to paint the divine face of Madonna Laura — an idea that is like an echo of the past from a poet of the Greek Anthology on Phidias.

In 1351-2 Filippo Villani wrote a book in praise of his own city, Florence, and among its famous men he included some painters. His are therefore the first "lives of artists" from the era of antiquity until then. And he feels the need to justify his treatment of the Florentine painters with reference to men of science and other painters. He revives the methods of the ancient histories, and also the legend of Prometheus, which he interprets in a mediaeval sense as an allegory of the power of artistic creation. Lofty talent, exceptional memory, and readiness of the sensitive hand belong to the artist. Pliny had said that among the Greeks painting was included in the first rank of the liberal arts. Villani does not hesitate to affirm the superiority of painters over masters of the liberal arts — that is, the scientists — thus: for the latter it is enough to have learned scientific principles from writings, but painters must translate what they feel with lofty talent and tenacious memory. Note that here is recognized in painters that superiority to scientists which will later be called *genius*. Villani probably repeated a current opinion, but that makes it all the more important that among literates and artists at the end of the fourteenth century was diffused the idea of a genial energy necessary for art, consisting in the translation of feeling by talent and memory, as we should say, into theoretical value. The aesthetic subject could not better be defined, in opposition to the scientific subject, which has no need of passing from feeling to creative power. Naturally the aesthetic object is not correspondingly defined: what happens, according to Villani, is that the creation of the painter is so natural that it seems to live and breathe, and the gestures of the figures are so appropriate that they express actions, such as discoursing, weeping and laughing. Physical realism and psychological expression: the object of art is not therefore to be distinguished from that of science. If the ancients had quoted Zeuxis, Policleitos and Apelles, Villani speaks of the Florentine painters. If anybody mocks he bids him be silent. For the Florentine painters revived an art that was bloodless and almost dead, just as Dante revived poetry. The first to open the new way was Cimabue, by means of the imitation of nature. Giotto placed himself in the open way and became equal in fame to the ancient painters, and even superior to them in art and talent; by which painting assumed afresh the ancient dignity and a renown that could not be greater. The absolute value of Giotto thus affirmed, Villani tries to determine his character, and seeks it in his culture — judge of history and rival of poets, and in his moral gifts — desire of glory rather than of gain. It is the humanistic ideal opposed to that of religious humility, indicated by Theophilus. Given Giotto's perfection, Villani is not able to indicate his individual qualities — that is to say, his individual perfection — different from those of others. But what he does not know how to indicate in Giotto, he knows in his pupils. Stefano was expert in anatomy, Taddeo Gaddi in the architecture of backgrounds. As to Maso, Villani feels that his value does not come from outside, nor from the object treated, but from his style, and he has no words to indicate his character. He can only express his admiration: he is the finest of all, and has painted with such charm, that it is not only marvellous but even incredible.

Pliny contributed, then, to Villani's notes on artists, but he was not the model for judgments of them. Therefore the idea of artistic progress is not to be found in Villani. On the contrary, after Giotto had caused painting to be reborn, the work of his followers was precious and placid. The sense of miracle, which belonged to the mediaeval tradition, helped Villani in not adhering completely to the ancient naturalism.

At the end of the fourteenth century Cennino Cennini wrote his "Book of Art" to contain the doctrine that he had learned from Agnolo Gaddi, son of Taddeo, who had been the pupil of Giotto. For the greater part, his book is a receipt-book of colours, according to the mediaeval tradition, but its meaning is new. He knows that Giotto "changed the art of painting from Greek to Latin, and made it modern; and had the art more completely than anyone ever had before." He knows that Agnolo Gaddi "coloured much more vaguely and freshly than Taddeo, his father." Now he wishes to teach Agnolo Gaddi's manner of colouring together with the doctrine of Giotto, although it may have been weakened in the course of two generations. Sometimes, then, his precepts assume the knowledge of the painting of his time; they refer to it and in it solidify themselves as judgments. Therefore the "receipt-book" of Cennini assumes the new aspect, as compared with those of Theophilus and the monk Dionysius. The aim of the teaching of Theophilus was the decoration of the House of God; the aim of Cennini was to teach how to become a painter. Sometimes this permitted Cennini to individualise the object of his criticism. The elements of the teaching are made much richer: the relation between pupil and master, between art and science, between art and nature, recognition of imagination and personal style, need for love and gentleness, the danger of eclecticism, the relation between colour and drawing, the mental value of drawing, the charm of colours, and the difficulty of their accord: these are the themes of the criticism of Cennini.

Also, for Cennini, one learns painting by copying the models of the master; but the conclusion is different: "It will happen to you, if nature has given you any imagination to see how to pick a manner of your own, and it cannot be other than good; because your hand and intellect, being always used to pick flowers, should know better than to take a thorn." Observe: from the practice of copying springs the personality of the artist, not by theory, nor by reasoning, but by force of imagination. With regard to science, Cennini does not, like Villani, dare to maintain the superiority of art, but contents himself with opposing to science the freedom of the artist and defining it as the freedom of imagination.

With regard to nature, Cennini knows "that the most perfect guide you can have and the best rudder is the triumphal door of drawing from nature. This is ahead of all other examples; and under this always trust yourself with daring heart, and especially when you begin to have some feeling in drawing."

Cennini considers that nature is the best master, but it is well that it should not be the first. "As early as you can, put yourself under the guidance of a master; and as late as you can, depart from the master." Feeling in drawing is style, which one learns from the examples of the master and with which one should confront nature. Neither drawing from nature nor copying the example of the master is art; nature must be corrected by the style, as the style by nature. Cennini helps himself by the passage from Quintilian on the visions that the Greeks called fantasias, and by which the mind represents to the eyes as present the images of things that are absent. Applying to painting this psychological observation, he draws from it a definition of painting: "This is the art one calls painting, that must have imagination, by the operation of the hand, to find things unseen (hiding themselves in the shade of the natural), and fix them with the hand, demonstrating that what is not, may be." It is difficult to insist enough upon the importance of this passage. In fact, for the first time the imitation of nature is understood as a production independent of and parallel to nature, as the reproduction of that which is not in nature, presented as if it were natural. It is the recognition of parallelism between artistic truth and natural truth (or scientific, if you like), and therefore it is the recognition of their distinctness. The artist must imagine, but it is necessary that his imagination should seem reality. Through the whole of the Renaissance there is not so lofty a voice, so transparent a knowledge of the character which belongs to art. It seems as if a virgin eye addressed itself to reality; maintained the mediaeval transcendency, as an ideal impressed upon the reality discovered, whence a synthesis (of ideal and reality) which will then disappear in knowledge. So Cennini defined, not art in general, but the art of which he speaks: the art of Giotto.

He knows that one does not come to art for gain, but through "natural love, through love and gentleness. The intellect gives delight to drawing, only as nature gives the same to that which is drawn, without any guidance of a master, through gentleness of heart." "Love" is used in the Dantesque meaning — inspiration; and "gentleness" is for Cennini nobility of feeling. Against cupidity of money the monk Dionysius opposes the chastisement of God; Villani opposes the desire of glory, of classical origin. The most Christian, that which most answers to style in fourteenth century painting, is the voice of Cennini: love and gentleness.

Florentine painting in the second half of the fourteenth century sometimes erred by eclecticism: there were not only Giotto and his greater followers, but also the Sienese painters who influenced the Florentine masters. Cennini disapproved of eclecticism, as a difficulty in the formation of an individual style: "If you are moved to draw from this master to-day, from that one to-morrow, you will have neither the manner of the one nor of the other, and you are bound to become fantastic, the love of each manner will distract your mind. Now you will wish to do in the mode of this one, to-morrow of that other, and so you will have neither perfect."

Theophilus had considered composition and the blending of colours, and not drawing, as fundamental to painting. The new value of drawing in Giotto is manifested in the demand of Cennini: "fundamental in art are drawing and colouring." For Cennini drawing is not only material drawing — drawing with pen — but also that "within your head"; that is to say, the capacity to feel and realise form. In this second meaning "drawing" is opposed to "practice," to craftsmanship. In order that the drawing may be masterly, it is necessary that it should become plastic form by means of light and shade, and the light

and shade must not have violent contrasts, but must be graduated by tempered light. But this love of form and light and
shade is contrasted in Cennini with pleasure in fine colour: he
knows that the folds of drapery are obtained with light and
shade, but he also knows that the light and shade injure the
beauty of colour. He loves fine blue in the garments of the
Madonna, and therefore he advises having in them as few folds
as possible. He dreams of blue and gold, and gold "makes all
the works of our art to blossom."

CHAPTER IV
The Renaissance

THE OLD conception of the Renaissance as an epoch opposed to the Middle Ages, by the disappearance of religion and the study of classical antiquity, has been recently modified. It is recognised that religion did not disappear in the Renaissance but was made more human, because it concentrated its faith in man, a microcosm in which the universe is included. And it is understood that the study of the antique writers, sculptors and architects was a consequence and not a cause of the new religion of man. Throughout the fifteenth century an intense faith in man, in his beauty, is his power, in his reason, is the basis of art as of science.

A faint beginning of the new world is found in the "Commentaries" written shortly before 1455 by Lorenzo Ghiberti. Translating and summing up from Vitruvius, Pliny and other ancient writers, Ghiberti proposes to draw new inventions from the rules of antiquity. He models the definition of the sculptor and the painter on that of the architect as given by Vitruvius, with some modification or addition to bring it up to date. He then recognises that sculpture and painting consist not only in the act (by material), but also in theory (by reasoning). To "reasoning" he gives particular importance. The Greeks "were inventors of art in painting and sculpture showing the theory of drawing; without this theory you cannot be a good sculptor or a good painter." Being a sculptor himself, he adheres to the standard of antiquity on the preference of form over colour. "Drawing is the foundation and theory" of both painting and sculpture: hence we see that the civilisation which produced Theophilus has disappeared. But the value of Ghiberti's criticism does not really

79

consist in the theoretical part, but rather in the historical part. He is the first artist since antiquity who has written on the best painters that he knew, and on two sculptors, one of them himself. Completing the series of Florentine painters indicated by Villani, he extends his glance beyond Florence, to Rome and Siena; everywhere the epoch of great art, which deserves to be recorded as comparable to the artistic civilisation of antiquity, is limited between the end of the thirteenth and the first half of the fourteenth century. Ghiberti indicates clearly that he considers his own age an age of decadence, in spite of Masaccio and Donatello, and in spite of himself, Ghiberti. In speaking of the painters of the fourteenth century he is stimulated by the example of Pliny: his justification is that of Villani. He tries to define the works of artists, works that he has seen and that have pleased him, to serve as a memorial to posterity. But Ghiberti is an artist, and therefore he does not refer to the judgments of others, but expresses his own impressions. The manner of his expression is primitive: he has not the ideas of the humanists, nor does he move easily among the categories of judgment. But his intuition is often happy, and is valuable to us. Thus he assigns the first place to the "discovery" of Giotto, "discoverer of so much doctrine which had been buried for nearly 600 years; he led art to the greatest perfection." We should note that this conception of Ghiberti is much more just than that which still prevails in various histories of art, which speak of a beginning, a progress, a perfection and a decline of art. Since art is connected with creative personality, the paradox is true that the beginning is always the perfection. It is true for Giotto or for Van Eyck, for Masaccio or for Giorgione, for Rembrandt or for Velazquez. The conviction of Giotto's perfection was commonly accepted, and we have noted it already in Villani. But it is certain that Ghiberti felt it personally. And in this way of conceiving, he may blend the reference to art of the mediaeval idea of miracle, with the humanistic sense of exaltation by man, of the omnipotence of man.

How does Ghiberti explain the greatness of Giotto? "He brought together natural art and gentleness without going beyond measure." If "natural art" and "measure" come from Pliny, "gentleness" indicates the affinity between Cennini and Ghiberti; that is to say, nobility of feeling. In Stefano, Ghiberti appreciates the effect of movement in a storm and the relief of a figure. In Bonamico he notes his natural facility: "he had art by nature, he endured little fatigue in his works; when he gave his mind to them his works surpassed those of all other painters; he was very ready in art, a man of great enjoyment." This is an embryo critical sketch, but observe that even the psychological motive of enjoyment serves to portray the born painter, who improvises that endless marvel; and when he engages in it is unsurpassed. Ghiberti defines the style of Maso: "He shortened greatly the art of painting." Pliny had called the manner of Nicomacus "summary painting," and Ghiberti translated: "This one followed the swiftness of the master and found certain abbreviations in painting." Of Maso, thus, Ghiberti wishes to say that his painting suggests rather than represents, executing impressions as forcible as they are broken. And in the authenticated work of Maso in Santa Croce at Florence we can understand that Ghiberti had seen justly.

Ghiberti feels a special enthusiasm for Ambrogio Lorenzetti: "most noble composer, most perfect master, a man of great talent, a most noble draughtsman, very expert in the theoretics of the said art." He abandons himself to admiration of the dramatic effects obtained by Ambrogio: figures "with soft hair dripping with sweat and with such anguish and such inquietude;" "the sky and the earth seem perilous, everything around appears to cover itself with great tremors," and so on. When he describes the reliefs that he himself, Ghiberti, executed for the doors of the Baptistery at Florence he occupies himself only with the representation. He is enthusiastic about art, thus, with the eye of the ingenuous artist, who, like the common man, takes painting for a natural object, and becomes impassioned, rejoices and suffers. So our children comport themselves when confronted with the heroes of novels. But see him free himself from this ingenuous commonness when he compares Ambrogio Lorenzetti and Simone Martini. "Master Simone was a most noble painter and very famous. The Sienese painters hold that he was the best; to me Ambrogio Lorenzetti seems much better and more gifted than any of the others." Naturally Lorenzo Ghiberti, in spite of his love of line, was always a Florentine, and he was a sculptor; therefore he could not abstract from the artistic elements the plastic qualities which made Ambrogio Lorenzetti a more concrete and solid painter than Simone Martini. Not of his opinion were the Sienese painters: a precious gleam of light that allows us to perceive at Siena a critical tradition well distinct from the Florentine, centralising its own admiration in the leadership of Simone Martini, just as the Florentine tradition gathered itself round the name of Giotto.

If the thought of Ghiberti may be regarded as still that of the transition from the Middle Ages to the Renaissance, that of Leon Battista Alberti expresses to perfection the ideals of the Renaissance itself. Not that the mediaeval religiosity and philosophy are dead in him, but rather that his explicit ideal is "to put the dictates of Christian wisdom into accord with those of pagan doctrine." What constitutes the point of the difference is the new conception of man, who is no longer a subsidiary focus, but stands in the middle of the universe; and has no need to go outside the circle of his activity to acquire knowledge of the real, because he comprehends everything in himself, like a little world that reflects the greater world. Between the religiosity of the Middle Ages and that of the Renaissance there is the same difference as between the denial and the affirmation of humanity. Religion of transcendence and religion of immanence are the two formulas which symbolise these two spiritual attitudes; to which it must be added that immanence, by its expansive power, surrounds itself with a halo of mystical transcendency. Art participates fully in the mode of spiritual life; and if already in preceding writers from Dante onwards it is possible to trace elements of this movement, it is in Alberti, among the writers on art, that for the first time the new condition of the mind fully appears.

His mental form and his motive in writing are both new. Born of a family of Florentine exiles, he came back to Florence a mature man. As a humanist he had learned at Bologna that the Greeks and Romans had had great artists; and he returns to his country to perceive that, through Brunelleschi, Donatello and Masaccio, a new art has come out there, which can be compared with that of antiquity. He is painter and architect, but above all philosopher; and eight years later, in 1436, he writes the treatise on painting which is intended to be the theory of the new Florentine art. He wishes to make painting arise from roots within nature. "We do not, like Pliny, recite history, but build anew an art of painting." Anti-historical in purpose, nevertheless he writes and makes history, since limited by the taste of his time, his principles are valid not of art in general, but only of the Florentine art contemporary with him. So strong is his influence that the Florentine painters adhere to his ideas until toward the end of the fifteenth century.

Painting, he says, is the section of the visual cone; that is to say, painting is a perspective solution of reality. Nothing could be more abstract than this. But it is necessary to remember all the sentimental value which science had assumed in the fifteenth century to understand how Alberti could consider perspective vision as a painter and not as a mathematician. He presupposes in the painter the Idea, of Plotinian origin; and the Idea will be executed with the hand. But that Idea is no longer transcendent, it is the mathematical knowledge of man. The origin of art is no longer legendary, as in antiquity or the Middle Ages; it is to be looked for in a mode of vision which renews itself every time that art is created; the origin of art coincides therefore in history and in the psychology of the artist, and has become the eternal now. To the same origin are referred not only painting but also sculpture and architecture: we are dealing with a principle of figurative style. Vision is substituted for technique. The advantage of such a conception is in the elimination of the technical receipt-book, in the contact between scientific intelligence and art. The disadvantage is in the projection into art of that scientific rationalism that should be reserved only for criticism. Alberti, however, does not exclude the mystical attainment of God through beautiful things, which speak to us of God, better than utilitarian things. And even in his pure sensibility he finds the tempering of his intellectual severity. "Beautiful are the planes that have the surfaces united in such a way that the lights and shades are agreeable and soft without any hardness of contour." Here is the contemplation of a beauty that has no mathematical reason, that excites ecstasy. And even his love of relief, of surfaces turning round, of the column and the sphere, is the love of a physical beauty which transcends the interest of natural truth. He loves light and fresh colours, he loves them so much that he wishes to abstain from them, as from a temptation. He rejects the gold that Cennini loved. Two reasons lead him to that. The disdain of materials already manifested by Petrarch has made its way: preferable to gold is the colour which imitates gold, which is the work of man and therefore intellectual. But the stronger reason is light and shade; gold does not accord with light and shade, with its reflections the light and shade become arbitrary, and without light and shade one cannot obtain the relief necessary to perspective vision. So the gold background disappears from painting: it was a delightful absurdity, well adapted to the ultra-worldly exaltation of the mediaeval fancy. But when painting accepts the limits of this our terrestrial world, the blue of the sky or the grey of a wall must chase away the background of gold.

Up to this point, the physical contemplation. Alberti interests himself also in moral expression for the sake of conformity, of the coherence of the representation. "The members of the dead are dead up to the nails." To the movements of bodies he adapts the expression of the movements of the mind. But he would avoid excesses, for the sake of dignity, and above all for the sake of loveliness, of grace. The interpretation of reality is not enough: there must be the ideal beauty necessary to contemplation. But compositions must not be crowded, for otherwise the plastic value of each figure would be lost. It is necessary to avoid excess of ornament, which is contrary to the essence of beauty. He imagines the parts of the picture consistently with his perspective principle. No longer suffice the drawing and colour which Cennini had indicated. There must be the circumscribed delimitation of zones, composition on the surfaces of the zones circumscribed, distribution of light and shade on the colours and forms in the zone. Here is the description of a Florentine painting of the fifteenth century, in which each zone is beautiful in itself, and is coördinated with the others in perspective vision, in which colour is subordinated to light and shade in order to define plastic form.

From the desire for plastic form arise other principles: the outline must be very delicate, like that of Parrhasios already defined by Pliny; the contour must be the "margin of the surface" and not a fissure; it is necessary to draw the nude figure before painting clothes upon it, and to define the bones and muscles before covering them with flesh. The perfection of plastic form is therefore that of man; the perspective space in which the human figure inserts itself is more properly a perspective void. But the positive elements of the representation must be those of man; he would even have the painter personify the wind in the figure of Zephyr, so as to justify the movements of the draperies. In such a manner was realised that ideal by which the whole cosmos was absorbed in man.

When, many years after the book on painting, Alberti wrote, in 1452, the treatise on architecture, the creative fervour of a new art was very much weakened, and the doctrine derived from Vitruvius and other texts played a great part instead of the direct study of the Florentine architecture of the fifteenth century. Nevertheless, perspective vision is demanded as the ordering of vaults and columns; and there appears a preference for circular planes which respond better to the plastic value of the edifices. But his critical masterpiece remains the treatise on painting, which was closer to the art of his time.

With it, then, Alberti realised in criticism the new conception of man, the new scientific theory of art, the new plastic ideal: it may therefore be regarded as the Magna Charta of the Italian Renaissance.

The passage from the fifteenth to the sixteenth century is distinguished in art by the end of the primitives and the appearance of a group of masters — Leonardo, Raphael, Michelangelo, Titian — who for a long time were regarded as the maturity and perfection of art. The artist then dominates not only technique but also the physical and moral knowledge of nature in a more complete manner than in the preceding century. But precisely in that moment of victory comes a crisis. Because the artist knows nature better, he has no longer the former confidence in the omnipotence of man (man is no longer the centre of the universe), and between man and nature appears an antithesis that is felt sometimes in a dramatic manner. Because faith in God is no longer vital, and scientific knowledge is made more certain, there begin to be felt the limitations of science and the doubt whether art and science lead to God. Because art no longer needs to conquer science, and is no longer a way to science as it was in the fifteenth century, but rather adopts the science acquired as an instrument, the need appears to recognise the nature of art in something that is not scientific; and the knowledge of a difference between art and science dawns. From that crisis, from those doubts, from those intuitions is born an ensemble of ideas on art, on artists and works of art, that was the essential element in the criticism of the seventeenth and eighteenth centuries, and is not even forgotten to-day.

The fifteenth century had not yet drawn to an end, and Leonardo da Vinci had already written the main part of his treatise, which is the fundamental program of sixteenth century art. "Painting," says Leonardo, "is not only a science, it is even a divinity, because it transforms the painter's mind into something similar to the mind of God." This is neo-Platonism, but with a new accent, because the painter, almost God, is opposed to the scientist who is simply man. Leonardo insists on the difference: "Science considers the quantity whilst art considers the quality of things. The artistic truth is the one which man conceives at the first step. The divine mind, the quality of things, the primal truth: these are characters which even to-day we consider proper to art. But the difference between art and science was not yet clear, and therefore Leonardo considered the primal truth of art as the preparation for the truth of science. "Painting is the origin of all arts and crafts, is also the source of all science." This is an autobiographical confession: all his life, indeed, Leonardo used his art, his drawing, in order to know anatomy, perspective and all the mechanical sciences that then were known.

In order that the painter may be worthy to originate all arts and sciences he must be universal. The knowledge of the human form is no longer sufficient. The painter must be clever enough to represent all appearances of nature, even fogs, clouds, rains, dust, smoke, in their different densities, the transparence of water, and the stars in the sky.

For such a purpose plastic form, which Alberti had theorised, was no longer sufficient. Leonardo's perspective is no longer a perspective of lines; he distinguishes three kinds of perspective: of lines, of colours and of remoteness. In the relation between the figure and its background, plastic form requires light on the figure and darkness on the background. But for Leonardo the relation is more complex: "When we look at an object which is darker than atmosphere, we see it becoming lighter as its distance increases; on the contrary if the object is lighter than atmosphere, it becomes darker as its distance increases." Whence he derived the vision of a dark figure on a luminous sky, or the admission of a landscape as a work of art in itself.

Looking at nature, Leonardo observes that shades are not black, as Alberti thought, but blue. The reader may remember that in the nineteenth century the question of coloured shades arose again, and that Delacroix discovered again the blue shades, without knowing Leonardo's critical experience. Leonardo knew that red and yellow have their splendour in light, but blue and green have their greatest values in shade. In short, Leonardo discovered the degree of luminosity in colours which the Greeks named *tonon*, the Italians *tono*, and Frenchmen colour values. Leonardo goes further, and prefers a rough surface in painting to a smooth one: that is to say, he wants touch in painting in order to paint as a colourist. Observe that with this idea he goes beyond his own painting, which has smooth surfaces, and foresees that of the late Venetians of the sixteenth century, or of the Flemings and Dutchmen of the seventeenth century.

But though he sees in nature the pictorial art of the future, he belongs to the Florentine tradition of the fifteenth century, and therefore he does not renounce plastic form. Though he sees very well the effects of tone in nature, he does not love colour. Imagine, then, a pictorial style which comprehends at the same time plastic form and atmosphere, which continues to assign the first place to the human figure, but wishes to see it in atmosphere: so Leonardo's manner realises the vision not only of an element — man — but of the universe of nature. What is it that must unite man and surrounding nature, that must fill the perspective void and envelop the figures? It is *shade*. "The essential parts of painting are quality, quantity, place and figure. Quality is shade, and all degrees of shade. Quantity is the size of shades, and the relation of size among them. Place means the composition of shades with regard to figures. Figure is the geometrical form of shade." This has the appearance of constructing from Aristotelian categories, to render objective his definition of painting, but in fact Leonardo expresses only his love of shade, upon which he insists many times. "Towards evening, passing along the streets, look at the faces of men and women when the weather is bad; what marvellous grace and sweetness is in them ... The sweetest beauty derives from evening, because a strong light is hard, a strong darkness is confused; a subdued light is the best." So Leonardo, as a poet and a theorist, thinks that beauty is a graduation of shades. It was sufficient to substitute for the door of a house in the evening a grotto among rocks, and to give the shade a delicate sense of mystery, and his masterpiece "The Virgin of the Rocks" was created.

The conception of shade, as the artistic quality of every form, is completed by the sense of the necessity for movement. Leonardo's idea that movement is the source of all life is a scientific explanation of nature and at the same time a statement of an artistic purpose. "As the bow's power is the effect of the drawing of its string, so man's power depends upon his movement."

The true movement in painting was realised by the colourists; it is enough to recall Tintoretto. All the colourists adopted individual lights. But Leonardo states that light must be *universal*, in order to obtain the grace of graduation, whilst limited lights produce dark shades. This was also a last homage to the form of the Florentine tradition.

But meanwhile he also opposes the Florentine tradition of loving solid form. Contour, in his opinion, must have a mathematical nature; that is to say, it must be so unreal as to become invisible. It is the Greek principle of which we have spoken already, but Leonardo carries it to extreme conclusions. Figure and background must be confused together in their limits, without any contrast. Leonardo wants delicate sensations, and his images must appear nebulous. Since the sixteenth century, art writers have been aware that Leonardo liberated painting from the hardness of style which depended upon precise contours. But to obtain a plastic form it is necessary to circumscribe it with a quite precise contour. A nebulous contour weakens form, and reduces it to a mass of atmosphere instead of to a solid body.

The great advantage of Leonardo's principles is the emphasis upon the necessity for synthesis, obtained by reducing all elements to shade. Technique also responds to the new synthesis. Leonardo states that a painter must sketch the whole figure first, and only afterwards may he complete the different parts. The necessity for sketching was unknown before him, when the parts of a painting followed the law of coördination. For Leonardo all parts were obliged to subject themselves to that first sketch, which was limited to the effects of shades.

Leonardo is the unique case of a great painter, and at the same time a bold thinker, who under the pretext of painting in general, has concentrated his thought upon the paintings he made himself, or prepared for the future. He presents the last development of the pictorial style as a need to conquer the whole of reality, but he expresses too, in words, his love for a moment of vision which allowed him to respect the Florentine tradition of form. At the same time he maintains and modifies the tradition, because he puts the form into relation with the atmosphere that envelops it, creating in the half-tone a principle of colour without colours. This conscious refuge in the shade answers to the desire to keep his life as an artist distinct from that science which, as the years went on, took ever a stronger hold upon his mind.

Michelangelo did not write a treatise on art, but sporadically expressed ideas on the subject; and the Portuguese, Francisco de Hollanda, collected his sayings. Compared with Leonardo's, the ideas of Michelangelo are those of a reactionary, for whom the sole artistic ideal is the plastic form of the fifteenth century Florentine tradition. Observe that this does not depend upon the fact that Michelangelo was before everything a sculptor. Donatello, a sculptor, realised a pictorial vision better than any Florentine painter of his time. And Michelangelo himself, in his sculpture, realised a form which is quite other than purely plastic, so that the contrast between his ideas and his way of feeling is not extraneous to the great drama of his personality as an artist, the drama of the surface left in the rough, the surface which appears unfinished.

Michelangelo writes: "I do say that painting must be good when it goes toward relief, and relief must be considered bad when it goes toward painting. Therefore, sculpture is the guide of painting; the former is the sun and the latter is the moon." Leonardo had stated that painting is far superior to sculpture, that a bronze relief containing perspective has a higher value than a marble statue. And Michelangelo opposes: "I consider the marble sculpture as the true sculpture, because the bronze relief is very similar to painting. And although both sculpture and painting derive from human intelligence, he who wrote that painting is higher than sculpture was ignorant as a maid servant." This is a direct allusion to Leonardo.

I have already referred to Leonardo's interest in landscapes, and to his aim of representing in painting fogs and clouds, waters and distant mountains. Now consider Michelangelo's judgment, mentioned by Francisco de Hollanda: "Flemish painting requires only the deceiving of eyes. It consists in ornaments, in old houses, in green meadows, with some trees, bridges and rivers. Flemish painters call all this a landscape, and they put into it some sporadic figures. Some people like such a thing. But it has neither reason nor art, neither symmetry nor proportion, neither intelligence nor choice, in short, neither solidity nor energy." All this is very clear. But when one thinks of all the importance in modern art of that which Michelangelo condemned, and of the decadence of Florentine taste in the second half of the sixteenth century, precisely from following the rigid principles of Michelangelo, one perceives how prophetic was the thought of Leonardo.

The ideas of Leonardo were known in the sixteenth century to a very restricted circle of persons, and it was not his ideas that accompanied the expansion of Italian art throughout Europe. Then the Italians were greatly admired for having brought proportions and perspective laws into art. Geoffroy Tory said that the Italians were the most perfect painters and sculptors in Christianity, because they had always the compass and the rule in hand. The ideas of Alberti then prevailed, and the ideas of other theorists of the fifteenth century who were always departing further from the consideration of art in homage to mathematical science: Francesco di Giorgio Martini and Piero della Francesca. The ideas of the latter were popularised by Luca Pacioli, in his treatise on "divine proportion," which had great renown. To this current attached themselves Jean Pélerin Le Viateur, author of "Artificial Perspective," published in 1505, and Albert Dürer. In his treatise on proportions, Dürer seeks to measure everything, with a precision and minuteness never used before, in order to give the rule of art according to Italian principles. He considers art as theory, in opposition to practice; and is convinced of the necessity of giving to art a mathematical law, in contrast to the German tradition of pure practice. But when he has arrived at the extreme conclusion of this desire of rational laws for art, he perceives that measurements are not enough, and that it is necessary for the artist to receive from God the gift to do in a day with the pen a better thing than another, with all the measurements, could do in a year.

"And if someone would wish to know what is beauty in images, perhaps one would answer that which is proved by the judgment of men, to which the others would not concede, and this is also my opinion, if the judgment is that of ignorant men. Now what can determine the cognition which must be in him who should be able to judge this well?" Nobody can find a perfection of beauty than which cannot be found one more perfect. Only the divine mind knows absolute perfection. Therefore the task that Dürer sets himself is only to prepare the mind, to give with proportions a way of drawing near to beauty. Then each one must do for himself. And if anyone should say that it is useless to tire oneself with science, if one cannot arrive at perfection, Dürer replies that it is necessary to seek the good even if one does not arrive at the best.

For scepticism with regard to absolute beauty Dürer is indebted to his consciousness as an artist who loves to paint figures of negroes and peasants; and from that scepticism he deduces a certain independence of the creative subject from the object represented, so that this is not the measure of the value of the work of art. In short, Dürer fathoms, with the impetus of his moral rigour, that crisis in the faith in objective beauty and human perfection, which was the faith of Alberti.

The artistic ideas of Leonardo were not continued directly, at least not in Florence, where the ideas of Michelangelo prevailed. Nevertheless an ideal continuation of them, or rather a development of Leonardo's presentiments on the future of painting, is found in Venice, in the writings of Pietro Aretino, Paolo Pino and Ludovico Dolce. From an aesthetic point of view their writings do not seem important; they do not further the theory of art beyond that of Alberti or Leonardo. But this is not the only time in the history of art criticism that an interesting effect results from a theory renounced, from the recovery of contact with the direct intuition of art. Remember the scientific foundation assigned to painting by Alberti: this was amplified by Leonardo, but its nature was not changed. It was a way without issue. To open it and go further it was necessary to formulate the theory of the irrational nature of art; that is to say, it was necessary to have a philosophical conception different from that of the sixteenth century. But he who felt the inconvenience of the rational conception, and had not the power to affirm an irrational conception, what was he to do? Occupy himself as little as possible with the rational conception and abandon himself to intuition. Of the two constituent elements of art criticism, the pragmatic and the cultural, the pragmatic prevailed at Venice in the sixteenth century. Toward the middle of the century the world perceived that there had emerged at Venice a kind of painting that obeyed different motives from those pursued in Florence and Rome, which nevertheless bespoke an important taste.

Venetian humanism is very ingenuous and primitive, if compared with the Florentine. The University of Padua continued to teach Aristotelian and Arabic philosophy, when for many years Florence had made neo-Platonism prevail everywhere. Florence produced painters and philosophers, sculptors and scientists; Venice, in contrast, besides great painters, produced only merchants, politicians and musicians. In such conditions how could a new Venetian criticism arise? The great Venetian painters could not write criticism; they had not the necessary culture for it. Aretino and Dolce were not artists at all, and Pino was only a third-rate artist. Aretino also acquired his artistic education in Rome, in contact with Raphael and Michelangelo. The true reason for his writing on Venetian painting was only the admiration he felt for some Venetian painters, because as a man of letters, he thought that he followed a similar taste. He stated the superiority of his prose, all vivacity and energy, to the very large and correct but monotonous prose of the humanists. In the same way he believed in the superiority of Titian's painting, free and realistic, to the pedantic drawing of the advocates of form. His ideas on art were sporadically expressed in his letters, like the modern articles in a daily paper, without any system.

Two years after Aretino's death Dolce published a "Dialogue on Painting" (1557), which he dedicated to Aretino; and, though Dolce had not such good taste as Aretino, he was compelled by the systematic form of his treatise to deduce some interesting conclusions from the premises of his master.

Nine years before, in 1548, Paolo Pino had published his "Dialogue on Painting." His culture and his intelligence are very limited, but his words are an echo of the discussions about art by Venetian painters. When we begin to read Pino's treatise we meet, together with the protagonist, some beautiful women; and the dialogue seems to be written in order to suggest how to choose the most beautiful among beautiful women. Venetians discussed art, not to discover a scientific truth, but to define sensuousness. Nor must we forget that the great Venetian painting of the sixteenth century began with the sleeping nude Venus by Giorgione.

The first consequence of such a condition of mind was a revolt against order. Florentine painting arose as a perspective order against the chromatic chaos of the Middle Ages. In Venice Dolce states that one begins to paint when he goes beyond order, and that variety imitated from nature must appear, not studied and willed, but produced by chance.

Pino raises exception even to proportion. He states that it is very rare for a painter to be able to follow proportions in a figure because every figure must be painted in movement, and movement destroys every abstract proportion.

For Michelangelo it was a real tragedy to leave some of his works unfinished. But in Venice people knew that it is necessary to avoid finishing too completely: finishing is the destruction of vivacity in painting. Aretino states that promptitude is always successful and he admires the promptitude of Tintoretto. Tintoretto paints more rapidly than other painters because he conceives an effect of light and shade in a more vivacious and energetic manner. Leonardo wrote that sketching is necessary to obtain synthesis. Aretino goes much farther: sketching is the favourite kind of painting; it is a reaction of freedom from the pedantry of grammarian painters.

Dolce and Pino agree in saying that the three principal elements of painting are invention, drawing and colouring. Invention is the art of composing lyrical or historical poems in painting, as a matter of content and not of vision. Dolce knows that the expression of feeling in painting is something additional, which must be produced by the imagination of the public. But he does not draw from this observation the necessary conclusion.

The experience of colouring was as much refined in Venetian criticism as it was lacking in Florentine. We know that, after being reduced to light and shade, colouring was limited to shade only. Dolce, on the contrary states that relief is a matter of colouring. In consequence relief is subordinated to colouring, and not colouring to relief. This is the strongest opposition of the Venetian vision against the Florentine.

"When a painter is able to reproduce the true colour of flesh and the true material of everything his paintings are alive and appear to possess all the elements of life but breath. The principal part of colouring is the contrast of light and shade. And there is a medium which enables the two elements to agree, in order to give the round effect to figures and their right places, near or far. Some people paint flesh so coloured and so hard that it seems of porphyry; its shades are too dark and sometimes it finishes in pure black. Some artists paint flesh too white, some others too red. I prefer a colouring of flesh quite brown, rather than too white. Above all no one must think that colouring consists in the choice of beautiful colours, like fine red, or blues, or greens. I believe that a certain neglect is necessary, because neither colouring must be too charming nor figures too completely finished: in every part one must see a gentle firmness. The greatest danger is to be too diligent."

It seems, indeed, that not Dolce, but Titian himself expresses Dolce's theory of colour, which is complex and refined, has its roots in the senses, but becomes an organism of a complete pictorial world, even to that fear of too much diligence which would have scandalised Dürer or Alberti, but which is nevertheless a sign of a detachment of the artist from the craftsman, of a freer consciousness of his own spiritual rights. Single colours have disappeared, forms have the appearance of aerial masses, light and shade are liberated from white and black, movement has become cosmic, because even a sitting figure is enveloped in moving lights.

All this announces that the crisis in Florentine humanism is on the way to its solution. The pictorial imagination of man is no longer isolated from the universe. The way has been found to fuse the imagination of man with those things which surround him and that way is called light and shade. Venetian painting realised this, and Venetian criticism had the merit of deriving it from the painting of its contemporaries. But to theorise, to interpret critically Venetian painting, it would have been necessary to have not only the lively senses of Aretino, but also the knowledge of how to reason like Alberti or Leonardo. And Venetian criticism was not capable of that. Pino considers that the perfection of art is the fusion of the drawing of Michelangelo and the colouring of Titian. For the first time eclectic theory appears in Pino's book. This was a sign of the decay of that individuality, which had appeared spontaneously in Cennino Cennini's refusal of eclecticism. The disappearance of individuality brought with it the decadence of art.

The "Lives" of artists, which in the fifteenth century we have seen already treated by Ghiberti, continue. Manetti writes a life of Brunelleschi, and in order to exalt his hero, outlines a history of architecture to indicate how that art was revived after the mediaeval barbarism. At the beginning of the sixteenth century the desire to write Lives of artists was increased. In Florence we know three essays of the kind; and elsewhere the same desire arose — in Marcantonio Michiel in Venice and in Pietro Summonte in Naples. But the work which overshadows all the others is the "Lives of Painters, Sculptors and Architects" by Giorgio Vasari (1550 and 1568). Vasari had prefaced it with his treatise on art, which is much more technical than that of Alberti, and indicates that, in Vasari, the desire to relate the biography of artists to the theory of art is in quite different proportions. Thus he affirms explicitly that in the "Lives," people will learn the perfection and the imperfection of works of art and the difference in the manner of artists. But what nobody had done before him, not even in antiquity, was to develop enormously the anecdotes of the lives of artists and the description of their works, so giving proof of a new historical interest. The history of Vasari also connects itself with the pragmatic type of Renaissance histories; that is to say, the practical force of individuals, without any connection with their ideal, as arbitrary agents, of whom the interpretation could only be psychological. Hence it happens that the artistic personality, as a synthesis of the perfection of art and of the single individuality, is understood by Vasari only in rare cases, when his critical intuition goes beyond his theoretical concepts. The concept of the imitation of nature, which, according to tradition, he sometimes intends as an operation parallel to nature, is accompanied therefore with the conception of artifice capable of all arts and sciences; which may be allowed to have freedom, arbitrariness, caprices; which has the right of artistic fury, but which, nevertheless, has always the limits of artifice. "Greatness of art in one is born of diligence, in another of study, in this one of imitation, in that other of knowledge of the sciences": too many origins, and precisely that which was wanting was the only authentic one — creative imagination. It is true that, beyond the imitation of nature, Vasari admits that one may arrive at art by means of the imitation of manners, in this contradicting the preceding tradition of Leonardo, for example, who excluded the imitation of masters and admitted as good only the imitation of nature. This, which is therefore the novelty of the Vasarian theory, is explained by his position in the world of art.

As is well known, Vasari was not only a writer; he was also, and believed himself to be above all, a painter and an architect. A pupil of Michelangelo, he is one of the many Florentine mannerists of the sixteenth century who learned the manner — that is to say, the external appearance of the style of Michel-

angelo and Raphael; and he repeated them many times hastily
without ever arriving at the expression of an imaginative personality. Their boast was design, father of the arts, which
rarely, however, was intuitive, as a value of plastic form, and
often signified invention; that is to say, the ability to compose
scenes with many figures, with many ornaments, with great
variety of everything, but with nothing felt. Being a Michelangelesque mannerist influenced Vasari's historical conception
even more than his theory. He made of Michelangelo his hero,
like the Prince of Machiavelli, and by the hero who represented
the perfection of art he measured all other artists. Just as Xenocrates had imagined progress up to Lysippos and Apelles so
Vasari imagines it up to Michelangelo and Raphael.

He distinguishes three ages, which correspond to the fourteenth, fifteenth and sixteenth centuries. In the first of the three
ages art was very far from perfection. And it deserved some
but not much praise because of its mistakes. In the second age
art improved from many points of view. Above all, it began to
know the rule and the order of architecture, because people
learned to acknowledge the proportions of ancient works, and
to represent very straight bodies with their perfect coherence
of limbs. Besides this, the second age improved its style, by the
custom of reproducing selected forms admitted as the most
beautiful, and of giving coherence to the various elements of
beauty, even if inspired by different models. The defects of the
second age were a too strict conformity to science, without
freedom of movement, an insufficient variety and abundance
of invention, the lack of the gift of grace joined to variety, and
of a lovable natural facility. All that the second age lacked, the
third attained. "By an exact rule, by a better order, by a right
proportion, by a perfect design, by a divine grace, by the variety of inventions, by the profoundness of art, the painted and

sculptured figures of the third age have attained perfection and true expression."

It is evident, then, that the ideal of Vasari as an artist is the standard of his judgments even on painters who had an ideal different from his; and therefore the sporadic but happy intuitions that Ghiberti had had of the absolute greatness of some masters of the fourteenth century were annulled. For example, Vasari reproves Giotto for having drawn eyes not round, but almond-shaped. This criticism depends not only on a naturalistic prejudice but also on an aesthetic prejudice in favour of the perfection of the sphere, according in the classical tradition. But precisely by these combined prejudices the marvellous intuition of Witelo was cancelled. Vasari, then, contributed to the ignoring of the debt that Renaissance art owed to the art of the Middle Ages, and to the imposition for two centuries of the idea that only in the sixteenth century had the perfection of art arrived.

The positive value of the criticism of Vasari consists in some happy intuitions that he had, above all on the art that he believed to be perfection attained. When he speaks of Michelangelo his standards of judgment no longer suffice him, and he turns to God. It is God who has sent Michelangelo on earth after He has seen in vain all the powers of craftsmen to achieve perfection; and He has furnished him with perfection in the design of painting and sculpture, in ornament and the practice of architecture, not to speak of moral philosophy and poetry. Such perfection Michelangelo has shown in the principal part of art; in the human figure, especially nude, with his grand manner, the proportion perfect, the movement of the attitudes, the expression of the passions. "And attending to this single end he has left aside the charm of colour, the caprices and the new fancies of certain details and delicacies which by many other painters are not entirely neglected, perhaps not without reason. Not sufficiently founded in drawing, these other painters have sought variety of tints and shades of colour, with various oddities and new inventions, and, in short, with this other way have made themselves a place among the leading masters." In the edition of 1550 Vasari had expressed only his veneration for Michelangelo; in 1568 he adds reservations through the influence of Aretino. Well, it is precisely these reservations which begin to make the Vasarian discourse, criticism. Criticism is limiting and the divinity of Michelangelo did not allow Vasari to see its limits. On the other hand, when he becomes aware that there is something more in the world of art than the human figure, a first limitation is made, and when he admits that one way to art is also afforded by variety in tints and shades of colour, Vasari recognises in the Venetian taste the right to live beside that of Michelangelo. No doubt the elements of critical definition are still material, but they have their value, and they are the best, in fact, that the Renaissance has given us.

Even more important is his judgment on Raphael. In 1550 Vasari regards the development of Raphael's art as a continuous progress, achieving perfection in his latest works, in which the imitation of Michelangelo is most pronounced. In 1568, on the other hand, he opposes the personalities of Raphael and Michelangelo, determining the limits of each. Raphael then makes him see that painting consists not only in drawing the nude; that he could attain a perfection of his own in invention, in perspective, in drapery, in "making alive and beautiful the heads of women and cherubs" and in portraits. "These things, I say, Raphael considered, and not being able to approach Michelangelo in that part of the nude, he resolved in these other parts to emulate and perhaps surpass him." From that is born a happy conclusion; Vasari sees that in the latest works, when

Raphael had assimilated Michelangelesque drawing, he "lost part of that good name which he had acquired." Now this judgment, which has been confirmed in modern criticism, surmounts the limits of Renaissance criticism in that it shows a knowledge of the artistic personality as such. It is evident in this instance that the criticism of Vasari is superior to the concepts that he could formulate. From the particular judgment Vasari ascends to the general precept: "Each one should content himself to do willingly those things to which he feels himself inclined by natural instinct, and not wish to put his hand, in emulation, to that which does not come to him by nature, so as not to fatigue himself in vain, and often with shame and injury." It is a precept in full accord with that which Aretino had written as far back as 1537: "Those painters, stupefied in gazing at the chapel of Michelangelo...wishing to imitate the greatness of his execution, in forcing themselves to make the majestic figures, movement and spirit, forgetting the firsthand knowledge, not only do not enter into his manner but also forget their own." Here is the condemnation of the Michelangelesque mannerism, and that Vasari should have accepted it is proof of the superiority of his criticism to his art.

To this height he is arrived, both under influence of Aretino, and because the problem of the two personalities of Michelangelo and Raphael in their different perfections stood in his heart as the foundation of his taste. But when he finds himself confronted with tastes more distant from his own, though contemporary, like those of Correggio, Giorgione or Titian, he is drawn to admire details but cannot understand the ensemble. He is disconcerted before Correggio because he perceives his greatness without being able to give reason for it; he is disconcerted before the frescoes of Giorgione because he cannot determine the subject, and before the latest productions of Titian because, on account of the large and broken touches, he can only see it well at a distance. When, in defect of understanding, he grasps at the principle of Florentine drawing and the imitation of the antique, he praises its benefits and bewails those who have not benefited by them. That is to say, his individual taste and also his personal interest veil his understanding.

Architectural criticism did not make during the sixteenth century that notable progress which the criticism of painting made through the work of Leonardo, Aretino and Vasari. Four treatises on architecture had a great success and numerous editions — those of Serlio, Vignola, Palladio and Scamozzi; but, born in the study of Vitruvius and the ancient monuments, they were unable to formulate the artistic problems of the architecture of their time; and are rather the mirror of practical and social needs. More important than the others is that of Serlio, who, though proposing to remain faithful to the laws of antiquity, through lack of culture, ingenuously exposes his own taste. He loves to insert the rustic order in the classical orders, in such a way as to spoil their internal logic; he considers the voids, not as an integration of depths, but as a value of atmospheric mass; he sees the distribution of the architectural elements more under the aspect of juxtaposition of colours than as relation of plastic forms. When he goes into France, more free from the classical severity of the Italians, he abandons himself to the caprice of variety, and tries to define the new combinations of architectural elements with abstract psychological categories: the hard, the soft, the delicate, the crude. That is to say, his fragmentary sensibility does not arrive at a rational theory of the sensibility itself; and therefore his criticism is in some respects parallel to the Venetian criticism of painting; like it, well directed as a tendency, but incapable of a theoretical formulation.

That Palladio was not the purely classical architect that tradition tells us, is perceived in the neo-classical criticism of Milizia and Goethe. But Palladio himself had no knowledge of the transformation made by him, with a Venetian accent, of classical architecture. Therefore, when one reads his treatise one finds in it only the ideas of Vitruvius, Alberti and Vasari. Even Palladio has a hint of architectural history. To him the restoration of good and beautiful architecture is not the work of Brunelleschi, as Manetti had believed, but of Bramante; and therefore the work of Bramante is classified as ancient architecture.

It has been said acutely that the true critics of the art of the Renaissance were the mannerists. And, indeed, by defect of natural impulse in art, they chose from the works of the masters most appreciated those elements that they believed to be art. Evidently they were mistaken as artists and as critics, because the chosen elements were all rather symbols of art than art itself; however, their attitude was a critical attitude, and therefore the treatises on art of the mannerists have a greater importance than their painting.

That which had the greatest fortune, translated into English and French, was the "Treatise on the Art of Painting" (1584) of Gian Paolo Lomazzo. He is a Lombard mannerist painter who, becoming blind, passed from the practice to the theory of his art. His taste is based upon that of Leonardo integrated with that of Michelangelo and Raphael. He appreciates the "chromatic alchemy" of Titian and of the Venetians in general, but excludes them from the model painters. He is proud of the Lombard tradition, and is moderately well acquainted with Flemish and German art. He is a mannerist painter on guard against mannerism. He formulates a program of eclecticism but indicates its dangers. His thought oscillates between empirical observation and the abstract concept. Therefore, according to him, art is the imitation of nature and the expression of ideas. He feels neither the value of form in itself, nor of colour in itself, and seeks the essential medium in movement-light, remodelling his ideas, therefore, on Leonardo. The appreciation of movement-light serves Lomazzo to understand northern painting (Correggio and Titian) better than Vasari, but not enough to make of it a unified single principle of appreciation. Therefore he prepares ideally the Carracci and not Caravaggio.

The treatise consists of three parts: theory, practice and iconography. This last is a literary exemplification of the subjects dealt with in painting. The theoretical part sets out to fix the science of pictorial possibilities, and quotes the "discoveries" that the various ancient and modern painters have made in art. The practical part indicates the preferences in the taste of Lomazzo.

Art is valid for that which it signifies, that is to say, by the truth contained; but the truth itself may be overcome by ornament, which is understood in the sense of caprice. Proportion and perspective constitute the grammar of painting, but it is typical of mannerism that the geometrical abstractions are assumed as typical entities, instead of as those modes of interpreting reality which Alberti had indicated. Movement and light are the culmination of painting. In movement is resolved the psychological expression of the object represented according to the creative impulse of the craftsman. Good lights can save even bad drawing (this is perhaps the most acute intuition of the art in formation at his time.) For light Lomazzo renews the mystical exaltation of the mediaeval tradition: light is God. Movement gives the psychological relief as light gives the physical relief. Colour depends upon the other parts of painting and completes the realistic illusion. Like the proportions, the movements and the lights, the passions are also considered abstractly, so that he outlines a treatise on the passions.

All this is said with frequent references to this or that artist, without Lomazzo perceiving however, the artistic personality existing behind the abstract figurative or psychological elements of which he speaks. The greatest importance of the work of Lomazzo is precisely in its having systematised the elements of abstract form. Lomazzo aspires to philosophical speculation and distinguishes art from the theory of art. Alberti and Leonardo give the rules for artists to direct them in their work; Lomazzo tries to legitimise what the artists have made. Therefore the abstract elements of form and colour are no longer among the technical instruments of work for artists, but among the schemes of interpretation for critics. We may therefore admit that Lomazzo seems to be a precursor of the modern German science of art, with the caution that the figurative schemes, corresponding to the artistic ideal of Lomazzo, gave him no knowledge of their limits with respect to art.

This was, however, the maximum result of Italian mannerism of the sixteenth century.

CHAPTER V
The Baroque Period

A GENERAL glance over the conditions of art in the seventeenth century reveals to us a wide-spread reaction to Italian mannerism which had reached all countries, a reaction which led to an exceptional flourishing of art.

Not to speak of minor figures, there were Caravaggio in Italy, Rubens and Van Dyck in Flanders, Rembrandt, Franz Hals, Ver Meer and many others in Holland, El Greco and Velazquez in Spain, who created not only a series of masterpieces but also a new pictorial civilisation. Sculptors and architects, in spite of their immense and sometimes important production, did not reach the exceptional artistic level of the painters just mentioned. These did not renounce the very rich artistic experience of the sixteenth century even when they had clear consciousness of opposition to it, as in the case of Caravaggio. But they profited by that experience in a different way from the mannerists: instead of Raphael or Michelangelo, they interrogated with particular attention Titian, Tintoretto or Paolo Veronese. But above all, instead of executing in haste and distractedly the formal and chromatic elements they had learned, they impregnated their culture with a personal mode of feeling physical and psychological reality, full of that free and primitive power without which art does not exist. Theirs was a new order which repaired the material and moral disorder into which art had been thrown by arbitrariness of theory, facility of hand, false emphasis on feeling and superficiality of intentions.

Their reaction to mannerism was direct, born of the very need to create according to the personality of the individual; and therefore they were the complete and perfect artists of the seventeenth century. But theirs was not the only reaction to mannerism.

Others sought a less natural and sensible way, more critical and learned; that is to say, they drew from all the great models of the sixteenth century those elements that they thought coincided with the best of art. They were reformers of mannerism, not because they opposed it, but because they amplified mannerism itself to such a point that they were constrained to find a critical accord between the various elements assimilated. Lomazzo had appreciated Venetian colouring by a Lombard tradition already old. The Carracci reversed the terms: they attempted to emulate the colouring of the Venetians because they judged that the lights and shades of Titian are more artistic than those of Raphael. Therefore they are no longer mannerists, because between the manner of the models and their own there is a zone of critical judgment which was wanting in the mannerists; and they were called eclectics. In this they were preceded by Paolo Pino who, in 1548, demanded the drawing of Michelangelo and the colouring of Titian. Their mode of reaction to mannerism was therefore indirect, born of the need to know the values of art rather than to create them, so that they allowed their personalities to develop on the basis of their doctrine rather than on their mode of feeling. As is natural, they rarely and only partially reached the level of art. Poussin, the French painter, was the best of these learned reformers, because he felt his doctrine so seriously as to live it dramatically, and therefore to make of it a new material of art. However, though their production in general is very inferior to that of the artists mentioned in the beginning, they were the more appreciated and exalted, the conquerors of the seventeenth century.

The Baroque Period

After the Council of Trent moral preoccupations appeared, lest painting and sculpture should offend with the nude the dominant hypocrisy, and lest poetical license should induce dogmatic errors. Gilio (1564), and Ammanati (1582) wrote precisely to avoid errors in history and unseemly representations. Cardinal Paleotti even published a kind of iconographical code (1582 and 1594), which differed from that of the monk Dionysius because this suggested to the painter what he should represent, while the intention of Paleotti was to define what the painter should not represent, and to assume for himself the office of *controller* of the conscience. He wished to induce the painters to be mute theologians, silent preachers, because human weakness cannot rise to the contemplation of divine things without the support of the senses; that is to say, these theologians attempted to divert art towards rhetoric and rationalism. Hence the moralistic literature on art, such as the "Sacred Painting" (1634) of Cardinal Federico Borromeo, or the "Treatise," written in collaboration by the Jesuit Ottonelli and the painter Pietro da Cortona (1652), have no direct aesthetic interest. They tell us, it is true, that the pure contemplation of physical beauty no longer suffices, whatever might be the reason, and that a need had arisen of moral beauty, often false and hypocritical, but sometimes even true. Immediately one prejudice disappeared; that the foundation of all beauty was the nude human figure, seen as a canon of abstract form; and there was encouraged the search for the beauty of clothed figures, to the advantage of concrete chromatic effects. But having a rule given for religious representation took away all possibility of spontaneous religious expression, so that Caravaggio, perhaps the only religious painter among Italian artists of the seventeenth century, was sometimes refused by the churches because he was felt to be *unusual* — that is to say, under suspicion of heresy. At the same time, the rhetorical aim of teaching given to pictorial delight took away from aesthetic pleasure all autonomy, and impressed upon it an undertone of sensual pleasure, veiled with morality. One result was the incitement to represent the physical sufferings of the martyrs of the faith, so as to excite that particular sensuality, which was called pleasure, mingled of grief and joy, and which interpreted in a manner indecorous enough the tragic *catharsis* of Aristotle.

With the moralism of the Counter Reformation was combined Cartesian rationalism. Science had found its method by means of the mathematical spirit, with the absolute domination of reason in the study of external nature. In Italy the artistic tradition was too much alive for rationalism not to become circumfused with a halo of transcendency, and not to become Platonic or neo-Platonic. Take, for example, Bellori's conception of the *Idea*, that "even if it originates from nature, it surpasses its origin and becomes original in art, measured by the compass of the intellect it becomes the measure of the hand." But in France the scientific spirit in general, and the genius of Descartes in particular, indulged a more exacting rationalism, hence the omnipotence of rules and the poetical art of Boileau. Therefore a contemporary Italian, Antonio Conti, was right in pointing out that the French judged art independently of the qualities of sensibility and confused the progress of philosophy with that of art.

In antithesis both to the moralistic aesthetics and to that of rationalism, there was diffused the conviction that art is an affair of sentiment. Therefore, to the concept of reason, was opposed the concept of "*taste*" as the judging faculty of beauty. Here they perceive that the so-called laws of art are not axioms of arithmetic or geometry, and therefore they tolerate exceptions and defects. To the scientific intellect is opposed *talent*, which in the following century will be called *genius*, the artistic creative faculty. There arose the distinction between artists who have "genius without taste" and others who have "taste without genius." These thoughts are so widely diffused that it would be difficult to indicate the original author, but they are all a reaction from moral and intellectual rules. Particularly clear is Du Bos in his "Critical Reflections upon Poetry and Painting." "The first aim of Painting is to move us. A work which moves us greatly, must be excellent on the whole. For the same reason the work which does not move us at all, does not engage us, is worth nothing; and if criticism finds in it nothing to reprove in the way of faults against the rules, it means only that a work may be bad without having faults against the rules, as a work full of faults against the rules may be an excellent work." "Now sentiment teaches very much better that a work is moving, than all the dissertations composed by the critics. The way of discussion and analysis with which these gentlemen regale themselves is good for the truth, when this consists in finding the causes which make a work please or fail to please; but only sentiment can decide this question." It is indubitable that such a way of conceiving art criticism not only represents an advance upon that of the preceding age, but that it also contains an absolute and eternal truth, which later aesthetics will formulate much better, without modifying its essential motive.

As far back as 1644 Sforza Pallavicino sought, on the other hand, to define the imitation of nature as a process of verisimilitude and not of the illusion of reality. One does not paint to deceive the birds that pecked at the grapes represented by Zeuxis, according to the ancient legend, but in order to obtain a lively representation, by which to excite in a delightful way desire, and in an ardent way passion. In which, even if there is a residue of sensuality, the negation of the moral and rationalistic laws of art is clear.

Finally, in 1684 Leibnitz observes that painters and other artists, though judging well the works of art, do not know how to render an account of their judgments, and when they are asked, they are accustomed to reply that what they condemn leaves to be desired an "*I do not know what.*" Given his differentiation of knowledge, he defines that such judgment is based upon a knowledge that is clear but not distinct, that is to say, is not rational; it justifies itself with examples and not with demonstrations, and therefore has importance as a standard of taste or of the qualities of the senses only. The reader will remember that we have found similar ideas in mediaeval thought, but in the seventeenth century they display a much higher knowledge, so that they lead on, without further interruptions, to the foundation of aesthetics in the following century.

In short, during the seventeenth century, moralism, rationalism and aesthetic sensism were juxtaposed or interlaced without any one of them predominating, and therefore the judgments on art were various and often contradictory.

Two principal currents of criticism indicate, nevertheless, the direction of aim:

The rationalistic current which departs from the Carracci, finds in Bellori its greatest Italian expression and in the French Academy its most systematic manifestation.

The sensistic current, which starts from Venice, has Boschini as its most ingenuous and convinced representative, while De Piles is the representative best informed and most just.

The Roman abbot, Gian Pietro Bellori, occupied himself

with archeology and with Raphael, and wrote "The Lives of Modern Painters, Sculptors and Architects" (1672). He dealt with few artists, only those who lived in his own century and had importance in taste, and he chose them not only from among the Italians but also from among the Flemish and French, responding thus to that need for universality in the knowledge of art which at that time one could only feel at Rome. Bellori's exactness of information is very remarkable, and the seriousness with which he sought a relation between facts and ideas is admirable. His critical position is against naturalism and against mannerism: of the first he considers the protagonist Caravaggio, of the second the Cavalier d'Arpino, and indicates Annibale Carracci as surpassing them, exactly like the truth compared to two errors. In condemning the mannerists his motive is simple: copying only the masters, the works of the mannerists are bastards and not children of nature. But against the naturalists the arguments were more complex, because they had to oppose the public who "praise things painted naturalistically, because they are accustomed to see things so, appreciate beautiful colours and not beautiful forms, which they do not understand; weary of elegance, they approve novelty of popular subjects, despise reason, follow common opinion, and remove themselves from the truth of art"— which depends upon the idea. According to Bellori, there exists a science of art of the learned, that consists in the Idea, in reason, in truth, in elegance, in beautiful form, and is opposed to the ignorance of the common people who occupy themselves with colour and novelty. Naturally the Idea, reason and truth are divine things, and God Himself providentially sent Raphael on earth (substituted on this occasion for Vasari's Michelangelo), and since after Raphael the craftsmen degenerated, behold God again sent a restorer of painting in the person of Annibale Carracci.

In a sonnet by Agostino Carracci, approved by Albani, the theoretical program of the school of the Carracci was the following: assimilate drawing from Rome — that is to say, energy from Michelangelo and proportions and harmony from Raphael; assimilate from Venice movement and light and shade with which Titian had attained the true; assimilate from Lombardy the colouring with which Correggio had attained the purity of an aristocratic style. Bellori approves, accentuating that which Annibale Carracci had derived from Raphael: invention, expression of the affections, grace of imitation — finally the union of the Idea and nature. Everybody to-day has a clear knowledge of the impossibility of realising art with an eclectic programme. But the programme of the Carracci, which could not be an artistic programme, could at least be a critical programme, in so far as it sought to identify the elements chosen in each master with the character of his artistic personality, if it were not that it contained an error which for a long time compromised the criticism derived from it. The lights and shades of the Venetians were in function of colour, while the colour of Correggio was in function of plastic form. By believing that Lombard colour was superior to Venetian, the Carracci were prevented from understanding what was the true possibility of the only chromatic tradition of their time, and therefore they misunderstood both the movement and the light and shade of the Venetians: so sacrificing everything to the desire of social order, dignity, purity and aristocratic elegance that they saw in Correggio. That is to say, precisely through not understanding colouring as an artistic form, independent of Greco-Roman plastic form, both the Carracci and Bellori deprived themselves of understanding the vital demands of their time. They made work the judgment of Vasari, who had before him the newborn phenomenon of Venetian colouring – and had less theoretical severity but greater artistic sensibility.

Therefore Bellori theorised the art of Caravaggio as a rebellion against Raphael and the antique statues in accord with the colouring of Giorgione, and, while admitting the goodness of his colouring and imitation of nature, condemned his lack of invention, decorum and drawing – in a word, of science. Domenichino is for Bellori a great artist because nobody better than he conceived histories; but Rubens, in spite of his readiness, certainty, freedom and colouring, lively mind and universal talent, lacks good drawing of natural forms and charm, and appeals to the crowd; and Van Dyck, in spite of his colouring and his fine portraits, is inadequate in composition and drawing.

Of all these above-mentioned prejudices the gravest is that of *choice*, because it derives from the classical aesthetic, and is always tenacious, down to our own day, because it is founded on an enduring social prejudice. Given the confusion worked by the Counter Reformation between pomp and religion, the idea of beauty was interpreted according to social choice, and moral beauty was not seen independently of physical perfection. Therefore, the identification of moral beauty with plebeian forms was only possible in Protestant lands through the work of Rembrandt.

The artist who perfected the system of the Carracci and incarnated the ideal of Bellori was Nicholas Poussin, the philosophical painter: and in order to exalt him Bellori described the scenes represented, accentuating the allegorical value of the figures and rarely pointing out the figurative elements. Thus Bellori demonstrates, not only in theory but in critical practice, that he needs to have recourse to abstractions outside art in order to recognise a value in art itself.

In the Renaissance, next in importance to the "Lives" of Giorgio Vasari, may be counted some treatises; for example, those of Alberti, Leonardo and Lomazzo. In the seventeenth century, on the other hand, the form of the "Lives" prevails. In the categories of judgment on painting it is not sought to give a theoretical systematisation; but it is preferred to exercise judgment on the individual works and the individual artists. We have already seen how the Carracci had indicated the relation between categories of judgment, such as symmetry, colouring, and so on — and put some artists as models of perfection in each particular category. Since each of those artists had had affinities with others, Domenichino thought to systematise those groups into schools and distinguish and characterise them: the Roman school, for the imitation of the antique; the Venetian, for the imitation of nature; that of Lombardy, for an imitation more tender and facile; and that of Tuscany, for a minute and diligent style. Observe that, in spite of the critical arbitrariness of such distinctions, they are still maintained in many picture galleries and cabinets of drawings.

The arbitrary polarisation of judgment was bound to degenerate into absurdity. In fact, there was no reason why the same abstraction imagined to define the diverse perfection of any personality might not be adopted to destroy it. Nor were there wanting those who catalogued the defects of famous artists: Raphael, hard and cutting; Titian, deprived of drawing; Correggio, ill-bred; Veronese, weak and too undefined; Michelangelo, without decorum; the Carracci, timid in workmanship, and so on. In which one may see a sort of parody of Carraccian criticism.

He who refers to these judgments is Passeri, who wrote the lives of artists who had worked in Rome and died between 1641 and 1673. He did not possess the choice and the erudite severity of Bellori, but he had a certain vivacity and simplicity, and reflected the artistic gossip of his time. More simply, he does not know that the invention of artists is the Platonic idea, and therefore, poor little man, he confuses it with caprice.

In every city in Italy which had had a school there sprang forth biographers of their artists, and generally they assumed a polemic position against Vasari, whom they accused of having been partial to the glories of the city of Florence. The Florentine Baldinucci hastened to reply and to demonstrate that Florence had had a great art before the other cities. Baldinucci's principal work is "Accounts of Professors of Design," the publication of which began in 1681. The title is significant because those capricious painters and sculptors whose lives Vasari so lightly recounted, are become professors, on account of their academical taste. They are certainly professors of the Idea, but they are also called professors of drawing; conservative character in Florence manifests itself indeed in art as well as in criticism. Baldinucci is an erudite man, precise and serious; he divides his material, not according to style or school, but according to the decades in which flourished the artists of whom he speaks. He does not write a history but a chronicle; he is not a critic, and limits himself to referring to the judgments of the competent. It is interesting, therefore, to know how the Florentine artists reacted when there came to Florence a picture by Rembrandt: naturally they were aware of the fame that he had acquired in Holland, but they did not understand it, and they saw him as "most extravagant, with a manner without contours or circumscription of lines, internal or external, all made of rough or repeated touches with great strength of shades, but without obscurity." They understood that is to say, that the shade of Rembrandt is luminous and different from that of the Caravaggio school, but they saw the contours lacking even more than in the most daring of the Italian luminists, and the lack of contours disconcerted them. The interesting thing is that the etchings of Rembrandt were much more appreciated at Florence than his paintings, because in engraving the local tradition was not so rigorous as in painting, and there were seen purely pictorial engravings.

Through lack of theoretical rigidity Baldinucci succeeds, nevertheless, in appreciating Bernini, before whom Bellori turned up his critical nose. Baldinucci understands that Bernini knew how to give unity to painting, sculpture and architecture, and indicates his stylistic synthesis in a freedom of touch which is a miracle. "The effect of this freedom is that he has worked singularly in that kind of drawing that we call caricature, or dashing strokes, deforming in ill-mannered jest the effigies of others, without taking away their likeness." In which we learn the origin of the genus of caricature, when it had not yet its practical, moral or political aim and was a spontaneous effect of freedom of touch.

Two writers, Scannelli and Scaramuccia, published two treatises in 1657 and 1674, demonstrating the transformation which has occurred in the world of criticism. They have no longer the intention of dictating laws, but of expounding their historical experience of painting; rather than treatises, they are critical discussions on the values of painting with reference to this or that artist. Scannelli speaks above all in the name of Correggio, Scaramuccia in the name of Raphael, and both have a certain knowledge of the personality of the artist. Scannelli is opposed to Paolo Pino in his programme of the union of Michelangelo's drawing and Titian's colouring, and affirms that Titian did not in fact need another's drawing in order to reach the perfection which was his. If the great painters have sometimes made defective works it is due to the accidents of human nature; but this takes nothing away from the perfection of their most beautiful works. Scaramuccia also protests against comparisons which would belittle the great artists. If Raphael has not made any daring foreshortenings like Titian, it is because he has not esteemed it appropriate to introduce them into his compositions, not because he could not draw them. It is true that he then spoils this critical truth by declaring the principle that, in order to avoid errors of judgment, it is necessary to speak well of all artists, thus annulling criticism in indifference.

The ideas of Nicholas Poussin on painting are in part transcribed by Bellori: Since painting, through the limitations of nature, is an idea of corporal things, the imitative practice of the painter is valid only if it is controlled by a rational doctrine. The subject of painting is the action of man, and in a subordinate way of animals and other natural objects; and by action he means mimicry, which, as a rhetorical artifice, is to painting as diction to poetry. In order that the painter should have the *splendid manner* the subject must be great; heroic actions, for example, and be represented without details, with the exclusion of all vile motives, with the concept of the essence, with natural composition and with a definitely individual *style, manner or taste*. Form is reduced to expression — for example, of laughter or terror; colour is only an attraction to persuade the eye. Poussin formed his ideas and his style at Rome, looking, above all, at Domenichino, Raphael and the antique statues, and a little also at Titian, whom he understands less well than the others; but already in his notes he shows a detachment from the Italians, even the classicists, a greater rigidity and a more rigorous severity of principles.

To the Academy founded in Paris in 1648 was added in 1665 the French Academy in Rome, to offer to French artists the way of "forming there the taste and the manner." Poussin was the example to follow; it was necessary at all cost to become Romans, even as the most classicistic among the Roman classicists. Fréart de Cambray (1662) writes a treatise against licentious painting; that is to say, painting pleasing in colour but without geometry, perspective or anatomy. A libertine, then, equals a materialistic heretic. Chantelou charges Bernini, on a visit to Paris, with producing the architecture of a libertine. Bernini judges that the manner of the French artists is sad and mean, and that he needs to give them the sense of grandeur. It is the same idea expressed by Poussin as the *splendid manner*, which will soon be called *grand goût*.

Even the terms which comprehend painting, sculpture and architecture are changed. Vasari had called them arts of design, attributing to design their unity. Likewise he had spoken of "the finest arts," and Baldinucci of "fine arts in which design is adopted," and Scamozzi of "fine arts." But it is only in the milieu of the Academy of France that the term "beaux-arts," is in general use, and the term then remained. For unity of design, is substituted that of the ideal of beauty.

The artistic programme of the Academy is indicated by Félibien, in agreement with Le Brun, who was for some time its dictator, in his "Conversations on the Most Excellent Painters, Ancient and Modern" (1666), in which discussions of principles accompany the lives of artists.

Correct nature, he says, by the study of antique statues, and cling to composition in order to arrive at ideal beauty. Only composition is spiritual, because it is made in imagination and precedes execution. Drawing and colour belong to craftsmanship and are the less noble parts of painting. Drawing predominates over colour. Drawing is essential for the representation of history, fable and expression. But colour is not, and it cannot be regulated scientifically. Since the picture is the imagination of actions, expression is essential; it is the soul of painting. With some reserve Félibien agrees with the physiognomy of Le Brun, that is to say, with his little book of engravings in which were drawn the types of anger, fear and so on, and which would enable pupils to avoid the disturbance of consulting nature. He draws a distinction between beauty and grace, in which beauty has the part of proportion, or physical harmony; while grace regards the sentiments of the mind. He eulogises nobility in the subject and pleasure in the execution. Félibien recognises that there are no rules for beauty, and that only the light of reason can attain it, even if against the rules; and he recognises the force of imagination and the necessity of abandonment to "genius"; but after genius has fixed the composition the drawing needs to be corrected according to examples. He recognises that there is no resemblance in wax casts, because artistic resemblance is given by the representation of the mind. In short, his principles are learned but not rational; that is to say, he often confuses social habit with the demands of reason. Hence the obsequious hierarchy: since the figure of man is the most perfect work of God, he who paints man is the most excellent among painters; next comes he who paints living animals rather than dead things without movement; then he who paints landscapes, and finally flowers and fruits.

Principles like those of Félibien were too rigid to be applied, and therefore a certain tolerance was necessary — for example towards Rubens, in spite of his sins against *decorum*, and towards Rembrandt, in homage to whom Félibien admitted differences of taste; on the other hand Velazquez was not worth attention. With regard to Raphael, he considers the "Transfiguration" his masterpiece, in spite of the genial reserve of Vasari. In short, Félibien's book is a compilation of judgments and notes drawn especially from Poussin and the Italian writers, and juxtaposed with little or no criticism, but interesting because reflecting the classical ideas, flowing together at Paris in the second half of the seventeenth century, in their effective disorder, in spite of the pretence of rational severity.

If the exposition of seventeenth century criticism were limited to the results described here, it would give us little satisfaction. In fact, it gave effect to a transcendent standard of art, called Idea, and at the same time to a classification of the manners of artists, in respect of which the critic professes indifference or chooses arbitrarily. The relative coincidence between the principle of the Idea and the art of Poussin remains without a sequel, in spite of the Academy of France; because, as has been said, to the philosophical painter, Poussin, succeeded the non-painter rhetorician, Le Brun. Indifference of taste is also widely spread, in spite of the apparent rigidity of principles. Nothing remained, then, except to seek a choice among the manners, which was subjective but not arbitrary. It was necessary that the judgment should coincide with an effective art, that the manner chosen should not be abstract but concrete, not a scheme but a taste, not a game of the rationalising intellect but an experience of art as lived.

To this demand responds the Venetian, Marco Boschini, author of the "Map of the Picturesque Journey" (1660) and the "Rich Mines of Venetian Painting" (1674). He is much less cultured than Bellori, and also less intelligent, but more sensitive to painting. A sensist is he who formulates a theory according to which all knowledge derives from the senses; and Marco Boschini is not a sensist, because he does not formulate any theory, and accepts the current theory in its most common form. But his judgments do not depend upon ideas accepted from outside, but altogether from his mode of feeling painting, which is a happy mode. Therefore his judgments coincide with the sensitist theory mentioned, which corrected the errors of neo-Platonic and moralist ideas, which felt the need of autonomy of art, and therefore approached confusedly the foundation of aesthetics; coinciding therefore with what was more promising in thought upon art and with that which was more vital in art. When it is said that for the abstract ideal form of Bellori, Boschini substituted an abstract colourism, it seems as if he had cast out the devil with Beelzebub, but, in effect, he sustained polemically that single tendency in which was recognised the better theory and the only art, at that point of convergence which is a single taste historically determined. In this sense the "baroque taste" assumes its positive significance, of appreciation rather than of contempt. If you should ask why the colourists then could make art and the formalists could not, I should answer that I do not know why, but that I could recount to you the history of art from Michelangelo onward as a demonstration by examples.

The unique perfection of Venetian painting, represented above all by Titian, Tintoretto and Paolo Veronese, is for Boschini axiomatic. Rubens and Velazquez are perfect painters (and this is the earliest recognition of their art), because their style is linked with Venetian painting. Boschini cannot deny the mannerists nor distinguish in the Venetian painting contemporary with him the living forces from the dead, but he felt the decadence after Tintoretto and Veronese. His position is parallel to that of Vasari, who was inspired by the model of an authentic artist, Michelangelo, rather than to that of Bellori, who was inspired by a defective artist, Annibale Carracci. But Boschini has more polemical sense: unjust toward the artists foreign to the Venetian taste — Raphael, for example — he derives from his own sectarianism an exceptional force of conviction. Even the much vaunted antique statues are not an obstacle to his faith; they are dead and Venetian painting is alive; and he justifies this affirmation with the international success of Venetian painting. Like Vasari, Boschini is also ambitious to be a connoisseur; that is to say, to distinguish the good from the not good in a painting, together with the character of the authors and the manner of working. To know the good and the not good, according to Boschini, it is necessary to know how to paint, and so arrive at knowledge through practice, but he does not deny that those who are gifted with "good talent" may also arrive at it without practice. In other words, he does not trouble to determine how knowledge is arrived at, but rather what knowledge means. Theoretically, according to Boschini, drawing is the foundation of painting, in practice it is only a guide: what gives life to drawing is colouring, and without colouring drawing is body without soul. He concludes: "the painter forms without form, or rather with form deforms the formality in appearance, seeking thus picturesque art." This is perhaps the best definition of pictorial form that has ever been given, and it will be convenient to stop and explain it in other words. He says that pictorial form is not plastic form; it is rather a deformation with the intent to find a new form, that is only the appearance of things, in which pictorial art consists. It is a programme that Manet or Renoir would have been able to accept, if they had known it.

And when one thinks that this was written at about the same time that Bellori fixed his ideas of classical form, we can grasp the antinomy of the plastic and the pictorial in the clearest way possible. As regards colouring, here are the "essential ideas." One works by impasto, and it is a foundation — that is to say, it serves as a sketch; by spots, and it is a manner — it serves to liberate you from natural objectivity; by union of the colours, and it is tenderness of shading; by tinting or flattening, and it is the distinction of parts — that is to say, it makes them stand out; by raising and lowering the tints, and this is rounding, or volume: by the rapid touch, and it is boldness of colour — this is the art of tone; by veiling, and this means retouching to unite more completely, for chromatic harmony. Certainly nobody of his century has given such richness of aspect to colour. For that which concerns invention, on the other hand, Boschini says nothing new.

Boschini wished to write the lives of the artists preferred by him, but not like the Venetian, Ridolfi, who in 1648 had published the "Marvels of Venetian Painting." Boschini wishes to occupy himself neither with marvels nor with happy thoughts; he wishes to expound only the *pictorial process*. In fact, he never speaks of the subjects treated without putting them into relations with figurative appreciations. Not even Bellori had known how to follow with such severity the main lines of a critical history of art, and Boschini was able to do it, not by greater strength of talent, but by greater attention to art.

So he describes the manner in which Titian finishes his pictures: "The enlivening by the last touches was to go here and there uniting with a rubbing of the finger the extremes of light, bringing them nearer to the half-tones, and uniting one tone with another; at other times with a stroke of the finger he put a touch of dark in some corner to reinforce it; at others some reddish strokes, almost like drops of blood to invigorate any superficial feeling; and so he went on reducing to perfection his animate figures." Of Bassano he notes the arbitrariness of the lights, the abandonment of the universal light demanded by Leonardo, and the consequent effect of a medley of indistinct colours, despising all diligence and polish. So he understands the value of that way of colouring; he interprets it as poetry, without obscuring it by classification of kinds. Boschini does not make hierarchies of kinds, as would the Academy of France. Bassano paints dogs and other animals "because he has applied his genius to the representation of *pure humility*." Anybody who is acquainted with the polemics about kind in the nineteenth century cannot but feel the stroke of genius in Boschini. Tintoretto seems to him a "lamp, a thunder, or rather an arrow which has cloven all the most sublime heights of the picturesque world." Veronese is the treasurer of painting, since from him have been imparted all the jewels of his precious casket. Movement, finally, is noted in style, rather than in action: "one sees the architecture march." Metaphors, certainly, and of the baroque style; but they have a critical content and serve to individuate the style.

The classicist doctrine of Poussinesque origin prevailed at the Academy of France when two polemics broke out to shake it. The first derived from the apology for Rubens made in 1676 by Roger de Piles (greatest representative of the amateurs independent of the official artists), which ended the struggle of the *Poussinists* in the name of drawing, the antique and the *grand goût*, against the *Rubenists*, who championed colour, the moderns and the *truth*. The second polemic derived from a principle formulated as far back as 1620 by the Italian, Tassoni, according to which the arts are per-

fected by assiduity and study, while their beginnings are
rough and imperfect. Between 1688 and 1697 Perrault wrote
his "Parallels between the Ancients and the Moderns," main-
taining not only the superiority of the Italian painters of the
sixteenth century over the artists of antiquity, but also the
superiority of the painting contemporary with him over that
of the sixteenth century. The polemic spread and was particularly developed by the writings of Boileau and Fontenelle. It
was badly directed because it was founded on technical progress; nevertheless, from the conflict of opinions arose two
favourable results: that of liberation for some time from the
superstition of ancient art; and that of reflecting upon the
difference between science capable of progress and artistic
values which come "at a blow and like a flash of fire," as Ronsard
had said already. To the same effect Deimier also said that the
poet "must be in his poems as nature in the production of
flowers," which was a non-classicist way of considering classic
art.

Roger de Piles was the author of numerous writings on painting, among which the best known is the "Abridgment of the
Lives of Painters" (1699). If we consider his theory we do
not perceive a complete revolution; on the contrary, all the
classicist ideas codified by Félibien are found again in De
Piles. But, side by side with these, others break out which are
very different. Without genius, which is a light of the spirit,
a special native talent, one does not make art in spite of all
the rules and examples of the masters. Artistic licenses are
apparently against the laws, but in fact they become new
laws when they are well-timed. Only the great geniuses are
above rules. A man of mind, even if not instructed in the principles of art, can judge a picture, only he does not always give
a reason for his feelings. There is a taste of the mind, as there

is a taste of the body, and it is natural, spontaneous. With artistic culture it may be perfected, but also corrupted. With the repetition of judgments this taste becomes a habit, and the habit may be transformed into ideas, critical in principle. Very important in criticism is the absence of preconceived ideas, and, if it is opportune to listen to the wisest painters and the cleverest connoisseurs, it is also necessary to listen to them not as oracles, but as people who may well be mistaken and whose opinions must be followed after they have been personally controlled. The rules of painting must be stabilised, not by the authority of any writer or by the example of any painter, but only by force of reason. It would appear that De Piles aspired to be the Descartes of art criticism, but his talent did not succeed to that extent because he continued to accept many traditional ideas which could not be checked. De Piles is preparing the taste which was to help Watteau in his art and the new direction of French painting in the eighteenth century; which was a marvellous result, rare enough for a critic at any time.

With regard to the elements of art, the treatment of colouring is the most different from that of the French tradition. Roger de Piles is inspired by Boschini, even to the words. He adds that if drawing precedes colour in painting, that is not to say that it is more important, it is rather a material which must receive from colour its perfection, its essential form. The values of colours (tones) do not reproduce the tints of things, but are made in such manner as to seem to have them. He quotes the saying of Rembrandt that he was not a dyer but a painter. Against those who occupy themselves with invention, as with a pure effect of the imagination, he opposes that the best painters look at Giorgione, Titian and Veronese, as the most perfect examples.

Rubens is for De Piles what Michelangelo was for Vasari, and Raphael and Annibale Carracci were for Bellori – that is to say, sent from Heaven. He links Rubens with Venetian painting, and finds that he has more facility than Titian, more purity and science than Veronese, more majesty, calm and moderation than Tintoretto.

De Piles buys a portrait of Rembrandt's which he admires, but he dares not deny the reserves which everybody made about his art. Nevertheless, he understands that Rembrandt is a master of colour, that his touches express flesh and life, that his portraits have a surprising force, suavity and truth; and he recalls, not without a touch of malice, that Rembrandt used to say: "old armours, old clothes – these were my ancients."

De Piles respects the antique, Raphael and Poussin, but not without independence. "The antique is admirable, but on condition that it is treated like a book that one translates into another language, in which it suffices to transfer well the sense and the spirit, without a servile attachment to the words." Poussin, through having looked too much at the antique "was turned to stone and lacked something human."

Not even the prejudice of kind is retained by De Piles; thus, he appreciates Peter Brueghel, and, with regard to landscape painting, makes the following observation: "If painting is a species of creation, it bears the marks of it even more sensibly in pictures of landscapes than in others." The landscape painter is obliged to "specify taste and character and to give as much more spirit to his work in proportion as it is less finished, ... and to extraordinary sensations the truth and simplicity of nature."

These and many others are the happy intuitions of De Piles, not the "scales of painters," in which, for erroneous pedagogic reasons, he imagines it possible to give a mark of merit to each painter for his drawing, his colouring, his composition and his expression. That is to say, his preoccupation with equity made him lose sight of the artistic personality.

In the seventeenth century, besides Italy and France, other nations publish treatises on art and lives of artists: Spain, the Low Countries and Germany. But these writers have no original critical ideas, applying Italian ideas to the artists of their own countries. Nor do the treatises of architecture present any important novelties, apart from the interest in scenography, and the new knowledge of freedom from classical proportions, expressed in a noisy manner by Claude Perrault (1676). Even for the seventeenth century painting was the principal inspirer of critical motives.

CHAPTER VI
Illuminism and Neo-Classicism

THE BEST painters of the eighteenth century maintained, with modifications, the direction of taste of the best painters of the seventeenth century. In the name of Rubens and the Venetians, Roger de Piles had opened a new way to French taste. Immediately there appeared the artist who suppressed the Poussinesque tradition — Watteau. It fell to Chardin and Fragonard, the two absolute artists that France had after Watteau, to impress their personalities upon pictorial problems, as Watteau had done. The minor artists, of the Van Loo kind, found a compromise between the academic tradition of the seventeenth century, and the demands of the new taste. In the meantime, at Venice, the recovery of the sixteenth century Venetian tradition, foretold by Boschini, and the influence of Flemish and Dutch painting, were the conditions of taste favourable to the rise of two artists like Tiepolo and Guardi, whose level of greatness Italy had not produced since Caravaggio. Outside Venice, the other cities of Italy continued in compromises between the Carracciesque tradition and Venetian, Flemish, Dutch and Spanish influences. Germany, Flanders and Holland in the eighteenth century were silent. England, after several centuries of artistic silence, made her voice heard with Hogarth, Reynolds and Gainsborough; that is to say, with a taste derived from Flanders and Italy. A great flowering of decoration accompanied the pictorial movement of the eighteenth century, transforming the baroque into *rococo*, losing in passion what it acquired in finesse, and going so far as to discover some new architectural rhythms. Sculpture, meanwhile, yielded to the prevailing pictorial movement, so far as to obtain with Houdon new values. In short, rococo was a belated baroque, by means of which freedom of imagination made its rights valid even in the face of classicism.

But towards the middle of the eighteenth century there came a reaction against the pictorial and the rococo. It was moral and intellectual. Moral, because the rococo was too much associated with the aristocratic classes and the artificial life that the French Revolution was soon to destroy. Therefore artists like Greuze interested themselves in sentimental expression, with a didactical pretence. It was an intellectual reaction, because the new excavations at Pompeii and Herculaneum, and the more intense interest in Greco-Roman art, brought an understanding of the seriousness and greatness of antique masterpieces. Then arose the type of philosophical painter, and it arose in Germany where there was preparing a very lofty philosophical civilisation, without, however, a close and beneficial relation between artistic ideas and the best aesthetic of the time: this type was incarnated in Mengs. Precisely because it was regarded as a "philosophical" reaction rather than artistic, and was conducted on principles, prevailing over modes of feeling, it created a detachment from tradition so great that it is difficult to find the like again in the remaining history of art.

The two typical representatives of the reaction, after Mengs, were the French painter David and the Italian sculptor Canova. Well, Mengs died hardly nine years after Tiepolo, Fragonard had time to see the absolute triumph of David, and Guardi was received at the Academy of Venice after Canova. That is to say, the generations of the rococo and those of neo-classicism were to some extent intersecting: but the two tastes were opposed in a definite manner. Distaste for their own age, and faith in Greco-Roman art, suggested to the artists a detachment from contemporary life that was nearly fatal to them. It needs

the genius of Goya to re-immerse in political and moral life
that art which an erroneous aesthetic had placed in a too rarefied atmosphere.

The movement of thought relative to the arts was accele-
rated in the eighteenth century and arrived at calling by the
name of aesthetic a new philosophical discipline. Remember
that in the preceding century there were already contraposed
two conceptions of art. One was rationalistic and derived from
Descartes. But with the Cartesian elements were interwoven
others of a mystical character, of Platonic and neo-Platonic
derivation, in agreement with some followers of Descartes, first
among them Malebranche. Truth of art was then identified
with truth of reason, but that reason reposed in God, according to the neo-Platonic Idea. Bellori, Poussin and the classicism of the Academy of France obeyed the Idea and its laws.

In spontaneous reaction against the use and abuse of the
Idea, arose the statement that art was a matter of feeling, and
that therefore, not laws, but sensibility and taste must be the
judges of art. Hence a vague and sometimes arbitrary state of
mind, substituting for the laws of art the principle of the relativity of taste.

It was inevitable, however, that philosophically educated
minds should object to the theory of feeling, because of the
latter's passivity and to seek the nature of art outside reason,
and not in feeling, but in an activity of the mind that was creative, and not rational but imaginative. In the middle of the
eighteenth century this was accomplished. Shaftesbury, in consequence of his neo-Platonism, understands the creative character of the artist; he puts an end to the concept of imitation
and conceives a philosophical criticism of art — that is to say,
a criticism capable of irradiating feeling and taste with pure

knowledge, without touching or modifying their essence. Vico, reflecting upon the history of poetry, distinguishes poetical from scientific logic and assigns to art the auroral moment of knowledge. Finally Baumgarten, who was a master in the analysis of scholastic logic, recognises its limits. He bases himself on the law of *continuity* by Leibnitz, on the sequence of obscure, confused and distinct perceptions. Leaving obscure perceptions to the senses, and those which are distinct to reason, Baumgarten recognises that confused knowledge — that is, artistic knowledge — has its perfection close to the distinct knowledge of science; and therefore he considers art as an active mode of knowledge, even if anterior to and different from scientific knowledge. In such a way he assigned to art its own field in the system of the human mind, accentuating it with the name of Aesthetics which appeared for the first time and remained the name of the new science.

These were very important discoveries, pregnant with consequences for art criticism in the nineteenth century, but much less in what remained of the eighteenth century. The aesthetic of Vico or Baumgarten originated in the desire to illuminate feeling, and therefore belonged to the reaction from Cartesian rationalism. But in art criticism, Cartesian rationalism, fused with neo-Platonic mysticism, prevailed as the aesthetic of ideal beauty, and a little after the middle of the century took the offensive against the artistic sensism inherited from the previous century. Instead of taking for examination the feeling of the work of art, and illuminating it ideally, art criticism preoccupied itself above all with ideal beauty, and reduced to secondary value, if not enslaving, the artistic feeling. Consideration of sentiment remained alive in criticism up to the middle of the century, but then weakened and almost disappeared, together with appreciation of the great artists of the century, from Watteau to Guardi. Formal beauty, identified with the beauty of ancient Greece, remained the sole ideal of criticism. This was the moment of the uncontested dominion of neo-classicism. The century had not ended, however, when there exploded the re-action against the ideal aesthetic, in the name of primitive art, supporting itself upon the ideas of Vico, Baumgarten and, fi-nally, Kant; and this reaction was so strong that it impressed itself upon the whole of the nineteenth century. This was ro-manticism. As a matter of fact, neo-classicism also continued into the nineteenth century; but the romantic movement had taken away from it all active power.

If the eighteenth century created aesthetics, in name and in fact, with a place of its own in the system of the mind, it also created the criticism and the history of art. As we know, the occasions of art criticism have to be sought hitherto in trea-tises on art and lives of artists. But, with art exhibitions, espe-cially in France, the eighteenth century furnished opportunities for critical reports; that is to say, art criticism found a form which was no longer extraneous. It was no longer a case of in-serting judgments between the facts referred to and the rules, but of writing solely to give the personal opinion upon a group of works and artists. Since these artists were contemporary with the critic, the desire was imposed to go back to principles, from the direct impression of the work, to test by the work the truth of the principles, to understand the work through the totality of the personality of the artist, and to understand the personality in the variety of contemporary tastes; there was imposed, in short, the desire to find a relationship between the synthesis of the work of art and all the elements of which it was constituted. In other words, it imposed art criticism, even if hasty and superficial, as a criticism of actuality. But within these limits, criticism of exhibitions would not have been possible without the philosophy of illuminism, and its new interest of finding the reason of the fact in the analysis of the facts themselves. Up to the beginning of the eighteenth century philosophy "considers the problems of nature and historical questions as a unity which cannot be divided into separate parts. It seeks to apply to one and the other the same means of thought; wishes to adopt the same way of stating the problems and the same universal method of "reason" for nature and for history. There is a common adversary, transcendence, against which natural knowledge and historical knowledge must both defend themselves. The weapon of defence is immanence, founded on leaving nature and history each within its own circle and fixing each in its own centre. That is science in so far as one refuses to admit anything which transcends nature or history" (Cassirer).

Such a programme was realised only partially, whether in the criticism of the eighteenth century or in that of the following century, because the "transcendent deities" of art criticism remained in the form of the so-called laws of art. These laws limit the judgment, both of a Diderot, the greatest critic of exhibitions in the eighteenth century, or of a Winckelmann, then the greatest historian of art.

The special importance of Winckelmann depends, however, upon the more lively interest, the more intense attention, that he gave to objects of ancient art as compared with his predecessors. To this contributed in great part the erudite work upon ancient art, which in the eighteenth century becomes enormous. The aesthetic ideas of Winckelmann are without originality, traditional, of the current neo-Platonism; his taste is not sure; but such is his faith in his historical knowledge of the ancient objects that he believes he can refute, and he expressly refutes, the conclusion of aesthetic philosophy. He is no erudite indifferent to judgments, but he believes that he can draw aesthetic conclusions directly from works of art or from testimony of ancient writers. Before him the best lives of artists were preceded by treatises on art in the form of introductions, and the judgments expressed in the lives were understood to apply the rules established in the treatises. Winckelmann turns the system upside down; he looks at the works of art with the intention of finding in them the reason for his judgments. Or rather, he identifies his judgment with that which he believes to be peculiar to the Greek artists belonging to the "beautiful style." That is to say, he identifies art with one of its historical moments. It is natural that, by his doing so, the works of art which he examines lose their individuality to become types of art. Therefore Winckelmann goes beyond the mark, both under the historical and the aesthetic aspect. But, meanwhile, he has found something on the way. He has left behind him the *lives of artists* and found a type of the *history of art;* and thus is called his book on ancient art published in 1764, the first time a work has been so named.

It is indubitable that Winckelmann fused the judgment of values and historical perceptions. While art criticism found its social position in reports of contemporary exhibitions, it accentuated research into ancient and distant works of art. In the meantime arose the constitution of an aesthetic or theory of the arts, as a branch of philosophy. Therefore one might think that in the eighteenth century art criticism had had an exceptionally flourishing period. A notable progress was undoubtedly made, especially in the sense of an extraordinary enrichment of critical points of view, of psychological analyses, of theoretical suggestions. The judgments, however, were often erroneous, and they encumbered unfavourably the criticism of the nineteenth century. The principal reason is the distrust, in the second half of the eighteenth century, of modern art; the blind faith in the unique beauty of Greek art; the detachment from contemporary life, a detachment expressed by art as well as by art criticism. Such an error had not been committed either in the Renaissance or in the baroque; it was unknown from Vasari to De Piles. To the "quarrel between the ancients and the moderns" there seemed to be given a definite solution in favour of the ancients. It was necessary, on the other hand, to think systematically about the problem of art, in order to avoid the too frequent caprices of sensibility and taste, but the systematic trend was such as to lose relations with the reality of everyday art. It was necessary to conceive ancient art historically, and not in a legendary way as the artists of the fifteenth, sixteenth, and seventeenth centuries had done; but the historical interest in ancient art became such that there was no place in it for the recognition of modern art. There must be added the prevalent scientific, moral and social preoccupations with which the century closed. So it will be clear that, in spite of the intensest interest in art, the like of which had not been seen since the Renaissance, the lack of recognition by eighteenth century criticism of the effective art of its own time contributed to that poverty of the figurative arts which marked the passage of the eighteenth to the nineteenth century.

The Academy of France, which constituted an incentive to discussion since the seventeenth century, maintains and extends its function in the eighteenth century, with greater vivacity, indeed, after 1747. In the same year comes out the essay of La Font de Saint Yenne, which is the first among the reports of exhibitions. It is a novelty badly received by the artists, who saw themselves criticised; it then is consolidated and assumes a special authority at the hands of Diderot. Publications on art become always more numerous, but for some time ideas and taste do not change. They continue to be those of De Piles — that is to say, obsequious in worship of the antique statues but also broad in comprehension of the greater artistic manifestations from the sixteenth century onward. There is, however, a difference between the tendencies of the men of letters, more devoted to the antique and the neo-Platonic Idea and praising the productions of the Academy, and those of the artists and amateurs who, without theorising, enjoy Flemish or Dutch colour, follow nature and prefer grace.

Watteau advises Lancret not to lose time with masters but to go out and "draw in the environs of Paris some view of landscape, then draw some figures, and of them form a picture out of his imagination to his choice." Mariette laments of his contemporaries that they love to find in pictures "actions which pass daily under their eyes in their households" and prefer a Teniers to a Poussin. Dezallier Dargenville alternates equity with indifference and accepts all schools and all artists; but even indifference is useful sometimes: in fact, against Félibien, he rejects the hierarchy of artistic kinds. In order to appreciate a pictorial composition of Paul Veronese as much as a poetical one of Poussin, Dubos makes a distinction that directly precedes Lessing: he notes, in fact, against De Piles, that *pictorial* composition regards "the general effect of the picture," and for this it is enough that "the groups should be well composed, that the light may be judiciously distributed upon them, and that the local colours, so far from conflicting, may be disposed in such a manner that there results from the whole a harmony agreeable in itself to the eye." On the other hand "the *poetical* composition of a picture is an ingenious arrangement of figures invented to make the action which it represents more touching and more convincing."

La Font de Saint Yenne proposes to interpret public opinion, and interprets, in fact, his traditional academic tendencies. "The historical painter is the only painter of the soul" and "the others paint only for their eyes." He believes there is a decadence of contemporary art, and in order to remedy it proposes the creation of a museum. To him are opposed others who, instead, are partisans for contemporary art. Count Caylus loves and collects antique objects and passes for a restorer of classical taste in the Academy. However, he appreciates Boucher and opposes mannerism in the name of nature, saying that "to love the beautiful works of the past is to be impregnated with their grace and simplicity, which one will then transfer, with hardly any doubt, to the imitation of living nature." He advises a young artist: "make nothing because some one else has made it: make for the reason that you think, feel and see." It is not, then, a case of perilous classicism, but rather of profiting by the classical to rediscover the grace of the eighteenth century. Finally, Cochin admires Tiepolo because "there is an almost infinite number of ways to make beautiful things, and all these ways are good."

Diderot began to write his Salons in 1759 and wrote them up to 1781. His theoretical and practical preparation for speaking of art is very limited; and the tone of his Salons is that of the journalist rather than the philosopher. Hence contradictions, due to momentary impressions, literary interest in the subjects, and judgments given without sufficient reflection. However, there is not wanting in him contact with the works he discusses, because he shares a public belief, which the artists also share, and which becomes a community of taste. He has no original aesthetic ideas; and when he outlines some they are without force. But he has a strong intuitive impulse, a full belief in it, and a very serious moral consciousness; all this takes to some extent the place of ideas, and keeps him away from too many prejudices.

The classicist Vien paints a "Raising of Lazarus," believing that "one has nothing to do but arrange the figures," and Diderot opposes to him the "Resurrection" of Rembrandt to remind him of the futility of the Academy and of the seriousness of art. Charles van Loo "neither thinks nor feels." Diderot's friend Greuze exhibited a "Portrait of Madame Greuze as a Vestal": "You mock at us. . . It is a mother of sorrows, but of small character and a trifle grimacing." The apparent justification of this judgment is in the defect of truth in the representation of the Vestal, but the real justification is in that "mock," in the lack of relationship between the picture and the artist's way of feeling. Of Boucher he says in 1761: "That man has everything except truth. But one does not know how to leave the picture. It holds you." And in 1765: "The degradation of taste (in Boucher), of colour, of composition, of characters, of expression, of drawing, has followed step by step the depravation of morals." The moral preoccupation is in this case favourable to artistic judgment; but not always — for example, when he admires Greuze for his artistic kind: moral painting. He feels the value of Chardin, superior to all. "It is he that is a painter; it is he that is a colourist. One can understand nothing of that magic. There are thick layers of colours applied one over the other of which the effect transfers from below to above." Before the first picture of Fragonard he adopts an attitude of favourable expectation; before the first picture of David he praises it "in spite of the too hard flesh tints."

As appendix to the Salon of 1765 Diderot places an "Essay on painting," which does not set out to be a collection of principles, for Diderot denies principles on the grounds of artistic freedom, but of more or less detached ideas, which he expounds in a lapidary style. "Nature makes nothing that is incorrect. Every form, beautiful or ugly, has its cause." Goethe observed on this sentence that it does not deal with incorrectness but with incoherence. So it is interesting to see how Diderot precisely makes artistic correctness consist in natural coherence. Against oratorical poses so frequent in the art of his time, Diderot affirms: "attitude is one thing, action another. All attitude is false and mean; all action is fine and true." He considers colour as the life of form and observes "excellent draughtsmen are not lacking; there are few great colourists." He looks for the chromatic expression of the passions, a different thing from chromatic mannerism.

With regard to finish, he loves it in works, but also respects the unfinished because of Rembrandt. About severity of proportions he puts questions which must have seemed embarrassing. He asks if the Vitruvian system was not invented to lead to monotony and to strangle genius, and if painting and sculpture might not have been destroyed if subjected to the same scientific severity as architecture. St. Peters at Rome was admired in his time because its proportions are so severe as to make it seem smaller than it is. He asks: "How can you call a harmony that which hinders the general effect? How can you call a defect that which makes the value of the whole?" And again: "The figure will be sublime, not when you shall have remarked in it the exactness of proportions; but when, on the contrary, you shall see in it a system of deformations well related and necessary."

In the above passages Diderot had the opportunity of giving the best of himself, the seriousness of his mind and his independence in the face of common prejudices. But others he accepts; from Winckelmann, with regard to the metaphysical value of art, and from the English moralists with regard to the subjects of treatment. He grazes error here, just because he had not the dialectical power to oppose his happy intuitive impulse to the presumed principles of art. However, he remains as a valuable testimony of the eighteenth century French taste, in his more serious aspect, in his demand for aesthetic laws, but at the same time capable of understanding and judging the more varied artistic temperaments which France then produced. The same attitude of provisional acceptance of traditional principles, accompanied by moral consciousness of the freedom of intuitive judgment, by recognition of the effective life of contemporary art and the control of good sense, is found in the chapters about art in the "Encyclopedia," as in the artistic dictionary by Watelet.

In Italy the conservative tradition of seventeenth century ideas lasted as long as in France. Ciocchi, Bottari and Algarotti do nothing but continue the tradition of Bellori, with greater equanimity and indifference, and with greater research for the graceful. Boschini is continued by A. M. Zanetti (1771), in a manner much more cultivated and socially refined, but also less creative and convinced. For example, Zanetti also admires Bassano, but leaves out Boschini's happy hint of his humility. At the end of the century was written the "Pictorial History" (— 1789) of Luigi Lanzi, who proposes the classification of artists as botanists classify plants, and regroups them according to regional schools (Florentine, Sienese, Roman and so on), according to individual schools (masters and disciples) and according to artistic kinds. His erudition is very broad and alert, his lack of prejudices towards the primitives is evident; his judgment is based on that of painters, but tempered by the comparison of contrasting judgments. He follows a common opinion and does not inquire into its contradictions, but accepts it with the control of good sense: therefore he believes that knowledge of all the schools serves to limit and therefore to define the merit of each school and of each painter. He gives great importance to the individuality of each one, but in the sense that he pertains to the tradition of lives of painters rather than to the history of art of the Winckelmann type. He knows the work of Winckelmann and admires it, but his aim is different. The centre of attention is no longer ideal beauty or the perfection of art, as in Winckelmann; it is, for Lanzi, Italy and her glory. In the eighteenth century there were doubts on the absolute greatness of Italian artists, on the part, for example, of the Marquis D'Argens: and the Marchese Venuti had replied in the name of Italian art in 1755. It was necessary to document the greatness of Italy under the aspect of painting: this was the aim of Lanzi. It is understood, then, that his work is valuable more under the erudite aspect and in general historical organisation, than under the aspect of art criticism. We must, however, note the great success of this work, not only through the various editions, but because, for a long time during the nineteenth century, it served as a basis for histories of Italian painting – for example, that of Stendhal. Italy of the eighteenth century gave two theorists of architecture of value. One is Carlo Lodoli (1690-1761), who was the first to consider the beauty of an edifice as the *representation* of its function, an idea revived, as is well known, in our own days, which then was a way of withdrawing from the picturesque emptiness of rococo architecture. Naturally his tendency was architectural rationalism, like that of Francesco Milizia, who was perhaps the greatest critic of architecture in the neo-classical taste. He is not averse from feeling the value of niceties, of graduations and of elegancies in the paintings and sculptures of the eighteenth century, but considers that his task is argument against the picturesque in architecture, in the name of that logical organisation which the classical orders transmitted.

In England there was a great movement of amateurs of art during the eighteenth century, and it was the amateurs who constituted a public opinion of the French or Italian type. But they did not give many critical results. The books of Richardson (1715, 1719, and so on) are a very serious report on the state of Continental criticism rather than a contribution of new ideas. The importance of the English aesthetic of the time did not have great effects on English criticism. An essay that was intended to be aesthetic, but instead is important only in the history of criticism, is the analysis of beauty by Hogarth (1753). He wants to determine what is the line of beauty, and, having observed that the curve is more adapted than the straight to ornament, indicates in the undulating line the line of beauty, and in the serpentine line, which presents still greater variety, the line of grace. All this has no sense if considered as a universal idea, but it is enough to think of Louis XV decoration to understand the meaning of Hogarth's words. In comparison with the antique, which was vaunted as the model of plastic beauty, he places the rococo as the model of serpentine lines; and draws the conclusion of his taste in the appreciation of Gothic architecture. It is, then, an example of a taste that should have passed from the rococo to the romantic, if it had not been for the neo-classical reaction.

The need of freedom from the rules is manifested in the taste and in the theorisation of the picturesque, above all by

Price, who saw in the picturesque a third aesthetic category close to that of the Beautiful and the Sublime, and by Payne Knight, who recognised in the picturesque a value irreducible to the phenomena of the visible.

If account is taken of the taste of the picturesque and that of the Gothic, of which we shall speak in the following chapter, it will be understood that neo-classicism was very much milder in England than on the Continent. There fell to Reynolds the task of representing that very diffused criticism, which had certainly a classicist tendency but did not wish to renounce the best of the baroque experience. Toward the connoisseurs of the rules Reynolds is ironical; he admits that taste becomes universal only when it is guided by reason, but insists on the affinity between taste and genius, and believes that the only difference is in the power to execute, peculiar to genius. Equally he is convinced that beauty does not consist in an idea but in nature; that the essence of taste consists in adherence to nature; that it is necessary to have faith in imagination and feeling, in which are hidden the principles of reason, of reason solid and concrete and different from that which is exclusive and abstract. He is against the illusionist imitation of reality, because he wishes that art should respond to the refining of the activities, and transform nature through the imagination. Equally, he is against eclecticism: "To wish to unite the beauty of two styles, to mix the Dutch school with the Italian, means to wed two contrary things, which reciprocally destroy their effect." "If I were asked if I thought that Michelangelo would have gained by a greater pictorial complexity, I should answer that his masterpieces would have been ruined. As they are, they are all genius, all soul." Reynolds believes that Raphael is great, but Michelangelo is superior; that Poussin exaggerates in theory. He is exalted by Correggio and interprets his light and shade as an effect of colour; he admires the greatness of simplicity of Titian and is enthusiastic about Rubens, his daring genius in compositions, the happy contrasts of his colours, the facility and animation of his sketches.

The greater part of these ideas were expressed after the neo-classical severity of Mengs and Winckelmann was already banished. Therefore the good sense of Reynolds, his taste, his pictorial experience, his detachment from the greater part of the prejudices of his time, seem to us like a protest launched against the archaeological adventure of taste, and in favour of a future, distant but certain. As often happens to conservatives, Reynolds must be considered as old-fashioned in his time, but one or two generations later he was certainly in the vanguard of taste.

Neo-classicism was founded at Rome a little after 1750 by two Germans, Mengs and Winckelmann. In various epochs and places classicist tendencies had prevailed, but neo-classicism properly considered is only that. We have seen that classicist tendencies spread everywhere, but Mengs and Winckelmann produced a revolution in taste. We have seen that the boast of the best aesthetic of the eighteenth century is precisely that of being freed from Cartesian rationalism; Mengs and Winckelmann, however, installed a new rationalistic severity in artistic taste. Mengs was a mediocre painter, Winckelmann an excellent archaeologist: neither the one nor the other was a thinker. It is, therefore, curious to state that the prime reason of their success consisted in the appellative of philosopher which was attributed to them: Mengs above all was considered as the painter philosopher. What impression Mengs had made on Italian culture is indicated by some words of Milizia: "Michelangelo succeeded, rough, hard, extravagant, coarse.

Although all the works of Raphael may be very beautiful: what good things do they say to us? Nothing." But compared with the precursors, "Raphael smiles, as Newton to the philosophers, his predecessors. And Mengs smiles; Mengs who, in order to become a painter, studies excellence of expression in Raphael, light and shade and grace in Correggio, colouring in Titian, all beauty in the antique; and becomes excellent." What is new in this attitude? Little or nothing. We know it in about the same terms from the time of the Carracci. Even the cult of the antique is not new. What is new is the more resolute attitude, the sense of polemical aggression against the more recent baroque and rococo tradition. Says Mengs: Perfection is of the Greeks not of the moderns. For the choice of the beautiful is necessary the philosophical mind, and Raphael had the philosophical mind in choosing the elements most important to express the passions. But the beauty of Raphael needs some reservations; his importance consists more in expression than in beauty. Absolute beauty is found only in Greek statues. The prototype of the vicious style is Rubens. Absolute beauty is justified in the divine transcendent Idea and is manifested in circular form and uniformity of colouring. Taste is relative beauty, imperfection, the only beauty of which men are capable. Taste is what determines the painter in his choice. And the best taste is the middle taste, not too coarse and not too delicate. And now think of the spontaneous adherence of Diderot to the painters of his age, think of the fantasies of Hogarth on the lines of rococo, think of the refinement of Reynolds in feeling nature; and you will perceive how Mengs is detached from art and attached to abstractions, to an ideal of beauty that does not exist either in Greek statues or anywhere else, and that is simply unthinkable. When he tumbles down from his flight into absurdity, he finds himself down below in the indifference of the

middle taste, neither too coarse nor too delicate. That the polemical motive which he obeys had its good reasons, that a reaction from the license and the too great facility of the late
baroque was opportune, nobody doubts. But through having
passed all bounds Mengs finds himself in the void.

Mengs and Winckelmann influenced each other reciprocally. The artistic ideas of Winckelmann are no better than
those of Mengs. He distinguishes in the artist an internal and
an external sense. The internal is feeling which must be ready,
tender and imaginative. The external is given by form and
colour. Form is the essential, because it can be exact and answer
to the truth of objects, while colour is arbitrary and varies
according to the individual who is looking. However, if in
the artist feeling is recognised, in the work of art there should
be only beauty, understood according to the neo-Platonic Idea.
It is easy for him to recognise beauty in architecture because
there it is given by the proportions. "At Florence beautiful
architecture is very rare, so that there is but one little thing
there that can be called beautiful." On the other hand, it is
difficult to recognise beauty in painting, on account of the colouring and the light and shade. The moderns are less good as
sculptors than as painters. To observe a work of art one should
reflect first of all upon the thought of the artist (which is not
identified with invention); then upon the beauty that consists
in variety and simplicity and is manifested in the human figure,
and afterward upon the execution, which should be well-
finished.

One could go on at length without succeeding in finding
either a generalisation or a detail new in the thought of Winckelmann. But, as not in the case of Mengs, the mediocre ideas
of Winckelmann and his abstract taste are founded upon a
profound historical knowledge of ancient art. And from the

relationship between his historical knowledge and his ideas is born a new interpretation of ancient art. He says: "The general and principal character of Greek masterpieces is a noble simplicity and quiet grandeur, as much in the attitude as in the expression." It is no longer, then, a case of nature and choosing from it, nor of the neo-Platonic transcendent Idea, nor of the proportions, nor of the technique. He refers Greek beauty to a particular state of mind in Greek artists. Historically this idea is open to criticism, because not all the Greek masterpieces respond to those statements, and, because it is valuable only if referred to separate individuals. The ideal of Winckelmann was noble simplicity and quiet grandeur; these characters he finds in the works that he prefers, and he attributes them to Greek masterpieces. Now it is exactly this identification of the personal ideal with those of the artists he loves best, which allows Winckelmann to impress a decisive progress on the history of art, to make it the history of art rather than the lives of artists.

Winckelmann divides his history of Greek art into four periods, inspiring himself explicitly, from the divisions of Scaligero for poetry, and of Floro for Roman history. Each period has its own style:

1. Antique, up to Phidias;

2. Sublime, which is the style of Phidias and his contemporaries;

3. Beautiful, from Praxiteles up to Lysippos and Apelles;

4. Of imitation, up to the death of the art.

Here is, then, a conception of progress from the first to the third style, and then the decadence. Winckelmann further institutes a parallel between the development of Greek art and that of modern painting:

1. Antique style up to Raphael;

2. Sublime style with Raphael and Michelangelo;

3. Beautiful style with Correggio and Guido Reni;

4. Style of imitation from the Carracci to Carlo Maratta.

Now it is easy to see in all that a legend without historical foundation, both because the idea of progress does not concern art, and because it lessens the absolute value of the artistic personality. It remains, however, that the two positive definitions of "sublime" and "beautiful" for the taste of two groups of artists have a significance in historical reality.

Otherwise, with regard to allegory, Winckelmann opines that the older Greek artists contemplated significance more than beauty, and made symbolical representations, and that only the more evolved artists considered beauty as the principal and highest aim of art. This is an important motive, which has its historical reality and was afterwards assumed and developed by Hegel.

These are the motives of more authentic history of art that Winckelmann was able to find; but he was distracted by an excessive naturalism by which the Greeks should have made perfect works because they were in the habit of seeing the nude bodies of the young; and by a desire of abstraction, whence the importance given to the artistic perfection of the typology of the gods; he was, then, distracted from considering the peculiar character of art. However, from knowledge of the antique works of art, from faith in their unique beauty, from anxiety to justify their value theoretically, Winckelmann found a relation between the work of art and its aesthetic value more rigorous than before.

A progress in the criticism of art was achieved by Lessing with his celebrated book entitled "Laocoön" (1766). The abundance of writers in the eighteenth century who were interested in the figurative arts and the predominance of the Idea among the qualities of the work of art had led the critics into an interpretation of the works always more generical, in which the psychological motives lost all contact with their realisation in form and colour. Thus, Spence and Caylus had theorised this mode of criticism, with regard to ancient art. Caylus had even indicated as the touchstone of poets the number of pictures that they offered to the artist. The result was to attach value to two kinds among the less estimable: the descriptive kind in poetry and the allegorical kind in painting. A reaction was necessary, and was, indeed, in the air; we have already found a hint in Dubos. But Lessing had the merit of taking the question to heart and of distinguishing clearly painting from poetry. The object of painting is bodies, which manifest themselves simultaneously, in space; the object of poetry is actions, which manifest themselves successively in time. The distinction had the merit of returning the observation of painting to its concrete reality, and not leaving to the imagination of the observer. Lessing stamped his discovery with a name: after him painting, sculpture and architecture were called *die bildenden Künste*, the figurative arts, while before him they were called beaux-arts, fine arts. Apart from polemics there was a truth in Lessing's discovery; but it was accompanied by various errors. First of all Lessing affirms that while Homer can deal not only with the visible but also with the invisible, the painter can deal only with the visible. Now, this is an error easily confutable. The simultaneity in space proper to painting and the succession in time proper to poetry, are both physical phenomena, and within their physical limits the distinction is just. But when one speaks of the invisible, the spiritual is intended, and therefore to deny the invisible to painting signifies to deny it the spiritual. Indeed, Lessing affirms that painting obeys the laws of beauty and not of poetry. But what beauty? The beauty of corporeal proportions. Since the beauty of clothes is inferior to the beauty of the naked human body, Vergil could speak of the garments of Laocoön, but the sculptor has represented him naked. Nor has he accentuated the expression of suffering; not, however, as Winckelmann said, for an ideal of noble simplicity and tranquil greatness, but for the laws of beauty which would have been destroyed by an expression full of suffering. Lessing, that is to say, admits figurative art only as a representation of physical beauty. Therefore he disapproves of modern art, which is occupied with the whole of nature and not only beautiful nature, and wishes to subject painting to the model of the sculptured group of Laocoön, which realised better physical materiality in its three dimensions.

It is clear, then, that the criticism of Winckelmann, which attempted to explain a Greek work with a moral ideal, was higher than that of Lessing, which reduced that explanation to a materially physical level.

One has a counter-proof of what is said above when one examines what Lessing said about ugliness in painting. On this question Aristotle had said a word of genius; that even an ugly figure may please us if reproduced in painting. Lessing wishes to oppose this, and makes distinctions: painting as imitative ability can express ugliness, painting as beautiful art will not express it. This a tautology. But can, or cannot, painting as art express the ugly? Lessing admits that we have the faculty of abstracting from the ugliness of the object represented and enjoying only the art of the painter. "But even this enjoyment becomes interrupted every moment by reflection upon the bad use that is made of art, and rarely this reflection will fail from drawing with it the disvaluation of the artist." In short, Lessing finds himself led into inextricable contradictions, precisely through not having understood the spiritual value of art, which can exist in an ugly figure; through not having had eyes for moral beauty, of a Rembrandt, for example, and through having interpreted in a physical manner the beauty of a Greek sculpture.

At this point we ask ourselves what grain of truth the distinction between figurative art and poetry can contain, if that distinction was accompanied by so much physical materiality. And in fact this can only be a truth of a different order from the aesthetic. The distinction of styles (sublime, beautiful, of imitation) was useful to the history of art for direction towards the determination of artistic individualities; for the same reason, the distinction of poetry and painting was useful to call critical attention to the manner in which each artist has realised forms and colours. Of what nature, then, are these distinctions? Certainly not philosophical, since they are not able to rise to the grade of categories, but philological. These distinctions are in fact elements of philological analyses, successive and provisory steps towards the interpretation of the individual. The later history of art has appropriated them and has recognised in them the reason of its superiority over the theories of art and the lives of painters in preceding times. And it has recognised in Winckelmann and Lessing two among its greatest founders, and has developed and multiplied the distinctions in order to draw nearer to the goal.

Illuminism and Neo-classicism

The way to arrive at the goal has been long. It has been necessary before all to recognise the perfection of art in artistic languages very different from the Greco-Roman; then it has been necessary to recover a relation between modern artistic creation and the mode of thinking upon art. Both these exigencies were not felt by neo-classicism, through defect of taste and through the resistance of an antiquated culture. The eighteenth century had not reached its end, and already the two corrections were on the way: the first with the romantic movement and the discovery of the primitives, the second with idealistic philosophy. The perfecting of the two corrections was, however, the work of the nineteenth century.

CHAPTER VII
Romanticism and the Middle Ages

THE period in which the movement in favour of the appreciation of Gothic architecture and of the artists of the late Middle Ages appeared and was developed, lasts from about the middle of the eighteenth century to about the middle of the nineteenth, except that it had a brief appendix in the last decade of the nineteenth century.

In England, Gothic remained the local style even through the eighteenth century. The Italian style of the Renaissance and baroque was an importation juxtaposed to the local style. For example, the architect Wren (1632-1723), though he did not love Gothic, constructed sometimes in the Gothic style when he was asked to do so. The Gothic Revival, however, begins by reaction against the importation of Palladian neoclassicism, the work of Lord Burlington and his friends, without taking account of the late and fragmentary Gothic tradition of Wren and company. The revival had, then, a polemical and critical value rather than a spontaneous and creative artistic value. The first so-called "Gothic ruins" in gardens are anterior to 1745. From then up to the Palace of Westminster, Gothic constructions were very numerous, and not only in England; but none of them rose from the documentary plane to the level of art.

From the end of the eighteenth century some painters also sought inspiration in mediaeval models, or at any rate wished to create primitive art. The first among them was the Dane, Carstens (1754-1798), who, in opposition to David and Mengs, exaggerated the rationalism of draughtsmanship up to the point of abstracting his contour lines, without light and shade. William Blake (1757-1827) produced figurate mysticism, besides poetical, without showing much artistic sensibility. So it fell to some Germans, in the early years of the nineteenth century, to give to the emancipation from the neo-classic a Catholic religious content and a primitivist form and tendency. Frederick Overbeck was the founder of the sect who called themselves the Nazarenes: they assembled in Rome from 1810 onwards in the cloister of S. Isidoro, surroundings chosen as adapted to mediaeval re-evocations and mystical abandonments. They were condemned by Goethe and Hegel and supported and defended by Frederick Schlegel. Between 1830 and 1840 disputes were revived among the Italians in favour of or against the ideas of the Nazarenes, and the painter Tommaso Minardi and the sculptor Pietro Tenerani adhered to the group of Italian "Purists." In France, in opposition to the School of David, arose the sect of the "Primitives," directed by Maurice Quaï. In England, in reaction against the dominant Academy, Dante Gabriele Rossetti (1828-1882), William Holman Hunt (1827-1910) and John Everett Millais (1829-1896) constituted, in 1848, the "Pre-Raphaelite Brotherhood," inspired, besides by the books of Ruskin, by the paintings of Madox Brown and the engravings by Lasinio of the paintings at the Campo Santo of Pisa. In 1851 the three Pre-Raphaelites seemed to be crushed under public scorn, when Ruskin, with two letters to "The Times", reversed the situation and established their fortune for many years.

To-day, however, criticism is agreed in recognising no artistic value, neither in the Pre-Raphaelites, nor in the sect of the Primitives, nor in the Purists, nor in the Nazarenes, nor in the Gothic Revival. That is to say, the movement toward the primitives had critical importance in so far as it could recognise artistic value in mediaeval monuments or other works of art, but came less near to its aim when some artists wished to make real and contemporary the art of the Middle Ages. The projection of spiritual life into the past destroyed the possibility of artistic creation, whether the past were Greco-Roman, or mediaeval art.

There were true and even great artists in the first half of the nineteenth century, who in some way represented romantic movement, but they were not touched by the primitivist tendencies; these were Goya in Spain, Constable and Bonington in England, Corot, Daumier and Delacroix in France.

That detachment, then, from contemporary art which had damaged the neo-classic criticism, damaged also the primitivist criticism.

The first manifestation of aesthetic thought on the absolute value of the primitives in art is Italian, through the work of Giambattista Vico. As far back as 1725 he proclaimed that the great poets (like the great painters) were not born formerly in epochs of reflection but in those of imagination, which are called barbarous: thus, Homer in the ancient barbarism; thus Dante, in the Middle Ages, in the renewed barbarism of Italy. "The first peoples, who were the children of the human kind, founded first the world of the arts; then the philosophers, who came a long while afterwards, and in consequence were the aged of the nations, founded the world of science; whence humanity was in fact fulfilled." This idea of Vico's is a myth, a historical legend. But its origin is founded in the knowledge of art, free from the limits of sense, as an imaginative activity, distinct from the intellectual or the rational, as the first knowledge of humanity, creator of representations rather than engaged in reflections. Vico goes on to affirm that "imagination is so much the more robust in proportion as the reasoning faculty is weak." In this thought was comprised in synthesis, not only the condemnation of the neo-classic "Idea," but also the whole aesthetic of primitivism, without need of any transcendency. But, as is known, the influence of Vico on European thought was very limited, and it is not known how much he influenced Hamann and Herder. However, in 1762, Hamann continued the same mode of thinking: "Poetry is the maternal language of the human kind: in the same way as the garden is more ancient than the ploughed field, painting than writing, song than declamation, barter than commerce. The most ancient men spoke by the senses and passions, and did not understand if they did not imagine. And of images is composed the whole treasury of human knowledge and happiness." And Herder in support: "The natural man paints that which he sees as he sees it, live, potent, monstrous: in disorder or in order, as he sees or hears he reproduces it. So ordered their images not only all the savage tongues but also those of the Greeks and Romans. As the senses offer, so the poet expounds; especially Homer." To the epic succeeds, in times of reflection, history.

Among writers on aesthetics, however, knowledge of the value of the primitive in art was due to experience of poetry. The consideration in England of Milton and Spenser as "Gothic poets" goes back to 1711; and Herder had studied Ossian and the songs of ancient peoples, Shakespeare, popular love songs, Hebrew and Oriental poetry, remaining vividly struck by the sensibility of poetry. When, on the other hand, the writers on aesthetics referred to figurative art they could not free themselves completely from a certain reverence for the technique of the period posterior to the primitives. Hence, Ermes Visconti ends his "Elementary Ideas on Romantic Poetry" by declaring that "classicism which is reprovable in literature must be admitted in plastic arts."

It was not, therefore, on idealistic philosophy that those

who felt the need of rehabilitating the art of the primitives must found themselves: but rather Frederick Schlegel must argue to this effect against Hegel. The basis of the revaluation of the primitives was due instead to moral and religious sentiment. Theoretical insufficiency was the reason of weakness in that criticism, and afterwards was the reason of the disfavour into which it fell. Instead of attaching to Vico and Herder, criticising Hegel, and defining the irrational, imaginative and mystical character of every true work of art, in whatever time it was created; instead of making a rational criticism of mystical art, there was a mystical criticism of art. Religious needs, the mysticism of nationality and effusions of sentiment often took the place of criticism. There were found various Protestants who became Catholics through need of an external rule, and works of art were appreciated for their religious efficacy, real or presumed, rather than religious works for their artistic value; and the Middle Ages were studied not in order to understand them in their reality but to present them as a model of noble feeling, chivalry and religion, to chant the marvels of fidelity, loyalty and generosity. In which ideas not only aesthetics but also history was lost.

Nevertheless, art criticism even today cannot avoid either the experience of primitive art, or the primitivist criticism of the romantics. When the writings of Winckelmann are read it appears evident that the religious and moral sentiment of the artist is not taken into consideration. At most, the moral or religious value of the scene represented is considered, but not the way in which it is represented. One could, therefore, appreciate the calculation of the proportions rather than the creative value of a statue; therefore the copy, cold and mechanical, of a Greek masterpiece was venerated as a model of beauty. Entirely taken up with the consideration of objectivity of the product, the neo-classicists renounced understanding the value of the creative subject. The romantics, on the other hand, through their intemperance and exclusiveness, had this merit of transferring criticism from the object to the subject, of retracing through the picture or the statue the personality of the creative artist, with his sentiments, his ideals and his torments. The whole life of the mind is engaged in criticism; reason is not enough. And to have impressed their criticism with religious and moral sensibility is the imperishable merit of the romantics.

During the seventeenth century interest in the Middle Ages is manifested in erudite research into the religious documents. The mosaics and other Christian monuments found an illustrator in Ciampini. The religious motive is accompanied in Italy by regional pride, by which the Florentine primacy in pictorial production affirmed by Vasari, came to be contested with the study of mediaeval works in Siena, Rome, Venice, Bologna, and so on. From the middle of the seventeenth century appeared in England historical studies on mediaeval monuments. But the first aesthetic judgment on Gothic architecture is found in Hughes (1715), who institutes a parallel between the classical writers and Spenser, and between Roman and Gothic architecture. "In the former there is doubtless a more natural grandeur and simplicity; in the latter we find great mixture of beauty and barbarism, yet assisted by the invention of a variety of inferior ornaments; and though the former is more majestic in the whole, the latter may be very surprising and agreeable in its parts." In 1725 Pope compared Shakespeare to a Gothic monument "more strong and more solemn", even if less elegant and less "glaring" than a modern (neo-classical) architecture. The judgment is no longer casual, and demonstrates a new direction of taste, in the "Anecdotes of Painting" (1762), which Horace Walpole wrote under the influence of Gray. In spite of prejudices by which every religious work was a fraud of priests to promote superstition, Walpole writes: "The pointed arch, that peculiar of Gothic architecture, was certainly intended as an improvement on the circular; and the men who had not the happiness of lighting on the Greek orders were, however, so lucky as to strike out a thousand graces and effects, magnificent yet genteel, vast yet light, venerable and picturesque. It is difficult for the noblest Grecian temple to convey half so many impressions to the mind as a cathedral of the best Gothic taste does." "I certainly do not mean... to make any comparison between the rational beauties of regular architecture and unrestrained licentiousness of that which is called Gothic. Yet I am clear that the persons who executed the latter had more knowledge of their art, more taste, more genius, and more propriety than we choose to imagine. There is a magic hardiness in the execution of some of their works, which would not have sustained themselves if dictated by mere caprice."

From these shrewd critical observations Walpole proceeded to imagining a chivalrous romance ("Castle of Otranto: a Gothic Story"), and to the transformation of a villa into a model of picturesque Gothic, with ruins in the Gothic style and a rococo disorder. The success of the romance and the fame of the villa contributed to a fashion in Gothic, and like all fashions this also became a motive for jests and oddities. More serious manifestations of the direct passage from the rococo and its Chinese variations, to Gothic are found in the book by Batty Langley, "Gothic Architecture Improved by Rules and Proportions in Many Grand Designs" (1742). He collected motives to give the way of repeating "the ancient mode, which will be exceedingly beautiful in all parts of private buildings." He bewails that the monuments of Saxon architecture which, according to him, must have been genial, have been destroyed by invasions. As for Gothic, he states: "Every impartial judge will see by inspection that their members both as to their heights and projections are determined and described by those beautiful proportions and geometrical rules which are not excelled (if equalled) in any parts of the Grecian or Roman orders." Hogarth in "The Analysis of Beauty," 1753, admires the great beauty of detail and its accord in Gothic architecture, while he considers Chinese architecture mean, and understands that Westminster Abbey expresses religious ideas to perfection. An anonymous book entitled "Investigator" (1755) sustained the superiority of barbarian art to classical.

The picturesque, the Gothic and the incipient romantic intersect continually in the tourists who follow the tracks of Brown (1767) and Gray (1769) to admire the horridness of the rocks and the violence of the torrents in the Lake District. The picturesque — that is to say, a natural motive seen under the aspect of pictorial style, and under the influence of the landscapes of Salvator Rosa, widely diffused in England — was united with the Gothic, because there was a general opinion that there was nothing more picturesque than Gothic architecture. It was enough that Gothic, instead of being considered as the expression of barbarism and violence, should become the symbol of the poetry and chivalry of the Crusades, that it should blend naturally with romanticism. This fusion appears to have happened already in the "Letters on Chivalry and Romance" (1762) of Richard Hurd. The heroic manner of Homeric and Gothic types are both interesting: "But I go further, and maintain that the circumstances, in which they differ, are clearly to the advantage of the Gothic designers."

Gothicism furnishes the poet "with finer scenes and subjects ... than the simple and uncontrolled barbarity of the Grecian." Shakespeare and Milton are greater when they use the Gothic manner. "If you judge Gothic architecture by Grecian rules, you find nothing but deformity, but when you examine it by its own rules the result is quite different." From which may be drawn some corollaries: the imaginative passion led to a concrete result, that of judging Gothic art; historically, and not according to an extraneous law; by Gothic was understood the poetical liberty of Shakespeare with respect to classic laws (Walpole wrote to Mariette that "a schoolmaster can observe the Unities, but it required a little more genius to write Macbeth"); and whatever might have been the intemperance of the enthusiasm, the discovery of the Middle Ages was the necessary result of an imaginative rebirth that expanded in a new poetical climate. For the problem of Gothic, the eighteenth century ends with the publication of the first two English books of effective archaeological value, "History of Winchester," by Milner, and "History of Gothic and Saxon Architecture in England," by Bentham and Willis, both brought out in 1798.

In England the critical interest in Gothic architecture derived from a supposed affinity between it and the national poets, from sympathies for the oddities of rococo, and from a national way of feeling which differentiated itself from the neo-classical way of feeling. In Germany, on the other hand, the taste for Gothic was preceded by a detachment from the neo-classical critical ideas of Mengs and Winckelmann. If England arrived at Gothic in a somewhat natural way, Germany arrived at it by polemical reason, not so much against neo-classical art as against neo-classical criticism. Mengs and

Winckelmann were the greatest obstacle to the romantic taste and at the same time the greatest incentive to the reaction. The romantic taste having arrived there later in the eighteenth century, and with greater difficulty, Germany knew how to formulate the theory of it with greater depth than England. Hagedorn was a friend of Mengs and Winckelmann, but he had learned at Vienna to admire Rubens, and therefore maintained a certain tradition of eclecticism according to the tradition of De Piles. The fame of Rubens was defended specially by Heinse, who, not without humour, helped to bring about the toleration of the fat women painted by him. Heinse demands freedom of imagination, of genius and of nature; he believes that there is a necessary relation between art and the people from whom it springs, and before nature he assumes a Rousseauesque attitude. Art, he says, is human and not Greek. Proceeding in the distinctions of Lessing, he is no longer content to distinguish poetry and painting; he distinguishes also between painting and drawing. One paints with colours: colour is then the aim, the beginning and the end of painting. He perceives that the opposite opinions of Winckelmann and Lessing depend upon the fact that they never had any colour sensibility. His letters on the Düsseldorf Gallery, which are of 1776-7, are intermediate in spirit as in date between the essay on imitation by Winckelmann (1755) and the work of Wackenroder (1794). Like Walpole, Heinse passed from criticism of the journalistic type to a romance, "Ardinghello" (1787), which is the first romance of artists.

Henry Fuseli (1741-1825) was an authentic artist even though Goethe classified him among the poetising artists; he had a double culture, German and English; he lived in England the greater part of his life, and there published his "Preludes" in 1801; he illustrated Homer, Aeschylus, Dante and Shakespeare, and through the greatness of their poetry he was able to approach more nearly than his contemporaries to Masaccio, Michelangelo, Rubens and Rembrandt. Fuseli institutes for the first time the relationship between Rembrandt and Shakespeare, both of the highest excellence and of unpardonable errors. He is able to note in effects of light and shade the characteristics of the style of Rembrandt. To understand how much of the romantic there is in such a critical attitude, it is enough to say that it was only taken up again by Delacroix in 1851.

The most convinced voice in the rights of sentiment against reason, the purest representative of the "Storm and Stress", was, as is known, Hamann. Hamann in 1762, in opposition to the eclecticism of Hagedorn maintains that spontaneity and imagination are everything in art, that genius is against all the rules, the "truth," the systems, the foundations of art. Herder takes up the ideas of Hamann, but would anchor them in historical ground. The genial individual of Hamann becomes for Herder the individuality of the people: both, however, in their different researches tend to recognise the originary rather than the civilised character of art, the moving rather than the correct. Shakespeare is considered the poet of northern humanity.

Goethe adhered to the ideas of Hamann and Herder when in 1772, hardly twenty-three years old, he wrote his essays on "Gothic Architecture" in honour of Strassburg Cathedral and in opposition to the "General Theory of the Figurative Arts" of Sulzer, published a year before. Goethe affirms that the fine arts show their true nature and their best effects in their origins. He does not believe in the theory of art, and trusts to the experience of his own sensibility. Hence he refutes the considerations of Gothic as barbarous in manner: "Gothic is not only strength and roughness, but also beauty. It is a different beauty from the weak and aestheticised beauty of the rococo. Art does not all fall under the concept of beauty. True, great art is more true and great than beautiful art. There is in man a figurative nature, which acts immediately when existence is made secure. Hardly has he no longer to preoccupy himself or to fear, when, behold, like a demi-god, he infuses his spirit in matter. The spiritual unity of the production of savages is given only by feeling. But whether it proceeds from savage rudeness, or from refined feeling, art is complete and vital. It is the art of the characteristic, the only true art. The genius must look neither at models nor rules, must not profit by the wings of others, but by his own." The sublime value of art, the creative character of feeling, the independence of genius from all rules are, then, the three principles with which the young Goethe explains his enthusiasm for the Gothic cathedral of Strassburg. He exalts it as German art, precisely because it is founded on its own national principles, not borrowed from classical art, principles according to nature, and not according to the school.

As is known, in later years Goethe had a very different conception of art, even an almost opposite one. However, his youthful enthusiasm for the cathedral of Strassburg was one of the clearest signs of the necessity for a revolt against the schemes of neo-classicism then dominant.

At this point occurred a new event, prepared for by Hamann, Herder and the whole "Storm and Stress", of which all the elements can be found in the past, but which is yet new by accent and tone. We speak of the "Effusions from the Heart of a Friar Enamoured of Art" by William Henry Wackenroder, published in 1797. The author was a sick youth, dead a year later, at the age of twenty-five. His tone is poetical rather than critical, and he inclines to poetise the lives of artists or the subjects of works of art, according to the manner of Heinse's "Ardinghello." This is certainly the weakest part of his work, but it is not a good reason for denying, as has been done recently, that Wackenroder has a place in the history of art criticism. To see a work of art there were the neo-classic rules, empty of content, and this was an impulse of rebellion against them on the part of the "Storm and Stress": that which Wackenroder bears like a gift of God is a new way of feeling, the humility of the faithful before the work of art, a religion that does not go beyond the demands of sentiment. All this is not yet a system of aesthetics, but it is the demand for a system of aesthetics that should be freer and purer than any rationalistic demand existing then or later. It was the transference of attention, with an intensity unknown before, to the artist's way of feeling. And this is the greatness of Wackenroder.

The artist works by "divine inspiration." Wackenroder knows that this divine inspiration is identified with spontaneity of creation. "If for a long time the artist cannot fix the imagination which a celestial ray of sun puts in his mind, there comes the moment in which without perceiving it he has a-chieved the work, and a clear splendour warns him of the miracle which has happened." The form is metaphorical and open to criticism, but the knowledge of the spontaneity of creation is here expressed. The "secrets of artists" do not exist, or at least they are not aware of them; they think "always more of the subject than of the mode of representing it." This is a marvellous metaphorical representation of artistic intuition, which possesses its secrets without knowing it, and does not re·flect upon modes of representation, which is the function of criticism, but abandons itself to the inspiring motive.

Every artist, when he is complete, has a manner of his own, which seems to Wackenroder born with him, not acquired with sweat and which "cannot be studied"; that is to say, it cannot be analysed for assimilation, as Mengs would do. "Oh sad wisdom! Oh blind faith! How can one believe it possible to reunite in oneself all kinds of beauty and every excellence of all the great artists on earth, and to master their mind and overcome all, only by contemplating and begging their so different gifts?" "The perfect beauty of art is manifested to us, in its fulness, only when our eyes do not turn to look at the same time at another beauty." Observe that, in that sense, must be understood the impossibility of studying the manner of artists: it is the affirmation of the absolute value of the artistic personality, that cannot be divided, that cannot be compared, that is valid only in itself. One must abandon oneself to contemplating the beloved artist by "embracing all his characteristic individuality," and not use the "pretentious severity of a judge," who, like the masters of morality, put "the artists in file according to the nature and importance of their merits." And if anybody opposed to him that a Greek statue excites in the mind the idea of beauty, Wackenroder confesses that he has no reason to contradict, but that he feels how, beside "the so-called high powers of knowledge, there stands in our mind a magic mirror that sometimes shows us things in a more powerful representation." This is a metaphorical expression of the intuition of the sublime. The judge of art lacks "tolerance and philanthropy"; art is the "flower of human sensibility." To the creator "the Gothic temple is as pleasing as the Greek temple ... Why do you not condemn the Indian who speaks Indian and not another language, and still wish to condemn the Middle Ages because its temples are not like those of Greece?" "Beauty: a marvellously strange word! Imagine a new word for every separate work of art! In each of these appears another colour, and for each one, other nerves have been created in the mechanism of man. But you take away from this word, with the arts of reason, a rigorous system, and you would restrict all men to feel according to your precepts and your rules, and you yourselves feel nothing." "Looking tranquilly at all times and at all peoples, we try always to feel the human in every sentiment and all its works."

Then, the divine inspiration, the spontaneity of creation and its non-rational character, the intuition of the artist who does not know the secret he possesses, the abandonment of the artist to the inspiring motive, the absolute value, outside all hierarchies, of the artistic personality, the necessity that the critic should be humble before the work of art, becoming its interpreter, without the self-sufficiency or the superiority of the judge, and love the work of art, and have human sympathy and tolerance for the sensibility of others; the sense of the infinite variety of art; and irony and disdain against the rules, against the pride of the elect, against the condemnation of the Gothic temple because it does not resemble the Greek temple: all these motives are certainly affirmed but not demonstrated, yet everybody feels that they are just and true, and therefore belong not to the abstract but to the concrete human reason. Nobody before the very young Wackenroder had felt them in their entirety, nor had expressed them; his mode of feeling, his "love," has brought them well within rational truth.

His immaturity appears generally in the historical application of his principles, because of too little knowledge, and he was very much more timid in dealing with the ideas of others than in expressing his own feeling. Before Dürer, however, he not only feels the artist's greatness, as nobody had before him, but gives the justification of his feeling with critical precision:

"Nobody stands there with half a mind, as often can be said of the mannered paintings of the new masters; everyone is taken in the fullness of life and so is placed on the canvas. Who should lament, laments; who should be enraged, is enraged; and who should pray, prays. All the figures speak, and speak loud and clear. Not an arm moves uselessly or only for the delight of the eye or to fill the space; all the members, all speak to us equally with force, so that we gather within us very firmly the sense and the soul of everything. We believe in everything that the artist represents to us, and nothing is ever cancelled from our memory... But the moderns seem not to desire in fact that one should take part seriously in what they represent; they work for rich lords, who do not wish to be moved and spiritually ennobled by art, but at the most astonished and tickled." As you see, the moral sensibility of Wackenroder has led him not only to discover the values of art but also to justify socially his own discovery.

The influence of the few pages of Wackenroder was very great, above all upon the Schlegels, and through them, upon the whole of romanticism and the Nazarenes, the painters already mentioned, who tried to realise the thought of Wackenroder without succeeding. Under that influence, Frederick Schlegel and his friends rediscovered the German and Flemish primitives, and with them rebound artistic taste to the Germanic national movement. They preferred them, therefore, even to the Italian primitives, because they believed they saw in them a greater religiosity, whereas they dealt only with a different religiosity. However, Frederick Schlegel understood the beauty of Bellini and Perugino, found it superior to that of Fra Bartolomeo, admitted that he loved the older Italian school, and saw the parallelism between Dante and Giotto, with which he contraposed that between Albani and the Cavalier Marino.

Hence he finished by disapproving not only the taste but also the art of the Carracci. This was the greatest consequence of Wackenroder's intuitions. Frederick Schlegel emitted this judgment in 1802-4, two centuries after the Carracci had given the impression of having restored painting. During the nineteenth century the judgment of Frederick Schlegel was shared by the best critics, but to-day there is a return to appreciation of the Carracci. Is it a regression? If so, as we believe, it is necessary to carry to extreme conclusions Wackenroder's mode of feeling.

Frederick Schlegel had also to defend the Nazarenes against the attacks of Goethe and Meyer. He set himself to oppose to the neo-classicism of David and his theatricality, the pious intentions of the Nazarenes. A delicate task for a critic. The results of the Nazarenes were not, in fact, artistic. And Frederick Schlegel must have felt it, because he had previously written that it was necessary to be resigned to not seeing art arise together with the new ideas, through fault of the rationalism of the century, which dried up feeling.

The principles of Wackenroder were totally transformed by idealistic philosophy. Therefore the successors of that truth which was inherent in the moral demand of Wackenroder are to be found rather among the writers who, instead of recovering themselves by philosophical principles, spoke of art in the name of the religious renewal that romanticism carried with it.

In Italy during the eighteenth century important studies on mediaeval art were not wanting. In 1757 Lami wrote a dissertation on the painters and sculptors from 1000 to 1300, to oppose the disparagement of the "Byzantine manner" in painting as of the "Gothic style" in architecture. In 1766 a mathematician, Frisi, wrote an essay on the constructive technique of Gothic architecture which was greatly appreciated and translated into German by Herder. In 1779 Baretti exalted the Gothic architecture of the cathedral of Asti, with ideas assimilated from the English surroundings in which he lived. In 1785 Della Valle opposed Sienese painting to Florentine, as poetry to science, as imagination to thought. In 1813 appeared the first volume of the "History of Sculpture in Italy" by Cicognara, in continuation of the work of Winckelmann. He rejected the epithet of "barbarous" given to mediaeval art, regarded the spirit of religion as the former of that art, recognised the infinite original beauties of the fourteenth century, and arrived at saying, "in the best times of the arts as much as the style gained in mastery and energy it lost in truth and purity," and that "the precious results of science restrict the genius of the arts, bridling the imagination and diminishing the force of a potent help, the marvellous." Which did not hinder him from admiring Canova.

The presence in Rome of the German Nazarenes excited various discussions between 1830 and 1840, which expanded into the "Manifesto of the Purists," of 1843, written by Antonio Bianchini, and which tended, not so much to imitate the primitives, as to impress painting with a greater moral and religious seriousness. Selvatico and Father Marchese adhered to Bianchini.

France was the country of Seroux d'Agincourt, who even before the French Revolution had prepared the monumental history of mediaeval art, from the fourth to the sixteenth century, which was published only in 1823. He showed a lively interest in the mediaeval masters for their own sake, and spread their work by means of engraving; but his ideas were not different from those of Winckelmann. Indeed, at one point, he explains his work thus: "Winckelmann showed artists what they should imitate, I will point out to them what they must avoid." The collector, Artaud de Montor, translator of Dante, delighted in the fresh colouring and certainty of brush of the primitives. Paillot de Montabert (1829) exalted the Italian primitives against the men of the sixteenth century, and affirmed that the sixteenth century is a beginning of decadence.

The most famous of all is Rio, the author of "Christian Art," the publication of which began in 1836, and which was regarded as the code of Christian ideal. The novelty of the historical treatment consists in the chapter on the mystical school, dedicated to Blessed Angelico. Rio states the critical problem thus: "Here ends the competency of those commonly called the connoisseurs, because to appreciate the works of Angelico requires a different organ from that which judges ordinary works. Mysticism stands to paintings as ecstasy to psychology. It is not enough, then, to determine the traditions of the school; it is necessary to associate one's self, with a sympathy strong and deep, with certain religious ideas which pre-occupied this artist in his workshop or that monk in his cell, and put them into relationship with the spiritual life of their time." The demand was just but insufficient: deep sympathy and comprehension of the spiritual life are valid not only for the mystical school but for all the schools, and, on the other hand, knowledge of the religious life, in itself, does not suffice to guarantee to the critic that the artistic realisation is achieved. So that Rio gives the impression of being very much more interested in religious history and the triumph of religion than in the history of art.

The resurgence of the Gothic style in France is linked with the name of Viollet-Le-Duc (1814-1879), architect and critic. There is no doubt that his love of the Middle Ages was great, but unfortunately, his restorations of ancient monuments, like his writings, reveal the exaggerated rationalism of the engineer rather than the moral sympathy of the critic. The same principles which, according to him, rendered necessary the use of Gothic served his adversaries to restore a species of neo-classicism.

We must turn to England to find in the nineteenth century an important critical work on the art of the Middle Ages. The true continuer of Wackenroder, even if he never read him, he who was able to translate the forebodings into a great critical edifice, is Ruskin (1819-1900). His spiritual origins are purely English.

Outside architecture the experiences of mediaeval art were not very important, except for the collectors. One of them, William Young Ottley, had published in 1823 "The Italian School of Design," in which he affirmed that the perspicuity of Giotto "has perhaps never been surpassed." In 1836 a committee decided to buy for the national collections works of art anterior to Raphael, because they were of a style more pure and elevated than the eminent works of the Carracci, and to that decision is due the unique character of the National Gallery. The success of Rio's "Christian Art" was great in England, and in 1847 appeared Lord Lindsay's book of a similar type, which served Ruskin as a guide to the knowledge of Italian art.

In the meantime the mode of Gothic architecture was widely spread in England. An architect and writer, Pugin, exhibited a new state of mind from that of the eighteenth century. In his "Contrasts," written in 1835, and "True Principles of Christian Architecture," published in 1841, he affirms that Gothic is not a style but a religion, and is worth more than the

Greek style because the Christian religion is worth more than the pagan. In honour of Gothic he becomes Catholic, and even dreams socially of the restoration of the Middle Ages. From him originates in England the attempt to judge the work of art from the point of view of the morality of its creator, hence the obligation of the most absolute sincerity and truth, according to which the essential elements of construction must be clearly revealed in the architecture.

Ruskin's "lamp of truth" is found, then, already determined by Pugin. But Ruskin does not appreciate Pugin; he has a much stronger and purer artistic sensibility. Therefore he detaches himself from the contemporary mode of Gothic and seeks the pure old Gothic of Venice and Amiens. The true origin of his art criticism does not reside in either religion or morality, but in enthusiasm for art. "There is the strong instinct in me which I cannot analyse, to draw and describe the things I love – not for reputation, nor for the good of others, nor for my own advantage, but a sort of instinct like that for eating and drinking. I should like to draw all St. Mark's and all this Verona stone by stone, to eat it all up into my mind, touch by touch": so he wrote from Verona to his father in 1852. It was just this passionate sensibility which allowed Ruskin to overcome the limitations of his moral and religious education to arrive at the comprehension of art, as his contemporaries well saw and present day critics have ceased to understand. Certainly Ruskin's thought is not organised logically, any more than was Wackenroder's, but we are forced to recognise that whatever logical organisation Ruskin might have made would have caused the loss of some positive value in his intuitions.

He rebels against the "rules" of drawing and substitutes for them the principle of love: a thing, "if it be not drawn for love of it, will never be right, and if it be drawn for love of it, will never be wrong, love's misrepresentation being truer than the most mathematical presentation." Before nature the Greeks err by lack of sympathy. When we approach the things of nature, we feel that "a wilful fountain sings and that the kindly flowers rejoice. And then, puzzled and yet happy; pleased and yet ashamed of being so; accepting sympathy from nature, which we do not believe it gives; and giving sympathy to nature, which we do not believe it receives. . . . But the Greek never removed his god from nature at all; never attempted for a moment to contradict his instinctive sense that God was everywhere . . . What sympathy and fellowship he had were always for the spirit in the stream, not for the stream; always for the dryad in the wood, not for the wood. Content with this human sympathy, he approached the actual waves and woody fibres with no sympathy at all ("Modern Painters" IV, XIII, 13). This is the natural love of Ruskin, which he identifies with "the feelings of love, reverence or dread with which the human mind is affected by its conceptions of spiritual being." (Lectures on Art, 37). It is natural, then, that he does not love the religious painting of his time. In the Middle Ages "art was employed for the display of religious facts, now religious facts were employed for the display of art." ("Modern Painters" IV, IV, 11). He looks at the sincerity of the artist, and sees well that when religion is adopted for art there is moral indifference, the result is not true art; while when there is a true religious feeling, art may be spontaneously created. And thus Ruskin makes some reservation even about Blessed Angelico. "Adore a falcon as did the Egyptians, and paint it as never would he who sees in it a feathered biped, because the ecstasy which you have experienced will pass through your hands into the picture, and will give it the power to communicate to others the same transport." Observe how religious feeling can discover the essence of art in mystical communion with nature, in ecstasy.

Having thus illuminated the nature of art, Ruskin considers that of the artist: "The whole function of the artist in the world is to be a seeing and feeling creature, to be an instrument of such tenderness and sensitiveness, that no shadow, no hue, no line, no instantaneous and evanescent expression of the visible things around him, nor any of the emotions which they are capable of conveying to the spirit which has been given him, shall either be left unrecorded, or fade from the book of record... He may think, in a by-way; reason, now and then, when he has nothing better to do; know, such fragments of knowledge as he can gather without stooping, or reach without pains; but none of these things are to be his care. The work of his life is to be two-fold only; to see, to feel." ("Stones of Venice," III, II, 10). "What we want art to do for us is to stay what is fleeting, and to enlighten what is incomprehensible, to incorporate the things that have no measure, and immortalise the things that have no duration... All that is infinite and wonderful, having in it that spirit and power which man may witness, but not weigh; conceive, but not comprehend; love, but not limit, and imagine, but not define; this, the beginning and the end of the aim of all noble art." ("Stones of Venice," III, II, 23). This is the ideal of the artists, which Ruskin does not find again after the sixteenth century, on account of the triumph of science, and the consequent rational benumbing of minds. Intolerance of intellectualism in art warns him that even in the Renaissance there filters through some sin of scientific pride. "Raphael, Leonardo, and Michelangelo were all trained in the old school; they all had masters who knew the true ends of art, and had reached them; masters nearly as great as they were themselves, but imbued with the old religious and earnest spirit, which their disciples receiving from them, and drinking at the same time deeply from all the fountains of knowledge opened in their day, became the world's wonders. Then the dull, wondering world believed that their greatness rose out of their new knowledge, instead of out of that ancient religious root, in which to abide was life, from which to be severed was annihilation. And from that day to this, they have tried to produce Michel Angelos and Leonardos by teaching the barren sciences, and still have mourned and marvelled that no more Michel Angelos came; not perceiving that those great Fathers were only able to receive such nourishment because they were rooted on the rock of all ages, and that our scientific teaching, nowadays, is nothing more nor less than the assiduous watering of trees whose stems are cut through." ("Stones of Venice," III, II, 33). Even in Raphael the scientific defect appears. In the "Massacre of the Innocents" he has defined the degrees of pity and terror: one would say "that the philosophical spirit had prevailed over the imaginative ... Not so Tintoretto, knowing or feeling that the expression of the human face was in such circumstances not to be rendered, and that the effort could only end in an ugly falsehood ... Still less does he depend on details of murder or ghastliness of death; there is no blood, no stabbing or cutting, but there is an awful substitute for these in the chiaroscuro." ("Stones of Venice," III, School of S. Rocco, 4). This is a great critical discovery, of a new type, in fact, in the history of art criticism: the drama does not become painting, with the raw elements of nature like the discolouration of death, the drama can become painting only if dissolved into visible elements, like light and shade full of terror. It is moral sensibility, and not a clear aesthetic idea, that leads Ruskin so far: but it is the result that counts.

To define the Gothic style, Ruskin does not limit himself to resorting to the usual constructive schemes of the pointed arch and the crossvault, or of the thrust and counterthrust. All that he analyses with his usual accuracy, but he goes further toward the "states of temper and the moral feeling" of artists. He has, moreover, knowledge of the unity of taste in painting, sculpture and architecture, and affirms that true architecture, when it is not pure engineering construction, is the work of potential sculptors and painters and must be observed as painting and sculpture. He admits that the Gothic architects are rude and uncultivated, but precisely to this is due their absolute freedom in ornamentation and spontaneity of creation, free from any pride of perfection: "All admit irregularity as they imply change; and to banish imperfection is to destroy expression, to check exertion, to paralyse vitality." ("Stones of Venice," II, VI, 24-25). He admires in the Gothic artists their love of fantastic variety, distinct from love of knowledge, their love of nature, beyond all abstract laws, their taste for the grotesque, their "active rigidity, the peculiar energy which gives tension to movement and stiffness to resistance," and, finally, their generosity, which produces "redundance, the uncalculating bestowal of the wealth of its labour." Whoever knows the masterpieces of Gothic art will feel Ruskin's moral indications as critical illuminations.

Always for a moral reason Ruskin opposes the celebrated Greek principle of choice from nature. A choice, in fact, appears insolent to Ruskin. He loves and adores nature, the whole of nature. To choose implies to have rejected, to have despised an element of nature, and it is therefore sacrilegious. But if all nature is worthy of representation it cannot all be represented in a single picture by a single artist. Therefore the artist must not choose among the things of nature, but among the elements of his art; he must not choose a piece of nature arbitrarily considered beautiful but must choose to express his love of nature in lines rather than colours, in light and shade rather than form, or the other way about. The standard of choice is thus transferred to the artist's way of seeing, from the object to the relation between subject and object, from nature to art; and this, too, is a flash of genius.

Ruskin's mysticism does not hinder him, then, from seeing clearly the figurative process of the artist, which is a necessity for all art criticism. Rather, to the figurative schemes he gives for the first time a historical content, raising them from the technical plane to the plane of taste:

" 1. Line (early schools)

  2. Line and light (Greek clay)

  3. Line and colour (Gothic glass)

  4. Mass and light (Leonardo and school)

  5. Mass and colour (Giorgione and school)

  6. Mass, light and colour (Titian and school)."

(Lectures on Art, 139).

To transfer the abstract elements of vision to particular historical conditions signifies to maintain only one aspect of their abstraction, that relative to nature, and to make them concrete relatively to a moment of taste. In fact, Ruskin does not dream of taking away from the figurative elements their concretely human character. He sees a development of taste in three moments: 1) line, 2) surface, 3) mass, or space in depth; he sees also how man has proceeded in accomplishing such a development — that is to say, through two ways, that of light and shade and that of colour; and he identifies the way of light and shade with the scientific tendency of the abstract conception of reality, and the way of colour with the spontaneous, free, serene and sane disposition of artistic imagination. ("Lectures on Art," 147). This means to make a truthful history of taste. Precisely by this capacity of identifying the taste of the artist with one or more figurative schemes, Ruskin succeeds in liberating from the classical prejudice of the superiority of form over colour, to discover the beauty of line in Botticelli, to understand that the beauty of St. Mark's is a beauty of colour, and many other critical discoveries.

Liberation from neo-classical prejudices, justification of the value of mediaeval art, through a portentous fusion of aesthetic and moral sensibility, are such merits as to compel recognition that to-day, in spite of the general oblivion, Ruskin as an art critic is more alive than ever, and that many of his positions are not superseded.

It is therefore with a certain grief that there must be acknowledged the grave harm of detachment from contemporary art that romantic criticism caused by looking only at the Middle Ages, just as neo-classical criticism had caused harm by looking only at the antique era. The fact is that, before works of art contemporary to him, the aesthetic sensibility of Ruskin seems to be dissipated. He is, in fact, responsible for that misleading of English taste — and unfortunately not only English — due to the Pre-Raphaelites: it is true that they determined their manner apart from Ruskin, but perhaps, without Ruskin, nobody would remember them to-day. Also to the Gothic imitations of his time Ruskin sometimes gave his suffrage, afterwards however to repent and to be irritated by the architectural applications of his principles. During the nineteenth century the two best painters that England produced were Constable and Bonington, and Ruskin disparaged them in order to exalt Turner, so much inferior to them. Delacroix and the French landscape painters of 1830 were more clear-sighted than Ruskin. He was, then, too much shut up in mediaeval art — and that was his pride — to understand what was happening around him.

However, he was the culminating point of romantic criticism, which will probably remain as an eternal moment in the criticism of art.

CHAPTER VIII
The History of Art and
Idealistic Philosophy

IN THE two preceding chapters we have expounded the critical motives proceeding from two tendencies of taste: the one assigned exclusive value in art to rationalised form, identified in classical sculpture; the other recognised the right of religious and moral sentiment in the production and interpretation of art, hence the exaltation of mediaeval artists.

The neo-classical taste was the conclusion, carried to extreme severity, of the cult of ancient art, which, from the Renaissance onward, was almost uninterrupted, and founded upon illuminist ideas; the taste for the Middle Ages appears in reaction from the neo-classical, under the impulse of contemporary life and romantic literature, then being born. The origins of the two movements came at a few years' interval in the second half of the eighteenth century. The eighteenth century was not yet ended when already a new tendency appeared which sought a synthesis of the neo-classical and the romantic tastes: I speak of *idealism*, and its ambition to define art as the classical form of a romantic content. The maximum results of idealistic criticism came in the first decades of the nineteenth century, at the moment when art was above all dominated by neo-classicism. But idealistic criticism continued until toward the middle of the nineteenth century, accompanying the development of romantic art. In the second half of the nineteenth century, idealistic criticism and romantic art both declined from their directive function. Romantic art, properly speaking, did not re-appear. Idealistic criticism, on the contrary, re-appeared at the beginning of our century and seems to be developing.

187

On the other hand, we have noted that, for the first time in the history of criticism, both the neo-classicists and the romantics look by preference to the art of the past rather than to that contemporary with them. They look at it with a nostalgic mind, the neo-classicists as to an unattainable perfection, the romantics as to a lost Paradise. Both of them propose the restoration of art, hence they become proclaimers of the imitation of the antique or of the Gothic revival. Therefore both lost contact with the authentic vein of contemporary art, a vein which, on account of its own detachment from the dominant ideas, must for several decades run in the dark of incomprehension. The idealists were too wise, and too conscious of the limits of their function as critics, to nourish illusions of an artistic restoration, but that did nothing but aggravate the detachment between criticism and contemporary art. Too much nourished on thought to approve romantic fantasies, too much aware of the eternal creativity of history to confuse entirely the classic and the neo-classic, they ended by occupying themselves seriously only with the past. The most paradoxical expression of this detachment is found in Hegel's famous theory of the death of art, which was the expression, of the *enfant-terrible* type, of a conviction widely diffused. An evident absurdity, and one which weakens his whole conception of art.

One consequence of such a state of things was that the greater artists of the first half of the nineteenth century — Goya, Corot and Daumier — had no relations with idealistic criticism. The idealists appreciated David, who in 1793 affirmed: "The artist must have studied all the springs of the human heart, he must have a great knowledge of nature, he must in a word be a philosopher. Socrates, able sculptor; J. J. Rousseau, good musician; the immortal Poussin, tracing on canvas the most sublime lessons of philosophy — these are so many witnesses who prove that the genius of the arts must have no other guide than the torch of reason." For the neo-classicists of the Mengs type reason was not a *torch;* and the "springs of the human heart" recall the treatise on the representation of the passions of Le Brun rather than the theory of indifferent beauty by Winckelmann. So much did he, even David, on account of the French Revolution, feel himself constrained to impregnate with romanticism his neo-classicism, just as did the idealists. Equally the pure neo-classicists would have with difficulty subscribed to the prophecies of the architect Detournelle, made in the same year, 1793: "In two years one will see born a sublimity which will surpass all that we have admired, sometimes with prejudice for the antique; we shall not be Athenians, nor Romans, slaves who use the name of free men; but Frenchmen, free by nature, philosophers by character, virtuous by feeling and artists by taste." Alas! *sublimity* was not born in 1793, nor for many years to come, and the triumph over neo-classicism remained one of the ineffectual illusions of the French Revolution. When with the political restoration in France, neo-classicism was abandoned, it was not German idealism which influenced the change of taste, but German mysticism, which Ary Scheffer translated into sentimentalism, the poetry of revolt of the Byronic type, which seduced Delacroix, and the picturesque erudition of Walter Scott, which Delaroche continued in figures.

In Germany some painters were more or less reasonably inspired by idealistic thought, painters who had to some extent relations with the Nazarenes: for example, Cornelius, Kaulbach and Bethel. Raczinski, a prudent admirer of Cornelius, wrote in 1838: "He considers the subjects which he treats from a very elevated point of view. Study of nature and the technical part of art occupy him less. Also, it often seems with him that the figures most impressed with force and grandeur lack something of life; one would almost say that in his personages the circulation of the blood is arrested." It was inevitable that this should happen to all the painters of ideas, these involuntary abortions of idealism, very rare except in Germany.

In concrete judgments on contemporary art the classical prejudice allows idealism to see very little more than the face of death, and even spoils historical conceptions of the art of the past, for it is evident that one cannot understand the spiritual life of the past without experience of the present. However, the positive value of idealism in art criticism is of another nature: aesthetic and thought in general have been greatly enriched by it, and the conception of history, as development, has given the maximum impulse to the study of the development also of art, in its double movement as individual creativeness and as the objective necessity of style. Hence it can be said without exaggeration that in German idealism the critical history of art finds one of the eternal moments of its method.

In the transition between the era of illuminism and that of idealism stands Kant, who justified systematically the judgment of taste. Taste, which judges whether a work is beautiful or not, has the pretension that its judgment is universal, without being able to furnish the rational demonstration of the rightness of its judgment. For this reason one cannot give any objective rule of taste. Every judgment derived from this source is aesthetic: in other words, its determining cause is the feeling of the subject, not a concept of the object. The search for a principle of taste, which shall be the universal standard of beauty by means of determined concepts, is a vain fatigue, because that which is sought is impossible and contradictory in itself. There is not a science of beauty but only a criticism of it, and there are no fine sciences but only fine arts. Before a production of fine art it is necessary to realise that it is art and not nature; but-the finality of its form must appear free from all restraint of voluntary rules, as if it were simply a product of nature, a spontaneous product and not willed. Fine art is the art of genius. Genius must be original, but, in order to avoid being arbitrary, it must produce a pattern, without knowing how its task is fulfilled.

In such a manner Kant realised the distinction between the subjective and the arbitrary in art and in artistic judgment; rejected all rules in art; fused the concept of beauty with that of art; distinguished art and science, art and nature, sense and imagination; and accentuated the spontaneous and original character of genius productive of art. Principles these, so true that they have become the common patrimony. On the other hand, Kant understood that art also belongs to a tradition that it is necessary to *follow* not to *imitate*, because detachment from tradition would mean to fall back on crude natural capacity, and on the other hand to imitate would mean to renounce the originality of genius. This was a mode for understanding the tradition of artistic civilisation proper to his time and for rejecting the imitation of the antique.

Herder, the adversary of Kant, also limits neo-classicism. He admires Winckelmann, but feels the need of a more deeply founded historicity. Taste has a sensible character, but grows through experiences; like imagination, taste also belongs to a setting historically determined. For Winckelmann art is a gift to the whole world of a chosen people, the Greek; for Herder art is the apparition of God in the historical development of humanity. Nevertheless the classical prejudice leads him to admit that the forms of sculpture (Greek, understood) are eternal, because they respond to pure human nature; the figures of painting, instead, change with the times, because painting depends upon effects of light and shade, in which the spirit of the artist may vary freely; and Herder is not aware that in such a way he assigns the character of art to painting and denies it to sculpture.

Herder was warned by the theory of Riedel (1767) of the danger inherent in neglecting the universal idea of art and in interesting oneself only in its historical aspect. Riedel, in fact, maintained that taste changed from people to people according to climate, custom, fashion and other things, and changed also from century to century, even from person to person. Hence to oppose a good taste to a bad one was an error of transferring the standard of the true to the beautiful, which was no standard, coinciding with pleasure and displeasure. To refute Riedel it would have been sufficient to oppose the Kantian concept of subjective taste with universal validity. Herder opposed to Riedel the need of liberation from national, temporal and personal limitations of taste in order to enjoy the beautiful wherever it is found, in all times, in all peoples and in all kinds of taste: everywhere, detached from all extraneous things, to enjoy and feel it purely. The sphere of taste is infinite, like the history of humanity; its periphery extends to all the centuries and to all the works, and taste and beauty stand at the centre. Who has no taste, in the full sense, cannot have even a Greek taste. In this Herder well saw the coincidence between the historical and the theoretical character of art criticism.

In his celebrated essay: "Naive and Sentimental Poetry," Schiller sought to make admissible the value of modern poetry, in spite of its different aspects from ancient poetry, and to define that value in the character of infinite rather than finite, spiritual rather than corporeal. But for the figurative arts he depends on Lessing, who said that sculpture defines in space, and Schiller admits that a work for the eye finds its perfection only in corporeal limitation: hence the superiority of ancient sculpture over modern. He does not speak about painting.

Sculpture and painting were distinguished by Herder thus: "Sculpture is truth; painting is dream: *that* is all representation, *this* the work of an enchanter. The most beautiful painting is romance, dream of a dream." Painting would therefore share the modern character, denied to sculpture.

Humboldt goes further: ancient poetry makes the same impression as the beautiful fragments of Greek sculpture. Modern poetry, on the contrary, produces on us rather the effect of melodious and moving music. The enthusiasm of Winckelmann for Greek statues, and the definitions of plastic value given by Lessing, had as a reaction the neglect of sculpture and a growing tendency towards music in the modern life of art. Let us remember that many years after Humboldt, Walter Pater theorised precisely the tendency of all arts toward the musical condition. Humboldt seeks, then, to explain the difference psychologically: the Greeks had an external sensible intuition, which directed them towards proportion and harmony; the moderns have an internal sense which makes possible stronger contrasts, brusquer transitions, discords unresolvable by the reason itself. When Humboldt presses closer his conception of the external sensible intuition of the Greek, he falls into the old error of seeking the idea of form, leaning upon mathematics and anatomy, and vaunting Greek art as aided by science. The happy ideas of Kant and the courageous romantic movement no longer inspire. Very much more worthy of note are Humboldt's explanations of the creative character of art, by which composition of extra-artistic elements results through work of the artist in something entirely new; his refusal to recognise beauty in the values of the object — that is to say, in elements extraneous to creation; and, finally, his refusal to admit hierarchies of the kinds: form being the essential element of art, the painter of history will be greater as a man than the painter of flowers, but one is no less a painter than the other.

Kant, Herder, Schiller and Humboldt are interested above all in their ideas on art; Goethe interests himself more in works of figurative art, but in the manner of a poet and artist rather than in that of a critic. In Rome, he pleases himself in the study of drawing, more than in analysing the works of art; and dreams of a type of critic who can surrender and subordinate himself to the object, which is certainly necessary for anybody who wishes to understand, but is not enough, because the critic, instead of surrendering himself, must precisely put his own ideas and feeling into relation with those of the artist of whom he speaks. We have said already that as a young man Goethe participated in the romantic movement, exalting Gothic as German art; but later, his need of universality on one side, and his complex experience of all technical matters on the other, led him to appreciate Greek art above all, and to speak ill of Gothic. His classicism is, nevertheless, often imbued with the direct experience of modern art; for example, he believes that all plastic art tends to painting, and exalts Rubens and the Dutch painters of the seventeenth century. He believes he can resolve the question of the ancients and moderns by exalting Raphael, who never Grecises but conceives as a Greek. He does not, with Lessing, admit that the ancients represented only the beautiful, nor, with Winckelmann, that they expressed only the silent greatness of placid tranquillity; they represented the *characteristic* under all possible forms. It is the need to specify, to define, to make concrete in art, which suggests to him the acceptance of the distinction of the arts by Lessing. The arts, he says, have a certain tendency to merge one into the other; but the duty, the merit, the dignity of the true artist consists in putting every art and every kind of art on its own basis, and in being able to isolate it as much as possible. Goethe is less original when he touches on history, he imagines a "psycho-chronological" development of art, which is nothing but the notion of perfection followed by decline, which we know from Bellori to Winckelmann.

During his journeys in Italy Goethe has various happy personal intuitions — for example, on Palladio, Paolo Veronese and Titian; and also repeats many commonplaces without checking them. There is an interesting contrast between his intuition and the commonplaces at Bologna, before the pictures of Guido Reni: "While the divine genius of Guido and his brush attract you, you would turn away from certain subjects so horribly stupid that there are no words reproachful enough to condemn them. Guido treats his spiritual heroes like mannikins to drape them in fine mantles with imposing folds. Nothing that presents a human idea. Also, to consult history, in this my moment of bad humour, I should be tempted to say: faith certainly resuscitated the arts, but superstition has become master and has again led them to ruin." That is to say, Goethe felt truly that those works of Guido Reni were not art; but since it has been repeated to him a thousand times that Guido Reni is a divine genius, he attributes the bad result to the Church: in which coincide in an exemplary manner the weakness of the critic and the acuteness of the poet.

In conclusion, Goethe, in spite of his love for figurative art, accepted the traditional judgments, and profited by the new ideas, vivifying both with some happy intuitions.

Before Hegel, William Schlegel tried to fuse theory, history and criticism of art. He tried to distinguish from aesthetics a *philosophical theory* of the arts, that should define the autonomy, sphere and limitations of each art. History must deal only with reality, but it has lost its character of chronicle by the fact that theory is present in it. Theory furnishes history with the relation between the individual appearance and the idea of art, while history furnishes theory with examples for its concepts. The work of art is complete in itself, and yet history can be made of it, because it is subject to national limitations and relationships. Time and ambients furnish matter for the eternal spirit of art. Individuals of genius are understood only as single appearances of the great genius of humanity. Therefore the historical conception of Winckelmann, with the unique perfection of one period of Greek art, is overcome; even the apparently barbarous periods are a necessary dissonance of the art of humanity. As for criticism, that stands midway between history and theory: the critic has need at the same time of the theory and the history of art. Therefore he must reject criticism of the beautiful parts of a picture, which is atomistic and anti-historical.

All this has remained fundamental to the critical history of to-day; but the concrete critical judgments of William Schlegel are much less interesting. Because of the concept of the autonomy of sculpture, he believes that it is in decline since Ghiberti adopted the pictorial relief; since it does not make use of a natural model, architecture should be imagined according to a peculiar original idea of the human spirit; negative appreciation for classical reason of Gothic architecture is not wholly abandoned, even though Gothic is German art. Finally, William Schlegel contradicts himself, now appreciating and now disparaging Correggio and Rembrandt.

The History of Art and Idealistic Philosophy

Frederick Schlegel, also, occupies and preoccupies himself with the history of art; he goes even further, and does not admit any other theory of art than an historical theory, without being able to indicate in what it consists. Under the influence of Wackenroder he opposes Mengs and his eclecticism, and takes a lively interest in Gothic and in the fifteenth century Germans, Flemings and even Italians. He is the first to call attention to the fifteenth century school of Cologne, and he calls the primitives Pre-Raphaelites. Sensible to Christian and national values, he opposes the *characteristic* of the fifteenth century to the *decorative grandiosity* of the sixteenth century, and refuses to appreciate the school of the Carracci. He proposes to himself the problem of the formation of a modern *Christian-national* pictorial school, but feels the impossibility of its solution, and attributes the blame to the rationalism of his time which has dried up feeling. Nevertheless, Frederick Schlegel opposes the condemnation pronounced by Goethe against the Nazarenes, and disparages French classicism of the David type in order to defend German artists·like Schick and Kock, who certainly rate lower than David.

He has knowledge of the importance of visual sensibility in order to understand the values of art, and occupies himself with colours, light and forms. But at the same time he values the poetical over the mechanical, imagination over vision, the problem of the theme treated over that of form; and therefore he ends in allegorical interpretation. He sees in Van Eyck Christian ideality, in Raphael pagan, and in Altdorfer the idea of German chivalry. Worse still, as much as William Schlegel, Frederick fails to distinguish the history of art from poetical description, and he indulges in historical pseudo-poetry. Therefore he does not succeed in giving to the great quantity of critical motives, both important and new, either an historical structure or a critical form.

The writers of whom we have spoken up to now prepare in various ways the idealistic aesthetic, which is then realised by Schelling and Hegel.

Schelling profits by a current idea on the work of art as a synthesis of two opposites, and specifies that the two opposites are the conscious and the unconscious activity, of which the opposition is infinite. But since these two activities must be represented as unified in the work of art, so by means of this the infinite will be expressed in finite mode. Except for what he has put there with a clear intention, the artist almost instinctively represents an infinity, which no finite intellect is capable of developing completely. Precisely the infinite expressed in finite mode is beauty; and the sentiment which accompanies the overcoming of the contradiction is catharsis, calm and serene greatness, even where these should have been expressed by the highest tension of grief or joy.

Art is distinguished from nature in so much as nature lacks of conscious activity; and therefore natural beauty is purely incidental. This cancels the principle of the imitation of nature; since instead of nature (which is beautiful by mere chance) giving rule to art, it is rather the perfection of art which is the principle and rule for the valuation of natural beauty. Art is distinguished from science, in spite of their having the same aim of knowing, because the artistic genius makes to coincide the finite and the infinite, the conscious and the unconscious, while science works without genius only on the finite and the conscious, and therefore science follows art.

The consequences of such ideas are expounded by Schelling in his discourse of 1807, "On the Relation between the Figurative Arts and Nature." He opposes the concept of Winckelmann of the imitation of ideal nature, which he substitutes for real nature without infusing it with creative life. The artist does not imitate nature, but rivals nature in creation. "The object of imitation was changed by Winckelmann, but imitation remained. For nature he substituted the beautiful works of antiquity, from which the imitation tried to take the external forms, without the spirit which animates."

Nevertheless the weakness of Schelling's aesthetic consisted in not distinguishing art and science, in respect of their aim. Because the active principle, without which the beautiful forms of nature remain empty of interest, is an idea, an order, a principle of reason. It was not enough to indicate the unconscious element which enters into every work of art, nor to understand by a flash of genius, that the idealisation of nature in art is not the contrary of reality, but is reality in its eternal moment, in its excellence purified from temporal accidents. Characteristic beauty is the root of beauty; but from the root one passes to the fruit, to the "true beauty" which is the dominating essence of form, to the beauty of the mind in itself, that is to say, to a beauty become concept, universalised, no longer individual. So much is true that although Schelling is aware of the erroneous uniformity of the concept of beauty in Winckelmann, he admits with him that expression is a collateral activity. Raphael, he says "not only produces absolute beauty, but is *also* able to break its uniformity with diversity of expression." Also the concept of the finite, which belongs to the artistic product, is materialised in the concept of body. Sculpture needs a body, can arrive at equilibrium between mind and body, but cannot elevate the mind at the expense of the material. Painting, instead, adopts "lights and colours, incorporeal and, in a certain degree, spiritual means." Hence the superiority of sculpture in the antique era and of painting in the modern. Michelangelo does not show enough plastic power, in search of energy and depth, and does not reach the plastic perfection of Raphael, who combined the power of genius with wisdom and measure. With the preponderance accorded to mind over matter, art could reach a new grade, not however more elevated, the grade of softness: it is the work of Guido Reni, whom Schelling called "the authentic painter of the soul." For the primitive masters, from Giotto to Raphael, cherished with respect "in spite of himself," as he confesses, he had consideration of the natural truth and seriousness with which they respected the limits of nature.

That is to say, Schelling loves the concept of art, but neither loves nor understands the work of art; rather than correct with his new concepts the traditional judgments, he assumes them as inalterable truth in justification of his own concepts.

George Hegel accepts the definition of beauty which his predecessors, and above all Schelling, had formulated: the true is the idea in itself, and the beautiful is the sensible appearance of the idea, the immediate knowledge of its exterior existence. In consequence, the aim of art is "to manifest the truth under the form of sensible representation." Hegel draws from these principles conclusions more radical than those of Schelling. He opposes the imitation of nature, and considers it an act of superfluity. "Neither is objective naturalness the rule, nor is the pure imitation of external appearances the aim of art." The sole task of the artist is expression of the ideal. With regard, then, to science or philosophy, he holds the opinion that scientific aim is the same as that of art, and insists upon the profound value of thought in recognising truth as compared with the apparent superficiality of art. Therefore art is a philosophical error or an illusory philosophy, with the consequence that art is to be considered as dead when true philosophy is born, not only in ideal order, but also in the temporal historical reality. Absurd, certainly, but a logical conclusion, whether of not having distinguished the aim of art from that of science, or of the opinion prevalent in art criticism, that artistic perfection is to be sought in some ancient masterpieces, rather than in the eternal human productivity.

Hegel is not content only with expounding his aesthetic ideas, with critical examples, but realises the identification of aesthetics, history of art and criticism, expounding a grandiose history of art, in which are well reflected the force and the limitations of his ideas. For the first time since Greek criticism the development of art is no longer considered as according to the imitation of nature (at first a beginning, then perfection, and then decline), but according to the representation of the ideal: at first representation is by abstract signs and it is *symbolical;* then it becomes more concrete, with the equilibrium of body and idea, and it is *classical;* then it becomes more intense, with a prevailing of idea over body, and it is *romantic.* To these three grades of art Hegel makes correspond the three figurative arts: architecture, which is symbolical; sculpture, which is classical; painting, which is romantic. It is not difficult for us to see how much false history was comprised in the Hegelian divisions; neither the fulness of knowledge, nor the artistic sensibility, which he had, succeeded in freeing him from these rigid partitionings. Given, indeed, the absolute perfection of classical sculpture, Hegel could not consider as perfect art either architecture, which was only symbolical, or modern sculpture, or painting, which, though it had more spiritual value, was nevertheless less art than sculpture.

The aim of architecture is the expression of a general idea by means of forms taken from inorganic nature, of masses proportioned and disposed according to the laws of geometry and mechanics. Its material forms can symbolise a mind, not contain it. The architecture of the ancient Orient, to which sculpture is attached, is independent of all practical utility, and symbolises religion. Greek and Roman architecture has, on the other hand, a practical utility, and it is therefore dependent; and sculpture is detached from it. Christian architecture is both dependent, because it serves cults, and independent, because it symbolises the Christian idea. The type of Greek architecture is the column; it is useful, because the sustaining force in it is reduced to the minimum of material means, and it is taken from nature, but with a regular and geometrical configuration unknown to nature. Greek architecture is more free than sculpture from organic forms; and it has no other laws than good taste and harmony. But from this statement Hegel does not draw the conclusion that since the creative freedom of architecture can be greater, its value as art cannot be minor or symbolical, but only different. The Gothic cathedral has a determined aim, but both in its grandiose aspect and in its sublime calm, it is elevated above every useful destination, to the level of something of infinity in itself; and corresponds well to the Christian spirit, both because it is a place of collectedness and silence, expressing Christian withdrawal within the consciousness, and because it is elevated almost to the infinite, as meditation is lifted to the Heavens.

Sculpture works an advance upon architecture, because, instead of adopting masses of inert nature, it represents the animate living body, and above all the human body, with which the mind is completely identified. Corporeal form is blended with spirit and becomes its living image. Sculpture represents neither the intimate feelings of the mind, nor the single passions; it does not offer individual character except in its generality, in the degree to which the body can express it, without movement, without living action, without development. It cannot bear colours, because the abstract form of sculpture is not an imperfection, but the limit which this art imposes upon itself. To sculpture fully correspond the pagan religion and the pagan conception of human life. The perfection of sculpture is naturally the work of the Greeks, because they understood the character of invariable indeterminateness in opposition to the incidental. Sculpture must represent the divine in itself, its infinite calm, its sublimity, eternal, immobile without contrasts of action or of situation. In man, also, sculpture must see only the invariable character, free from every extraneous influence. In such a way sculpture realises the perfect expression of physical beauty. Hegel goes on to analyse the ideal form of Greek sculpture, systematising but accepting fully the thought of Winckelmann, and hence, though appreciating the expressive capacity of Christian sculpture, he believes that the Christian spirit is not adapted to sculpture, coming from the infinity of the soul. He makes an exception of Michelangelo, but only to confirm the rule.

With painting is initiated the series of romantic arts, in which music and poetry participate. The mind does not limit itself to sensible plastic representation, but bends upon itself, descends into the depths of its nature, distinguishes itself from nature and from the body, acquires the feeling of its free personality, of its infinite nature, of its divine essence. Therefore the nexus between mind and body is loosened. The mind asks more ideal forms, less material, a vaster field of representation, richer and more varied materials, an expression more lively and profound. Nature itself becomes more spiritualised, everywhere presenting a reflection of thought, an echo of feeling, like a frame for the development of the mind. This is the object of painting, and for this reason the natural centre of painting is the Christian world. The Greek painters were not able to attain the conception of modern painters precisely because their paganism answered to the limitations of sculpture. The painter substitutes for reality an appearance that has need of a greater spirituality. Colour, which defines such an appearance, demands of the objects represented a more individual and living character, hence the multiplicity of situations, the movement, the variety which respond to the materials of painting. And, again, painting necessitates a more personal manner, more sensitive, passions more pronounced, a place for the particular, the individual, the accidental. Its field is very much more vast, because it embraces all the objects of nature, all the works of human activity, all the details of existence.

Here a parenthesis is necessary. The representation which Hegel gives of painting is the one most corresponding to the representation of art in general, according to the principles of the idealists, their spiritual knowledge, their animation of universal nature. To-day we interpret in such mode not only painting, but also sculpture and architecture. If Hegel was not able to do this, it is due to the domination of the thought of Winckelmann, which he still obeyed.

The form of painting, Hegel proceeds, is given by surface and colour, hence it must renounce material plasticity. But the apparent imperfection is a real progress. Painting no longer shows objects as they are in themselves, but transforms them into figures, which are a mirror of the mind. It is, then, that appearance which manifests the mind to itself, as an eternity of the fleeting. The spectator contemplates, in a manner more free from all objective reality, art itself, which is a spiritual manifestation in forms of the external world. The physical element which belongs to painting is *light:* chiaroscuro, effects of lights and shades, are not the materials, but the production, the creation, of painting; and light becomes the principles of *colour* which is the principal means of painting. Chiaroscuro has a plastic character, and is therefore a complement of drawing; but the contrast of lights and darks is pictorial. The colours have a psychological symbology and a harmony of their own, which depends upon the presence of the fundamental colours (blue, yellow, red, green), not attenuated as in Mengs and his followers, but harmonised with daring and energy.

At this point one would expect Hegel to recognise in painting a completeness of spiritual expression, but, unfortunately, it is not so. Painting, he says, is more incomplete than poetry, because, to express feeling and passion, it has at its disposition only the face and the attitudes of the body. Therefore the forms and the colours express nothing in themselves, but only with reference to human bodies and their movements. This is a last residue of illuministic naturalism in idealistic criticism.

However, Hegel understood that the sentimentalism of the pictorial school of Düsseldorf was a malady which must be cured, and he understood that the primitive Italians were true artists and that the Nazarenes were not so at all. He analysed happily the relation between religious piety and the calm of artistic contemplation in Italian painting of the Renaissance; and noted the complete independence and freedom of the artists with regard to the themes treated: even in portraits, they are figures of another world which the artists created, they are roses which flourish in heaven. The primitives, even. if imperfect as compared with the masters of the full Renaissance, are nevertheless appreciable for pure and innocent piety, for grandiose conception, depth of sentiment and ingenuous beauty of form. In spite of their technical imperfection, they have been too much praised to the disadvantage of the perfect painters. This was a concession to extraneous ideas, since it seems evident that according to Hegel, the problem should have converged on the sensible expression of the idea, and not on technique.

Finally, in Dutch painting of the seventeenth century, Hegel sees well that, if the motives are insignificant and incidental, even to grossness and banality, their representation is well penetrated with ingenuous gaiety and joviality; so that, not the motives, but the gaiety and joviality form the true theme and base of the picture. That is to say, the Dutch manifest poetical character in presenting true human nature, while in the recent historical pictures, in spite of every resemblance to real men and personages, one immediately understands that the painter knows neither man nor the humanity of man.

I hope that this enforcedly fragmentary and schematic exposition may be enough to indicate both the greatness and the limitations of the history of art imagined by Hegel. The greatness consists in the new spiritual consciousness of the work of art and of the development of artistic taste. Hence it can well be said that, not from the history of Winckelmann but from that of Hegel, must start any later attempt which would really fuse the history and criticism of art. The limitations are of various nature: before everything, he speaks of the perfection of architecture, sculpture and painting rather than of individual artists, and therefore he does not recognise the individual perfection of every true artist. His keen taste allows him to understand the Dutch beauty of the seventeenth century, like the Italian of the sixteenth century, but not that of the primitive painters, nor of the Christian sculptors, nor of the Gothic architects. If he is right in distinguishing the character of the various arts, he does not see that the distinction is valid only as a provisional scheme for understanding the distinctions of all artistic personalities; he considered as finite, distinctions which are in fact infinite. This error depends really upon the theory which universalises the idea of expression in art rather than individuates the ideals represented by each artist. Hegel derives another limitation from the neo-classical education, from faith in the universal and eternal perfection of Greek sculpture, by which he was obliged to confuse plastic form with artistic form, was obliged to reduce perfect form to the human body, and therefore to maintain a residue of naturalism in his idealism. He cherishes the most lively sympathy for painting, even for modern painting, and allows it more progress than sculpture, but since sculpture is the perfection of art the progress of painting is a recession from art and a step forward to transform art into philosophy. Whence the logical conclusion of the death of art in modern times.

One of the great merits of the idealistic aesthetic, as the awakener of art criticism, was the absorption of the concept of beauty in the concept of art. But this went further, and met with the obstacle, already encountered by Aristotle and St. Augustine, of the representation of the ugly. Kant had already juxtaposed to the analysis of beauty that of the sublime, and Frederick Schlegel had hinted at a theory of the ugly. The rationalistic impulse was too much present in Hegel to allow him to cultivate this field. Solger had an intuition that in the concept of the ugly there was something positive, that it was not a simple antithesis of beauty, in so far as the ugly sought to supersede beauty, but denied that the absolutely ugly could enter into the limits of art, and admitted only that in the passage from the sublime to the comic, beauty must pass very near to ugliness. Weisse from his corner insisted on the positivity of the ugly, in so far as it stimulates beauty, in a magical if diseased manner. Rosenkranz wrote outright an *aesthetic of the ugly*, as an integration of that of Hegel, in the name of the relativity of beauty. He maintains that the same elements which lead to beauty, the sublime, the pleasing, could take another, perverted road — that of the ugly, whether through spiritual mediocrity, or caricature, or lust for the repugnant. Therefore art comprehends the ugly not only in so far as it does not succeed in reaching the beautiful but also in so far as its aim can be precisely the ugly. Even the Greeks represented images of the ugly, and horrible and mad crimes; moreover, in Christian art the diabolical element makes part of the spiritual world, and could not be eliminated from it without understanding that world in a superficial manner. Moreover, he who makes the devil beautiful adds fraud to ugliness, and is to be condemned. It is therefore necessary to express the ugly by means of an intensification which is an idealisation. This ugliness, which makes an integral part of art, is admitted by Carriere, because it is an essential element of the characteristic, and therefore of the individual expression, free from any particular type of beauty. The true ugliness, that which partakes neither of art nor of beauty, is the false expression of free individuality. Here is a principle of the overcoming of the abstract opposition of the beautiful and the ugly: the synthesis of the two opposites placed upon the characteristic, no longer understood in the object created, but in the principle of the free and individual expression of the subject. Hartmann adds that the ugly and the diabolical are reflected in two different worlds, the aesthetic and the moral, with an apparent irrationality which participates in a final rationality. Through such a tortuous way some German aesthetes tried to explain the ever more imperious bearing of extraneous factors upon the neo-classical beauty in the art of the nineteenth century.

The new conception of history as development, due to Germanic idealism, gave new vigour to philological and positive studies in the history of art: an example of this new direction is the work of Rumohr. But we shall speak of him later.

Here, we shall touch rather upon the two writers on art who worked above all upon the basis of the ideas of Hegel. One is Hotho, for whom the true themes of historical research are the various conceptions which peoples present in the various arts. In this way he neglects personal character in the work of art, but illuminates well the ideal life of artistic periods. His history of German and Flemish painting (1842-3) is noteworthy as a vision of the whole, rather than as a criticism of separate works. Hotho also initiates the history of taste, dealing with the fading and revival of the fame of the Van Eycks. Toward modern art he, too, is little directed. Among the French artists he appreciates Horace Vernet and is silent about Delacroix.

A general history of art, under the influence of Hegel, assigning essential value to the religious and spiritual elements in the general aspect of art, was written by Schnaase (1843-1864). He proceeds dialectically to synthesis, and would embrace empiricism and speculation, art and culture, reflection and narration, even romanticism and illuminism. He conceives his history as universal history, which comprehends East and West, the ancient, middle and modern ages. He would deal with it in a philosophico-historical manner. He considers that art is the central activity of peoples, that in it are manifested feelings, thoughts and customs, and therefore he treats art as an essential document of the life of peoples. In every work he seeks its spiritual principle, and calls such a method physiognomico-poetical, counterposed to the optical-pictorial. His greatest merit concerns the treatment of mediaeval art, which is the art most dear to his heart, and in which he sees the most immediate expression of the deepest feelings. He tries to find the historical relation between the art and the life of mediaeval humanity. His interest in the spiritual tendencies of various artistic periods, rather than in single artistic personalities, is his character and also his limitation as an art historian.

The German idealistic system of aesthetics was diffused in France, but in a manner which lost, or almost lost, any critical vitality. Philosophically the diffuser was Cousin (1818); Lamennais interwove idealism and religion; Jouffroy, starting from Cousin, placed the idealistic metaphysic in relation with acute psychological observations: for him the task of art is to discover the invisible through the physical. In criticism, at the beginning of the nineteenth century, he took part in the controversy between Emeric David, who would reduce the principle of ancient art to the pure imitation of nature, and Quatremère de Quincy, who maintained instead the ideal value of art, identified with classical art, and opposed the doctrine of Winckelmann to the nascent romanticism. Guizot, in an essay on the limits between sculpture and painting (1816), starts from Lessing, but goes very much further to express ideas very similar to those of Hegel. But his interest in the ideal content of many historical pictures in the Louvre shows that he has not understood the more vital part of the Hegelian doctrine. The classicist tendency and a vague mysticism prevailed in the official French artistic literature for a long time, even after neo-classical art definitely was dead; and this was the chief cause of the detachment, ever more profound, between the official doctrine and true artistic life in France. The typical example of a belated classicist may be indicated in Charles Blanc.

Full of compromises with the official classicism was French criticism of a religious tendency, of which the two principal works are the "Treatise on Painting" (1828) of Paillot de Montabert, and the "Christian Art" (1836) of Rio. Rio writes with a prevailingly religious interest, and under the influence of Schelling's ideas, and even recognises explicitly the weakness of the aesthetic tradition in France as compared with German. But his temperament is more rhetorical than critical, and therefore he draws few conclusions from the best aesthetic preparation as compared with that of his contemporaries: nevertheless the interpretation of the art of Blessed Angelico and of the Sienese school is new and full of just observations.

Very much closer to art were, naturally, the artists themselves who wrote about art, even if they were the serfs of neoclassicism. A pupil of David, Delécluze, wrote a book on his master, in which is explained with great acuteness the effective value of neo-classical art and taste, and of the movement born in the same school of David, of the primitivists or religious painters. In it Delécluze distinguishes well the sentimental and intuitive needs of classical and religious art, from theories formulated by others.

The sources of inspiration of that French activity of the nineteenth century which counts in the history of criticism were, however, very diverse, both from the idealistic aesthetic and from the religious revival or the neo-classical experience.

In Italy also the idealistic aesthetics, of the Schelling variety, had various repercussions, and influenced Gioberti, who combined ideas on art with those on religion. Already at the beginning of the century Cicognara, in his "History of Sculpture" (1813-1818), had understood the perfection of some Christian sculptors and had insisted on the value of the religious impulse in art. As far back as 1806 Pietro Giordani had proclaimed that painters must be masters of philosophy, in order to convert private affections to the public welfare and reveal the hopes of humankind. Pietro Selvatico, who had read Hegel and Rio, who had visited Munich and spread abroad the principles of that "philosophical art" which he had praised in the Italian purists, published an "Aesthetico-critical History of the Art of Design" (1852-56). In this work he would take away from philosophy, and assign to history, the task of directing artists, of understanding the moral and religious value of the primitives, the moral degradation of baroque painting and neo-classical art, and also of feeling the ridiculousness of neo-Gothic nonsense. He fixed himself above all on the masters "who gave impulse and life to a given order of ideas and facts," and insisted on the unity of painting, sculpture and architecture, and of the need of an ideal inherent in all art. But his work lacks something of organisation, because the traditional motives of the lives of artists are stealthily introduced in the midst of idealistic problems.

So that we may conclude that the most coherent, comprehensive and fair history of art of the idealistic type may be considered even now that of Hegel.

CHAPTER IX
Philologists, Archaeologists and Connoisseurs in XIXth and XXth Centuries

IDEALISTIC philosophy gave a strong impulse to history by the concept of development in which were fused the idea and the fact, the divine and the human. The idea was no longer considered as transcendent to but as immanent in the fact, fused in the fact — for example, by Hegel. But, as we have seen with regard to his history of art, such fusion did not always take place, but rather there appeared a contrast between ideas and facts which could only end in a forcing of the facts. It was, therefore, natural that realistic minds should occupy themselves with the facts for their own sake, at first still mindful of finding a relation between the facts and the ideas, and then emancipating themselves from the ideas. Thus arose the philological method of history, which flourished particularly in Germany from the beginning of the nineteenth century. Such a method consists in verifying the source of evidence and decomposing it: that is to say, before accepting evidence, one tries to determine upon what it is founded, and then decomposes this source into its original separate sources. This external process of criticism of the sources accomplished, one passes to the internal process; that is to say, one seeks to determine if and to what extent the author of the evidence has reason to tell the truth or to modify or falsify it.

It was natural that the history of art should follow the philological method to verify its written sources. What Pliny recounted about the antique painters and sculptors was repeated, with occasional comments, before seeking to determine the sources from which Pliny had drawn directly or otherwise.

Begun by Jahn in 1850, and continued by Brunn, Furtwaengler, the two Ulrichs, Eugene Sellers, and by Kalkmann in
1898, the problem was in great part, resolved if not completely so, by means of comparisons of texts and happy intuitions.
So that it has been possible to identify the criticism of Xenocrates and in general the Greek criticism of the third century,
and distinguish it from Roman criticism at the end of the Republic and the beginning of the Empire. As much can be said
for Vasari, whose "Lives" are the chief source for the knowledge of the Italian Renaissance. Milanesi, Frey, Scoti-Bertinelli,
Kallab and Schlosser have established the sources of Vasari, so
that to-day we have an almost certain rule for accepting or
rejecting a Vasarian item of information. These are two typical
cases, and many others could be quoted.

While the traditional literary sources were being thus verified and often purified, there was an intensification of research
into, and publication of, primary written sources: inscriptions
and documents in the archives. Above all, these last have
brought about an extraordinary increase of information on the
Renaissance and the modern age, permitting us to define with
certainty the life and culture of the artists, the authorship of the
works of art, their date, the occasion of the production, the
external relation between the works of art and with life, religious, social and literary. In some cases the literary tradition
– for example that of Vasari – has been completely reduced
to powder, and the information on the life and works of artists
has all been founded upon the documents in the archives.
Publication of and comment upon these documents constituted
a good part of the activity of art historians in the nineteenth
century.

With the criticism of literary sources and the publication of
documents of the archives they have, in fact, accomplished

that task of philological criticism which was indicated to them by the political historians. But such a task for historians of art could only be lateral and secondary: the principal sources for philological criticism were the works of art themselves. For this, the aid of political historians was limited or non-existent. It was necessary to invent a method of interpreting the monuments of art. In order to appreciate a source, the philological historians had decomposed it into its elements. Similarly the art historians, of a philological tendency, decomposed the monuments of art according to certain schemes, among which the principal were: 1) the content of the work of art, considered not as the feeling expressed by the artist, but as the theme dealt with, whence arose a special discipline — iconography; 2) technique, a very vague concept in which were comprised the science of construction in architecture, the systems of working marble, wood and bronze in sculpture, the different ways of amalgamating colours (tempera, oil, water-colour) for painting, besides perspective, anatomy and the other means of naturalistic illusion; 3) style, understood in a material manner as the ensemble of figurative conventions which absorbed the artistic personalities or which they shared with their masters and pupils.

Winckelmann had studied the form and content of Greek works of art in order to define what was perfect art; Hegel had imagined a universal development of the mind to pluck from it the moment of perfect art; Ruskin had made his moral sensibility vibrate to discern true and false art: all three had moved heaven and earth to understand and judge art. The centre of attention of the philological critics was different: it was no longer art, but philology itself. The monuments of art were considered only as documents for the knowledge of the religion, the habits and customs, the characters of people, their intellectual and practical life — everything except their artistic imagination. Now without being aware of it, now with full consciousness, the philologists renounced the great conquest of the eighteenth century: the consciousness of the autonomy of art.

There was often in the philologists a sincere enthusiasm for art, and at times even an artistic capacity, which showed itself in drawings and paintings or in lyrical descriptions: what they lacked almost always was thought upon art. There was in that attitude a fashionable motive, aversion from philosophy, which was accentuated in the second half of the past century, in the period of positivism, and which ended in a renunciation of all authentic thought, whether of the philosophical or the historical order. But there was at the same time a very just demand; that of not losing sight of the facts, and of verifying their exact conditions and limitations before judging them. What a work of art meant to represent, what technique had been used in it, what relations there were between its stylistic elements and those of other works of art, whether by the same artist or by other artists associated in time and place: all this was determined by the philologists in an incomparably better way than before; and there would be nothing to object to it, except when they thought to draw from these statements of fact an historical reconstruction or a critical judgment of art. The critics, who were true historians, and the historians, who were true critics, were thus justly irritated, because neither iconography, nor the history of technique, nor the history of abstract figurative elements is the history of art. Art is something different from all these things, something nearer certainly to what Hegel saw than to what is seen by a philologist. So that, looked at in retrospect, the enormous philological labour on art of almost a century and a half appears to us very much more like an imposing mound of stones than an architecture in stone.

Nevertheless, philological labour on art had two important consequences upon critical judgment, even apart from the simple exactitude of the facts in reference. One of the two contributions is negative. Idealism, of the Schelling type, had exalted art as a mode of knowledge, but had attributed to art intellectual knowledge. Through explaining genius rationally, he had ended by rationalising genius. The philological historian of art explained instead the elements of a work of art, leaving genius aside; or rather, he ignored genius, sometimes granting it some civilities, but preferring to fly from it; and this is also a way of avoiding the rationalisation of genius — the only way, indeed, for anyone not convinced that thought is capable of understanding that which is not reducible to rationality. Bound to the facts, philological criticism observed its own limits, at least this was true of its more intelligent representatives. Its function was then that of *scepticism*, with regard to a definition of art like that of Hegel, which did not take enough account of the non-logical character of art; from which followed an agnosticism which established the negative conditions for a later and more comprehensive conception of art.

The other contribution was positive. Winckelmann had believed himself able to understand Greek and Egyptian art, although he knew, in fact, almost only Roman copies. The discovery of authentic Greek art began properly with 1800, when Lord Elgin despoiled the edifices of the Acropolis at Athens to carry the sculptures to London. If to-day one compares a recent history of Greek art with that of Winckelmann one finds that the ideas have hardly changed, but the works discussed are almost totally new. Whole epochs, like those of Mycenean or Minoian art, have come to light in course of fortunate excavations. Even more impressive has been the accumulation of a quite new knowledge of Egyptian art. The romantic movement in favour of mediaeval art led the philologists to discover with new eyes the monuments of Byzantine, Romanesque and Gothic art, and to explore the Christian catacombs. Knowledge of Asiatic art has been increased a hundredfold, above all in the twentieth century: to-day we distinguish very well the productions of Mesopotamia, Persia, Central Asia, India, Indo-China, China, Japan and many so-called barbarian people, like the Scythians, the Africans, the Mayas, the Aztecs and the Incas. Finally, even of the artistic periods traditionally better known, like the Renaissance and the modern age, an infinite number of lost works have been rediscovered and reclassified, and artistic personalities fallen into forgetfulness have retaken their place in history: Grünewald, El Greco, and Vermeer of Delft are typical examples of this. The gaps that worry philologists are, and will probably remain, infinite. But the enrichment of knowledge is such that, however little the artistic sensibility may be, certain errors preceding the philological mode are no longer possible. Winckelmann and Hegel had believed that the absolute perfection of art was to be sought in Greek sculpture of a given period: to-day such an error would seem ridiculous. Ruskin had believed that true art was connected only, or almost only, with Christian religiosity; and even this seems to us an oddity. Like Winckelmann, Hegel and Ruskin, though for different reasons, the philological critics too were interested in the art of the past and did not care for contemporary art. Indeed, on contemporary art philological criticism had nothing to say, neither the decomposition of the sources, nor virtuosity in attribution, nor iconographical research being requisite for it. Not being able to employ the only instrument at its disposition, philological

218

criticism abstained from intervening in the problems of contemporary art, thus giving a lesson in morality to both Winckelmann, who promoted the neo-classical Academy, and Ruskin, who defended the Pre-Raphaelite Academy. On the other hand, by having made known with ever more perfect mechanical reproduction the different forms of art of all times and places, the philological criticism of art has offered to artists experiences without number, and has definitely freed them from the classic as from the Christian myth.

The spirit of analysis prevailing in philology caused books of art history to be conceived as written museums, in which the works of art are arranged and classified. It was natural that completeness of information should be looked upon as the essential value. Therefore histories of art became histories of universal art, and monographs on an artist contained the examination of all his works. Classical archaeology sought to become something more extensive than a history of art. Beginning with F. A. Wolff in 1807, it started from the figurative monuments to find in them the relation with philology and linguistics, with aesthetics and the theory of art, with the history of culture, religion, law, with the practical life of the ancients. Archaeologists therefore invented the so-called science of antiquity, in order to justify their interest in all that which is not properly art.

The first "Manual of the Archaeology of Art" is the work of Müller (1830). He was a philologist rather than an archaeologist; he proposed a totalitarian history and projected a general collection of the monuments of ancient art. Such a cultural content can easily assume the form of an encyclopaedia: and Pauly-Wissowa for classical antiquity, Kraus for Christian antiquity, furnished in encyclopaedic form fundamental instruments of labour. In 1842 appeared Kugler's "Manual of Art History," which had the greatest influence, and not only in Germany. Kugler has full knowledge of the empirical character with which he works, and which he opposes to the idealism of Hegel; he is anti-romantic and does not occupy himself with the aims of art. But he does not renounce research into the intimate artistic character of the monuments; rather he regroups the monuments according to their formal characters, more than according to external schemes, such as peoples and the like, and he often has happy intuitions, as when he distinguishes the objective sensible tendencies of Florentine painting as compared with those more sentimental and lyrical in Sienese painting of the fourteenth century. Similarly, he is able to distinguish in architecture that which is artistic from that which is constructive practice. His tendency to universality is clear and therefore comprehends prehistoric art, demonstrating with facts the advantage of avoiding erroneous laws of taste. To him is due the partitioning of art into four moments: art of primitive peoples, classical art, romantic or mediaeval art, and modern art. The most popular manual, translated and republished even in the twentieth century, was that of Springer, which appeared in 1855. The approach to positivism is greater here: art is the imitation of nature, and is understood, not as an original activity, but as an institution changing according to the customs of peoples. The method of art history must be that of history in general, without being modified by the fact that its content is art. Springer understands that the development of the artistic personality is the major task of art history, but understands that personality as a practical activity. That depends upon the special limitation of his artistic sensibility, inadequate, in fact, to give life to his broad doctrine.

In France a theoretico-practical treatise which had great publicity was the "Grammar of the Arts of Design" by Charles Blanc (1880), in which the historical experience of art is distributed in a systematic manner, but in which the lack of any dominating thought is astounding. It deals with a classification of manners, without profound conviction and without artistic sensibility.

Among the more recent histories of universal, or almost universal art, is to be mentioned that edited by André Michel. It is natural that the multiplication to infinity of the monuments studied, without concern for ideas or rules of judgment, should tend to specialisation, and therefore that a history of art in all Christian countries from the fourth century to our own times should be no longer possible to a single individual. For that reason André Michel distributed the various chapters among various collaborators, and tried to obtain unity by means of conclusions written by himself at the end of each period. He thus defines his task (1906): "Our role is limited to observing and classing the facts, that is to say, the monuments which are the matter and the object of a history of art, and to trying to indicate in what relation they are found with general history." Therefore his "conclusions" do not consider art, but the thought and religion of the various periods, and the share of the several nations in artistic production. In the German "Manual of the Science of Art" founded by Fritz Bürger, and not yet completed, the process of division reaches the limit: it is a series of monographs, often good and sometimes less good, according to the value of the author of each, without there being any directing personality or any idea of the whole.

Philologists, Archaeologists and Connoisseurs

But the encyclopedic tendency of philological activity was the least capable of concrete results: the study of single aspects of the work of art, even if arbitrarily abstracted, could give better. The technique which claims the practical activity of the artist and is connected with the physical world must specially attract the attention of philologists, always anxious for material certainty. And, indeed, studies on the technique of all the arts were specially developed in the nineteenth century, and to them contributed the sciences of physics and chemistry. It is enough to recall the "Law of the Simultaneous Contrasts of Colours" of Chevreul (1838), which exercised so much influence on later painting, and the studies published between 1855 and 1877 of Helmholtz and Brücke on the physiology and psychology of vision. The technical aspect had special favour, or rather dominated all other aspects in works of architecture — for example, those of Viollet-le-Duc, Choisy, Dehio and Bezold; in all the manuals or treatises on the so-called minor arts — for example, in the "History of Industrial Arts" by Labarte, and also, though in less degree, in the studies of mediaeval art by Courajod, or in the studies on Greek art by Loewy. This last takes great account of ideal values, but the directive line is always that of ability to reproduce external nature.

It was Semper who gave general value and aesthetic pretension to technical motives. He is the adversary of all idealism and tends to natural science of the Darwinian type. He is not interested in the intimate life of art, but in the evolution of forms assumed as essential. He believes he is able to find in technique the origin of essential forms, of types and symbols in art. He occupies himself neither with painting nor sculpture, but with architecture and the decorative arts, textiles, ceramics, works in metal, and so on. Apart from the material of art he considers utilitarian character as the only aim of art. Even if repugnant, such a materialistic conception of art has, however, had its use: that of recalling the attention of the historian to the realisation of mind in matter, to the way in which matter had been sensibilised by art. Semper's culture was, however, too limited to enable him to draw from his own principles the stylistic conclusions in a historical sense, as they were later drawn by Robert Vischer and Alois Riegl.

The least cultivated among the observers of a work of art asks himself immediately what it represents, what is the "subject" treated; and even the most erudite among the scholars, when he is not interested in that which is peculiar to art, in avoiding Semper's mistake, falls back into the treatment of the "subject." He believes that only through the "subject" can the work of art be reunited to the spiritual world in which it is born. The first to develop the study of subjects were the archaeologists, beginning with Winckelmann. Since he believed himself to perceive the perfection of art in the perfection of types of gods, he arbitrarily identified art criticism and iconography. The philologists of the nineteenth century did not fall into the same error and were interested in the iconography of the gods, for its own sake, and in artistic mythology in general, considering the work of art as a simple instrument for achieving the history of myth – that is to say, of religious belief. Conze and Overbeck are specially illustrated in this field.

The Christian archaeologists had to be specially interested in iconography; indeed, the reason of their studies was very much more the illustration of primitive Christianism than the history of art. Cahier and Martin, Didron, De Rossi, Garrucci, Wilpert, founded their works on iconography. The same can be said of the scholars in Byzantine art, Kondakoff, Strzygow-sky, Diehl, Millet.

Very much more than the technical, the iconographical method is an obstacle in the understanding of art, because the types and compositions of mythological and sacred scenes may remain almost the same throughout the most profound differences in artistic civilisations and individual imaginations. Since to create in art does not mean to invent, the repetition of motives popularly accepted is clearly distinct from the personal contribution of the artist and the taste of an epoch or school. Peculiarly to iconography is due one of the worst prejudices in art history, that of the static immobility of certain artistic periods. The consideration of Greek art as of eternal aestheticism, of noble severity, is as absurd under the aesthetic aspect as it is false under the historical aspect. Such a prejudice is to-day corrected. But that of the century-old immobility of Byzantine art is not yet destroyed.

Where the iconographical method most clearly shows its weak side is when it turns to Romanesque, Gothic or Renaissance art, because the abundance of monuments allows us to know them better in their individual aspects: and the books of Mâle on religious art in France are a typical example of such weakness.

When, on the other hand, all the elements of the work of art — not only those relative to the subject treated, but also those which are technical and formal — are put into relation with the history of civilisation, the results are much better. Under that aspect, also, archaeology has given some typical examples: Perrot and Chipiez, for the art of the ancient Orient and of primitive Greece; Gardner and Collignon, for Greek sculpture; Klein for Greek art. Thode illustrated both: the new way of feeling nature, due to the mysticism of St. Francis, as the origin of the art of the Italian Renaissance; and the contrast between Christian religiosity and pagan form in Michelangelo, as the end of the Renaissance.

A special way of seeing the relations between civilisation and art was developed in France, above all with regard to the Italian Renaissance. The initiator was Stendhal, who presented a picture of the disorder, arbitrariness, and a-morality in public and private life in Italy during the Renaissance as a condition of the flourishing of painting. He instituted a relationship between the picturesque in life and art.

From the positivistic philosophy of Comte, Taine drew the idea of the ambient (milieu) as a determinant of art, and then systematised the intuition of Stendhal, treating not only Italian Renaissance but also Dutch and Greek art. Taine rightly considers that the work of art is not isolated, but that, to understand it, it is necessary to place it in relation with the other works of the same artist, with the school or group to which he belongs, with the world surrounding him and the taste of which conforms to his own. "To understand a work of art, an artist, a group of artists, one must represent to oneself with exactitude the general state of mind and manners of the time to which they belong."

Where error begins is when Taine believes that *ambient* is the *cause* of painting. It is a double error: first of all, it does not take count of the freedom of individual creation, and then it materialises the ambient as a physical fact. On the other hand, he is not free, as he believes, from the prejudices of idealism. He says that he accepts all schools and all tastes, even the most opposed. But, according to him, Italian painting reached perfection between 1475 and 1530; before it was imperfect, and afterwards it decayed. He carries back to Italian painting of the Renaissance the same errors of Winckelmann and in part those of Hegel. It is not, in fact, a case of accepting all tastes, but of discovering in all the presence of the creative personality.

Limiting, then, Italian painting to the so-called Golden Age of the Renaissance, Taine asks himself what was the cause, otherwise the *ambient:* race akin to that of Greeks and Romans, by which the Italians resisted Gothic, prefer melodious music, have the taste of "ordering," and understand man better than nature. To this permanent cause (race) are added others which are temporary: there was much culture in Italy in the Renaissance, but it was a culture based more upon figures than upon ideas (here Hegel comes up again); they wore picturesque clothes and did not take religion very seriously; and interest in the human body and its passions came from the lack of a stable government and the frequency of riots and human types like Benvenuto Cellini. In short, a picturesque state of mind half-way between figures and ideas, an abundance of energetic characters and violent customs, adapted to the knowledge and the taste for beautiful bodily forms.

To-day it seems to us grotesque that a talent like Taine could really believe that these motives, heterogeneous among themselves and above all heterogeneous to art, were its cause. It is certain that his very diffuse ideas have had their inconveniences in later culture. They have contributed, however, to the comprehension of the participation of art in social life, and have allowed to be seen, through social life, some aesthetic values formerly avoided and insufficiently appreciated, as for example, in Dutch painting.

Inspired by Taine is the "History of Art during the Renaissance" by Eugene Müntz (1888-1895). It is ordered thus: first it speaks of patrons (that is to say, the princes of each court); then of tradition (the cult of the antique); of religious life, of the studies of reality, of perspective, anatomy, caricature, clothes, methods of teaching, organisation of labour, and of the subjects treated; of style, or conventions of technique, and finally of the authors of architecture, sculpture and painting. It is an orderly and abundant picture of all the elements external to artistic activity, with an absolute indifference to individual imagination, and even to their effects upon taste.

Greatly superior to Taine and Müntz appears Jacob Burckhardt, not because he had a much better critical and historical method, but precisely because he was an aestheticising dilettante, with an artistic sensibility very much alive. His idolising of the Renaissance, as a civilisation completely separated from the mediaeval, with the habit of arbitrariness and caprice, has not withstood criticism. In particular, his famous concept of the "state as a work of art" is not sustainable, unless as a paradoxical suggestion. But the merit of Burckhardt is to have kept his treatment of the culture of the Renaissance distinct from the history of art. In "Cicerone" (1855) he limits himself to indicating what are the greatest works of art in Italy, pointing briefly to his own preferences. But in the "History of the Renaissance in Italy" he writes a true history of architecture and decoration. He then transcends both cultural information and the taste of the refined tourist, seeking to define the development of the forms of artistic representation. Idealism had formed the concept of plastico-constructive or organic, as that which was best adapted to make understandable the essence of Greek architecture. Subsequently it was believed that the same concept would serve to understand the Gothic cathedral. But a series of monuments were not comprehensible in that concept: late Roman, Byzantine, Romanesque, Italian Gothic constructions, and finally and above all, constructions of the central type of the Italian Renaissance. To distinguish this series from the preceding, Burckhardt formed the concept of the "style of space." This is a scheme which goes on bearing fruit, and which allowed Burckhardt to transcend the purely cultural stage and to attach himself to pure visibility.

Two German authors of artistic monographs who may be associated with the tendency of historians of culture are Grimm and Justi. In his life of Michelangelo (1860) and that of Raphael (1872) Grimm certainly exercised his poetical enthusiasm to produce a species of mythology of the two great personalities, without realising them in their effective art. To the mythological type of Grimm is opposed full adherence to reality in the monograph of Justi on Velazquez (1888). Justi was working in Rome in 1867 on his monograph on Winckelmann when he began his monograph on Velazquez. It is difficult to imagine a stronger contrast between the ideas of Winckelmann, who found in Justi his greatest illustrator, and those necessary to understand Velazquez. But it does not appear that Justi had full consciousness of that contrast: nevertheless, his full adhesion to his theme, his constancy of observation, the enormous amount of material collected, the acceptance of the common opinion of Velazquez as the purest painter among painters, the most faithful to truth and life, and above all the moral energy which Justi put into all his undertakings, allowed him to adhere to the painter in a vital way: certainly critical judgment has need of a greater detachment, and therefore of a wider horizon. A proof of Justi's critical insufficiency consists, besides, in his total incomprehension of the art of the nineteenth century.

Philological criticism of art showed its best qualities, not in the organisation of universal histories of art, nor in the materialistic treatments of technique and iconography, nor even in evasions towards the history of culture, but in researches into the individual. The *catalogue raisonné* of the works of each artist was the masterpiece of the philological history of art. And the best talents among art historians devoted themselves to this aim. Each one, according to his temperament, has reinvested this central aim with cultural informations, lyrical flashes, and with empirical principles of aesthetics; some have collected their experiences in grandiose histories of art, others in monographs, others in revisions of museums and galleries, others, finally, in simple catalogues: it does not matter, the essential aim has been the *catalogue raisonné* of the works of an artist.

From this aim has developed the type of the connoisseur, which has ended by prevailing from the close of the nineteenth century onward over every other type of art historian. Indeed, in the ability of the connoisseur, the art historian has found the reason of his distinction from other philologists and historians, the characteristic of his own method. It may easily be that the culture of an art historian is inferior to that of an historian of literature or civilisation in general, that his power of thought is less than that of an aesthetician, but neither culture nor thought produces the connoisseur. In popular conception the art historian is he, who, placed in front of a sculpture or a painting, succeeds in classifying it by the simple reading of the figurative elements inherent in the work, without needing to refer to written sources. Now it is evident that nobody can be a connoisseur of the art of all times and places; but even for limited epochs true connoisseurs, those who commit few errors, are very rare. The practice of the connoisseur is one which derives from the habit of looking and re-looking at the works of art of a certain period. By intuition those works of art are distinguished as belonging to individual groups, the individual groups are placed in relation to antecedents and successors, in the individual groups is seen the development of style from one work to another, and from the quality of a group is deduced if a work of art to be classified is worthy to enter it, or should be excluded; whether it be an original, and how preserved, or a copy, and of what time, or, finally, a forgery. Philological criticism of written sources must precede the judgment of the connoisseur: if there is not at least one indubitable work of the master, verified as such from written sources, the basis of the knowledge of that master naturally disappears. But when there is a verified work of the master, and the authentic part is distinguished from the part restored, the authentic part reveals the style of the master: the technical, figurative and iconographical elements allow the individuation of the artist. It is no longer a case of the empirical personality which answers to this or that name; it is a case of knowing the personality of the artist in his art; and then the comprehension of the connoisseur is truly the basis of art criticism. In fact, to make the judgment of a connoisseur be worthy of an art critic, it would suffice to have it founded on the knowledge of what is universal art and on historical culture. It would suffice; but of course it is not easy. If, until now, it has been rare to see the connoisseur and the art critic combined, the reason is in the prevailing mental direction towards philological criticism, rather than towards true criticism, and also in the fact that the task of the connoisseur is in itself absorbing, and rarely leaves enough energy for the necessary integration of thought and culture.

The earliest among the philologist-connoisseurs is without

doubt Rumohr, and since in him is found also a strong philosophical knowledge, under the influence of Schelling, it often happens that, beyond philology, he arrives at pure criticism. His "Italian Researches" (1827-1831) deal with Italian art from the time of Charlemagne to Raphael, not as a compilation of facts, but as a research of separate problems chosen for their critical interest. His criticism of written sources is acute and unprejudiced, and the observation of works of art is directed to both the spiritual and the technical aspect. He therefore perceives, for example, that Giotto was certainly an innovator with respect to the vitality and reality of figures, but that precisely by this he is removed from the ideals of the Christian tradition. Elsewhere he speaks of the spatial composition of Ghiberti. The intuition which best brings Rumohr close to modern connoisseurs is his conception of the *originality* of the work of art, as distinct from the copy, as the artistic aspect of the personality.

Under the influence of Rumohr, Passavant wrote his monograph on Raphael (1839). After passing in review all that had been written on the master he recounts his own researches thus: "In order to see as far as possible with my own eyes the works of the master I returned for a year to Italy where I had already spent seven years. I undertook a journey to England and another to Paris, where in youth I had admired the treasures of the Napoleon Museum, and in 1816 the Raphaelesque paintings which then belonged to Mr. Bonnemaison and now adorn the Prado museum in Madrid. I already knew thoroughly the galleries of Germany, except that of Vienna, which I wished to visit: so that I can say with all reason that I have seen and studied almost all the works of Sanzio. I was at Urbino, his country, in the places where he lived and worked; I ransacked the libraries of Italy, Germany, England and

France to collect documents. The most difficult part of my labour was the catalogue of works, to make which it was my business to examine everything which had been attributed to him: and I devoted six years of journeys to such verification. A still greater difficulty remained with the drawings. Nevertheless, the practice of a painter, the long habit of observing works of art, as much on the critical as on the theoretical side, made me sure of not falling into serious errors." This is a programme not only for Passavant's monograph, but for every work of a connoisseur: he must not only travel widely, see and re-see, but confine himself to the *catalogue raisonné*. And by having understood this, the work of Passavant, in spite of the fact that his critical opinions on Raphael are superseded, is still, nearly a century later, indispensable to scholars because of his *catalogue raisonné*.

Germany produced another type of connoisseur in Waagen, who did not embody his researches in a monograph but in some reviews of public and private collections in England, France and Russia. He visited England twice, in 1835 and 1850, and published in 1854 his famous "Treasures of Art in Great Britain," which is a mine of information, rectifications and suggestions not completely exhausted even to-day by scholars. He felt that his summary mode of judging art, that of the pure connoisseur, was insufficient, and that it was necessary to deepen the interpretation of the work of art; but he had not the mode of exhausting his special demand.

The development of the method of connoisseurs in classical archaeology has been slow. An important step was achieved by Brunn, who first collected all the written sources on the individual artists of antiquity, and then availed himself also of figurative comparisons. In such a manner he called attention to the individual personalities, though understood in an empirical sense.

It is natural, however, that the major field of the connoisseur should be Renaissance and modern art, because of the infinite number of works of art to be classified. And, indeed, a greater intensity of the spirit of connoisseurship is found in the books written by Crowe and Cavalcaselle in collaboration: "The History of Flemish Painting" (1857), the History of Italian Painting from its origins to the XVIth Century (1864-1871), and two monographs on Titian (1877) and Raphael (1882). Crowe was an Englishman of letters who gave to the joint work the cultural background. Cavalcaselle was an Italian painter and political revolutionary, who dedicated the greater part of his life to travel and to drawing the paintings he saw: round the drawings he wrote the stylistic characters. With this system he penetrated into the style of painters more deeply than anyone before him. Gifted with a tenacious visual memory and a noteworthy sense of quality in painting, he succeeded, with the aid of his own drawings, in comparing in a precise manner the style of works seen at wide intervals of time and place. Therefore he destroyed an enormous quantity of legends on value assigned to copies or imitations, distinguished masters, and pupils, and was able to indicate the succession in the production of the same master. His work is gigantic, and is a turning point in the whole history of art; many times reprinted, it is still essential for scholars.

That which was achieved by Cavalcaselle by the force of his memory and by his drawings of paintings, was achieved after him by the use of photographs of paintings and sculptures. Photography, as is evident, reproduces a single aspect of the work of art; but anyone who has seen the original can easily reconstruct it in memory by looking at the photograph.

Therefore a comparison between photographs, by anyone who is familiar with the originals, can give a certainty on stylistic affinities or differences, otherwise impossible. The first who drew from the comparison of photographs the occasion to correct many errors of attribution, some of which had escaped Cavalcaselle himself, was another Italian, Giovanni Morelli. He was a physician, a follower of the anatomist Döllinger, and therefore he had the taste for exact science; he was a collector, and he had an outstanding artistic sensibility. He was not a thinker, and so he was not aware of the important part that his artistic sensibility had in his judgments. He believed, rather, in the duty of mortifying sensibility and of reducing the history of art to the application of some empirical principles, called experimental, in order to give them scientific dignity. He professed to observe that the painters of the fifteenth century, so attentive to variations in the model, repeated conventionally the hands and the ears, and he generalised this observation so far as to make of it a law: the works in which hands and ears are drawn in the same manner are by the same author. It is necessary to remember the infatuation for experimental science in the years between 1850 and 1880 in order to succeed in understanding, not only how a man of talent could have been able to construct such a theory, but also how such a theory could have had a great international circulation, and an influence, even favourable to the scholars of art history. But it must be added immediately that Morelli looked at works of art with lively intuition and not with his theory. That which he brought to the art of connoisseurship was philological consciousness and a rigorous attention to details.

The form of his writings is a review of current attributions in some German and Roman galleries (begun in 1874); this was an occasion to specify the classification of the works of art of the greatest Italian painters. In this revision he had the opportunity to make some famous discoveries: for example, that of the Venus of Giorgione in the Dresden Gallery, considered to be a copy by Sassoferrato. Another correct and famous achievement of Morelli was the reconstruction of the early work of Correggio. His desire he stated thus: "I should like to revive in my mind all the great figures of Italian painting, I should like to understand them to the point of assimilating my mind with theirs." This makes one understand what an instinctive spiritual activity served as the background of his *catalogues raisonnés*.

The work of Cavalcaselle and Morelli allowed Italy to see studies of art history flourishing between the end of the nineteenth century and the beginning of the twentieth. I may be allowed to recall the "History of Italian Art" of Adolfo Venturi, begun in 1901 and arrived to-day at its twenty-first volume, in which the connoisseur, the philologist and the artist are interwoven successfully and in which all the problems of Italian art from the fourth to the sixteenth century are treated in a thoroughly new manner. By reason of the vivacity of his artistic feeling, the writer can appreciate a Byzantine mosaic of the seventh century, which was formerly considered as the culmination of artistic decay, or a Michelangelesque mannerist, when from the thicket of convention springs a creation.

In Germany, opposed to Morelli, was Bode, who wished rather to continue the connoisseur's tradition of Waagen and Cavalcaselle, and whose merits in knowledge of Dutch painting, Italian sculpture and ceramics, and Persian carpets are universally known. Wickhoff and the archaeologist Furtwaengler were inspired rather by Morelli. To-day Max Friedländer is not only the greatest connoisseur of German and Flemish

art, but also the greatest German representative in the connoisseur's tradition.

In Holland, Hofstede de Groot revised with the acumen of
a connoisseur the *catalogue raisonné* of Dutch art.

Morelli directed to the study of art history Berenson, who
has not only enormously augmented and defined the field of
knowledge of Italian painting, but has been able to give many
refined psychological suggestions on the intimate characters
of artists and, finally, has outlined some motives of pure visibility. A great connoisseur of mediaeval architecture and sculpture was A. Kingsley Porter, who also went beyond the knowledge of facts towards an aesthetic appreciation founded upon
moral sensibility.

CHAPTER X
Criticism of Contemporary Art in the Nineteenth Century

FROM the third century B. C., when Xenocrates wrote, down to, but excluding, Winckelmann, art history and criticism found the reason for their existence in the appreciation of contemporary art. Even when the art of the past was studied, it was judged always in relation to the art of the present. Vasari admired Giotto according to the standards of Michelangelo; Bellori admired the ancients and Raphael according to the standards of the Carracci and Poussin, and Mengs admired Raphael, Correggio and Titian according to his own standards; but Winckelmann reversed the position and judged modern art by the standards of the ancient Greeks. The perfection of art was displaced from the present to the past. The Romantics looked for perfection in the art of the Middle Ages rather than in Greek art; always they looked for it in a past art. The idealists drew from this premise the logical conclusion: in the modern era, art was dead because it was dissolved in philosophical science. Philologists, archaeologists and connoisseurs, emerging from idealism, continued to bend their attention upon past art and to forget modern art, both because they were convinced of the nullity of the latter and because their philological and analytical ability found problems to resolve only in the art of the past. With rare exceptions, if they perceived modern art, it was only to appreciate those among their contemporaries who were better able to imitate the things or the principles of past art; those, that is to say, who were less original as artists, less representative as contemporary artists.

Various conditions favoured on the contrary an exceptional development of criticism of contemporary art in France. In the nineteenth century, France had a series of great painters, superior to those of other nations, and well armed with theory: it is enough to recall Delacroix, Ingres, Courbet, Manet, Cézanne and Gauguin. They took part in critical discussions, not only with the spoken and written word but also with their pictures. Romanticism, moreover, excited a brotherhood among poets, novelists and artists which led writers to promote, explain and discuss the art of the painters: this was true of Stendhal, Gautier, Baudelaire, the Goncourts and Zola. Again: painting shared in the moral and political struggles which were so ardent in France in the nineteenth century and therefore attracted the attention of politicians, like Guizot, Thiers and Clemenceau. Nowhere so much as in France was developed the idea of the close relation between art and social life; a dangerous idea, certainly, and sometimes misleading, but capable of preserving the vitality of art. It may be added that exhibitions were regular — biennial or annual — in a capital so centralising as Paris, and that the reports on exhibitions were of the kind already developed in the eighteenth century, and dignified by Diderot. Every two years, or every year, a number of the best writers gave their judgment upon the works exhibited, and tried to generalise upon the conditions of contemporary art, or on the method of criticism, and even to draw from it prognostications on the tendencies of taste. All this work had often the defect of journalistic improvisation; it often lacked sufficient historical and aesthetic information; but it had the incomparable merit of being attached to art in the making. Often changeable with changes of taste, French criticism of the nineteenth century was fragmentary, but it nevertheless kept constant its aspiration toward universal aesthetic values. It never fell into the iconographical and technical absurdities of contemporary archaeological and philological sci-

ence, and it was also liberated from the limitations of the idealistic aesthetic, in a very simple way, verifying the presence of
art in the works that it saw made. In order to extricate themselves from the double yoke of classic and Gothic art, historians sought afar, discovering prehistoric or folk works from
the Far East and from ancient America. French criticism
sought within its own house, and found consciousness of the
art of the day. If it be true that all history is the present day
interpretation of the past, the consciousness of present day art
is the basis of all history of the art of bygone days.

The renewal of criticism in France is identified with its liberation from the classicism of David, and, forcing the date a
little, it can be made to begin with the Salon of 1831.

As always, the tendencies intersect, and neo-classical criticism has not entirely ceased in France, even to-day, after so
many revolutions in taste. But since 1831 it has lost all vitality, even if, up to 1863, it had an original and lively cham-
pion, Delécluze, a pupil of David, who wrote his first Salon in
1819 and from 1822 to 1863 continued to oppose ruthlessly and
with absolute conviction any new manifestation of art. Opposed to any effect of expression whatsoever, in the name of
classic sculptural form, and convinced that painting must
have been the product of sculpture, originated in its turn
from architecture, Delécluze, shut up in his own theory,
understood nothing of what was happening around him. He
did not understand that the only vital art of his time was painting, and that the sculpture belonged to the tedious kind, as
Baudelaire was to say. His critical function was therefore purely negative, and had its own importance by the exclusion of
any compromise whatsoever. In France, more than in any
other country, there was a struggle, without quarter given,

between the innovators and the traditionalists; and the innovators always ended by conquering, after having created a tradition of their own: to-day not only Delacroix, but Cézanne also, is in the Louvre. But, with rare exceptions, so long as the innovators were alive, they were never admitted by the traditionalists and received neither the honours nor the worldly advantages which the French State reserved for the traditionalists. The French innovators, therefore, were not drawn to compromises, as were the innovators in the other countries, and they remained severely faithful to their individual mode of seeing and feeling, creating thus the moral conditions of their greatness. For having created such detachment, Delécluze has in part the responsibility and the credit.

On the other hand, even before 1831, signs of a new direction of criticism were not lacking. The Salon of 1824 confronted the critics with the problem of Delacroix. Stendhal was averse from him because of his own classicism; he respected David and, unfortunately, appreciated Horace Vernet. But he was opposed to the followers of David, and even if he did not admit in Delacroix the right to oppose his own "unreason" to the "incapacity" of the Davidians, he noted the favouring of him in English criticism, and admitted in him the feeling for colour and movement. Moreover, he considered the landscapes of Constable magnificent.

In 1822 Delacroix exhibited his first picture ("Dante and Vergil"), and Thiers received immediately the revelation "of a great painter," of a "born superiority which revives the hopes a little discouraged by the too mediocre merits of all the rest." Thiers was an admirer of David and a confirmed adversary of his imitators; he justified the revolution of style, of the "grand goût" of drawing, against the "littlenesses, the falsities, the smirkings of the last century," but felt that now "one must give other rules and not praise exclusively the grand style, the *grand goût*"; he admired the power in David in renewing his colouring in accord with that of the Flemish and Dutch, but noted that that colouring did not accord with his style. For all that, he did not discourage those who sought to put "more life, more truth, more naturalness on the canvas."

In 1827 the picture "Marino Faliero" by Delacroix was pointed out by Vitet as the shock of the exhibition; nevertheless he admired the colouring "of an admirable strength and richness," but "you can count all the strokes of the brush, nothing is fused, nothing graduated." Vitet understood that this "lack of finish" was conscious, in order to avoid "the coldness which ordinarily accompanies a precious finish." One must, he said, admire the colouring of Delacroix, "but it is so hard, so dissonant, that sometimes it tires instead of pleases." With regard to the composition of the picture, while Vitet found in it a lack of unity (he was thinking of material unity), he admired "the page of history"; he found in it a great power of mind, a great flexibility of imagination, a profound knowledge of what we call historical art, but not, in short, a work of art. Thus as far back as 1827, Vitet put two of the fundamental problems of nineteenth century criticism: that of pictorial finish opposed to the finish of abstract form, and that of expression opposed to neo-classical composition.

In 1829 Delacroix replied to criticism with fine irony on the critics who "run to the defence of the principles avowed by people of taste." "On the one side the men of spirit new and bold, but capable of destroying the whole edifice of good doctrines, were roughly rebuked and called to order; on the other, with the aid of these salutary rules, the community of rhymers and daubers, a limited and short-sighted race, but docile to excess and easy to lead, marched without effort in a comfortable routine." Delacroix wrote thus in defence not only of himself but of art and criticism.

The year after came the Revolution of July, and in the Salon of 1831 Delacroix exhibited his "Liberty." The outcries against the ideal of ugliness, against materialism, and so on, were many. But one young man, Gustave Planche, applauded Delacroix was "of that new and grave race, born yesterday, so great and powerful to-day, charged with a special and serious mission, called to regenerate society, to renew institutions"; of that race who did not suppose that the triumph of the revolution should "remain without influence upon the arts of imagination." It is necessary to remember all the spiritual value of the French Revolutions of 1830 and 1848 to understand the significance of this parallel instituted by Planche.

In 1831 Planche began his Salons, which he continued to edit up to 1852. His intuition is happy, in spite of the fact that his standards of judgment are not noteworthy. He understood in 1833 the error of Ingres, who believed the development of modern art closed with Raphael, without taking into account Veronese, or Rubens, or Rembrandt; he understood in 1831 that the greatest personalities were Gros, Gericault and Delacroix; in 1838 he saw that Corot went beyond realism and in 1847 praised him highly, overcoming all prejudices against his execution.

Two critics who, between 1831 and 1834, tend to rise above the struggle of the neo-classicists and romantics are Lenormant and Laviron. The first, it is true, confuses that process with a compromise, that is, with eclecticism of the Horace Vernet type; while the second attacks Vernet and all the eclectics, including the Carracci. Both show that landscape is the only kind which had made progress and they consider it as the art of the future. The protagonist of the new type of landscape is Théodore Rousseau. In 1833 Lenormant and Laviron single out Rousseau. The former writes of one of his pictures: "The horizon is transparent, the building, through the trees, harmonious and clear, the ground in the middle distance admirably luminous. Mr. Rousseau is still far from his aim; but I would not give his future for the complete career of twenty of our renowned landscape painters." In 1836 the Salon rejected Rousseau, at which Laviron and Planche protested, praising the naivety and the compositional greatness of the master.

The resistance to the romanticism of Delacroix and the realism of the landscapists of the Rousseau type was the work of Ingres. Praised by Lenormant, criticised by others, the style of Ingres and his school found a very acute definition by Louis Peisse in 1841: "It is a sort of modern classicism. A little less insipid than the old, but more scholastic, perhaps, and above all more importunate, for it is not so modest. One easily recognises its productions by the following signs: composition poor; figures light-strewn and of half natural size; expression cold; drawing exact and stiff; execution studied and almost precious in modelling; absence of relief; grey tones, colouring weak and monotonous, flat light; touch uniform." If Peisse had understood the poetry of the line of Ingres his definition would have been perfect.

On the threshold of the fifth decade of the century, the opposition of the two schools — that of Delacroix and that of Ingres — was already defined, as that of two theories already done with; and the young began to look for a new tendency. Even if recorded later, the basic ideas of the two theories were then well known, were indeed points of departure for all later criticism.

As far back as 1824 Delacroix had written: "I think that it is only imagination, or, if you like, what comes to the same thing – that organic delicacy, which makes one see what the others do not see." The task of the artist is: "to draw from his imagination the means of rendering nature and its effects, and to render them according to his own temperament." A touch of naive inspiration is preferable to everything." "The finest works of art are those which express the pure imagination of the artist." He praises "picturesque licenses: Rembrandt's lack of finish, the excess of Rubens'." He naturally admires ancient art, but opposes it to neo-classical art, to abstractions, to virtuosity; he understands by composition the distribution of the chromatic masses, independently of the subject. In it the subordination of details to the whole must be complete. Colour, considered in itself, in its effects, in its varieties, pre-occupies Delacroix before everything: "I know very well that the quality of colouring is more annoying than welcome to the modern schools, which attach quality only to drawing and sacrifice to it all the rest." He confirms the irony of this statement in his study of colour, which is for him the necessary antidote, both to idealism and to neo-classicism, and is indeed the element essential to reach the imagination. The aspects of colour are for him infinite: "The more I reflect upon colour the more I discover how that reflected *half-tint* is the principle which must dominate, because it is effectively that which gives the true tone, the tone which constitutes the values, which counts in the object and makes it exist." Blue shadows; prefer-ence for juxtaposition of tints, for the synthesis of the lights derived from the tints; above all, the mixture of the tints them-selves, as studied in the different ways of colouring of Titian,

Veronese, Rubens or Rembrandt: all these were essential to the theory of Delacroix.

To the complex work, passionate, without measure and without limits, full of sensibility, peculiar to Delacroix, is opposed the calm, certain, dogmatic precision, the aridity and the restraint of the ideal of Ingres.

Here are some of his aphorisms: "The principal and most important part of painting is to know what nature has produced of the most beautiful and suitable for that art, in order to choose it according to the taste and feeling of the ancients." "Drawing is the probity of art." "Drawing includes everything, except the tint." "If I were to put a sign above my door I should write: 'School of drawing,' and I am sure that I should make painters." "Colour adds ornaments to painting; but it is only the lady's-maid, because it does nothing but make more lovely the true perfections of art." "Not too hot colour; it is anti-historical. Fall into grey rather than into hot colour." "Narrow reflections in the shadow, reflections along the contours, are unworthy of the majesty of art." "Any doubt concerning the marvels of the ancients is blameworthy." "There is nothing essential to find in art since Phidias and Raphael, but there is always something to do, even after them, to maintain the cult of the true and perpetuate the tradition of the beautiful."

The contrast between Ingres and Delacroix could not be more definite, and eclecticism between the two systems could only be given by works which were lacking in value. In the eighteen-forties there was already enough detachment to judge Ingres and Delacroix and to turn elsewhere.

To the Salons of 1845 and 1847 were directed the comments of the new men who breathed the revolutionary atmosphere which led to 1848, and who felt the empty rhetoric of the first romanticism and sought to found the new romanticism from which realism derived, which was sometimes a transcendental realism. Besides defining Ingres and Delacroix, they furnished the critical explanation of Corot, sympathising with Courbet and the social values of art, and finally understanding the greatness of Daumier. Baudelaire, Thoré, Proudhon, Champfleury, Gautier, Mantz, Fromentin — naturally they are of unequal value; but their combined effect is unique in the history of art criticism.

The first Salon of Baudelaire is that of 1845, the last that of 1859; all his ideas are already formed in 1846. For him art is the ingenuous expression of temperament. The rules are to be banished from art as from criticism. Criticism must be partial, impassioned, political, made from an exclusive point of view so that it may open the widest horizon. He believes that the more recent and more real expression of beauty is romanticism. It does not consist in the choice of subjects, nor in truth, but in a manner of feeling. We must find it within us, not outside, in intimacy, in spirituality, in colour, in aspiration toward the infinite. Baudelaire's artistic experience is founded on the two names: Ingres and Delacroix. The prevalent opinion was that Ingres was a strong draughtsman and a weak colourist, and Delacroix the reverse; but the division was material, and Baudelaire needed to rise above it. "There are different sorts of drawing. The quality of a pure draughtsman consists above all in delicacy, and that delicacy excludes the pictorial touch: now there are happy touches, and the colourist charged to express nature by colour would often lose more by suppressing the happy touches than he would gain by realising a greater austerity of drawing. Colour certainly does not exclude great drawing — that of Veronese, for example, who proceeds above all by the ensemble of the masses; but it excludes certainly the drawing of detail, the contour of little bits, in which the touch will always eat up the line. Love of air and choice of subjects in movement ask for the use of wavering and disappearing lines."

To arrive at artistic individuality it is necessary to feel art in its infinite variety. "What would a modern Winckelmann say (we have many of them, nature overflows with them, the idle dote upon them), what would he say before a Chinese product, a product strange, bizarre, outlined in its form, intense in its colour, and sometimes delicate to the point of swooning? Yet this is a sample of universal beauty." It is not necessary to believe in progress; it is necessary to look to the personality. "The artist depends upon nobody but himself. He promises to the centuries to come, nothing but his own works; he guarantees nobody but himself. He dies without children. He has been his own king, his priest and his God."

Baudelaire possesses, thus, the sensible experience and the theoretical concepts for judging Ingres and Delacroix. Ingres has an ideal "made half of sanity, half of calm, almost of indifference, something analogous to the classic ideal, to which he has added the curiosities and the minutenesses of modern art. It is this combination which often gives to his works their strange charm." From his work, though, one receives an impression of rarefied air, of the atmosphere of a chemical laboratory, of an automatic population "who trouble our senses by their too visible and palpable extraneousness." "He believes that nature should be corrected, amended, he often suppresses the modelling, or lessens it, up to the point of invisibility, hoping thus to give more value to the contour." For that reason he is "a man gifted with high quality, an eloquent amateur of beauty, but denied that energetic temperament which makes the fatefulness of genius."

"From his youth M. Delacroix was great. Sometimes he has been more delicate, sometimes more unique, sometimes more of a painter, but he has always been great." "Of Delacroix's drawing, so absurdly, so foolishly criticised, what must one say, but an elementary truth completely misunderstood: a good drawing is not a line cruelly hard, despotic, immobile, enclosing a figure like a straight jacket; the drawing must be like nature, living and palpitating; simplification in drawing is a monstrosity; nature presents to us an infinite series of curved lines, fugitive, broken; Delacroix's drawing has at least the great merit of being a perpetual and efficacious protest against the barbarous invasion of the straight line." His colour "thinks for itself, independently of the object which it clothes. Then his admirable accord of colour often makes us dream of harmony and melody." Finally, he is loved by poets because he is "essentially literary."

Strong in the experience of Delacroix, Baudelaire sees clearly the impotence of eclectics of the Vernet type, "the absolute antithesis of the artist." He condemns the sentimentalism of Ary Scheffer: "To seek poetry deliberately in the conception of a picture is the surest way of not finding it. It must come unknown to the artist. It is the result of painting itself."

Baudelaire sees in creative imagination the principal quality of the artist, and therefore he loves religious painting. But he condemns the didactic art of those who, like Overbeck, study the beauty of the past only "to teach religion better." He is opposed to the realist and positivist painters, and, in theory, has doubts about genre and landscape pictures. But he appreciates Courbet and sees his relation to Ingres. He is "a powerful workman, a savage and patient will. Politics and literature also produce these vigorous temperaments, these protestants, these anti-super-naturalists, of whom the justification is a spirit of reaction, sometimes salutary." He loves Corot and Rousseau. The last is "a naturalist drawn unceasingly toward the ideal." As for Corot, Baudelaire protests against the prejudice about his lack of finish. "There is a great difference between a thing *made* and a thing *finished* – generally that which is made is not finished, and a thing very much finished may not be made at all."

In homage to his romanticism, Baudelaire theorised caricature, and in a profound way understood its moral character. In this connection he admires Daumier. What distinguishes the latter is *certainty:* "He draws like the great masters. His drawing is abundant, easy; it is a swift improvisation; and yet it is never *chic*." "His drawing is naturally coloured. His lithographs and his wood engravings awake ideas of colour."

Here ends the criticism of Baudelaire; later he was favourable to his friend Manet, but he did not understand his art. However, Baudelaire is master of his experience of Ingres and Delacroix, Corot, Rousseau and Daumier. His intuition carried him a long way, and served him on occasion to improvise an aesthetic system, which is not really systematic but is controlled by reference to an art which his poetical intuition made him see as authentic.

Thoré, who assumed the pseudonym of Bürger, was an unquiet spirit, troubled by philosophy and religion, a follower of Fourier. Under the influence of Rousseau he interested himself in art criticism and went back from the modern age to the old, especially the Dutch and English, contributing to the discovery of Vermeer of Delft. For Thoré art is the love of nature. The decadence of art is due to losing the feeling for nature. The external expression of that feeling is the work of the complete artist; and therefore art is a language. "Art results from the impression produced on man by nature, from the reflection of the external world in the microcosm, in that little world which we carry within us." "Effect in nature is like the physiognomy of a passion." Different from science, which isolates, art "expresses being in its surrounding harmonies. The smallest corner of the country is a vista of the sky and leads to the infinite." But landscape painters who determine the exact form of the details do not take count of the atmosphere. "Subject is absolutely indifferent in art. The fantastic arabesques of the Renaissance have survived thousands of noble statues. A pot by Chardin is worth all the Romans of the modern imperial school. Ostade is as much king in his cottage as Raphael on his Parnassus." More than Baudelaire, Thoré withdraws from romanticism and makes a decisive step towards naturalism. He perceives that the vitality of naturalism depends upon its relations with the social movement. It is not true that the naturalists choose their objects by chance; they show "a decided propensity towards the classes which the academic schools have nearly always repudiated." Even confronted by the problem of finish he sees justly: the more a picture is expressive, the more it is finished.

He loves Rousseau and believes him to be the greatest landscapist of his time, though he perceives that his first sketchy manner is better than the later well-finished manner. He admires Corot, and realises that under the appearance of a confused sketch there is a spiritual world; he realises, too, that the ingenuousness of the drawing arrives even at elegance, and counsels him good humouredly to leave out of his landscapes the Greek divinities and replace them with Breton peasants. He admires Delacroix, but no longer considers him as the central problem of his criticism. The landscape painters on the one side, and Courbet on the other, allow him to understand the drama of taste developed during the Second Empire, which broke out in 1863 with the "Salon of the Rejected." He sees that official art has become mercantile, and satirises the conventions of the social taste and of the "Prix de Rome." He, instead, confirms the unity of tendency in the rejected, and makes it consist in taking art back to its origin. In their work there is a lack of drawing, in the sense of outlines; there is an unfinished look, there is a lack of details; but there is to the fullest extent the effect of a striking spiritual unity. The contrast between the public and the artists does not consist, as is said, in the subjects treated, but in the fact that the public wish to see in painting the object in itself, while the true artist offers them his own way of seeing and feeling. In spite of reserves, Thoré was therefore encouraging to Courbet and to Manet, who was then beginning.

From the revolution of 1848 dates the realistic campaign of Courbet. He wishes to paint "the common and the modern," and signs himself "Courbet without ideal and without religion." Round Courbet gather Champfleury, Duranty, Max Buchon, Baudelaire, Proudhon, Castagnary, Silvestre, Decamps, Daumier and Corot. The credo of Courbet is known: "painting is an art essentially concrete, and can only consist in the representation of real and *existing* things. An *abstract* object, not visible, is not within the domain of painting. Imagination in art consists in knowing how to find the most complete expression of an existing thing, but never in supposing or creating that same thing. Beauty is in nature and is met with in reality under the most different forms. As soon as it is found, it belongs to art, or rather to the artist who is able to see it there. Beauty, like truth, is a thing relative to the time when it is seen and to the individual fit to create it. The expression of beauty is in direct ratio to the power of perception acquired by the artist. There can be no schools, there are only painters."

As aesthetics, all this was worth very little; but as an introduction to the life of art it was an antidote necessary for a definite cure for the neo-classical academy, the romantic reverie, and the vulgar opportunism of the eclectics. The success of Courbet's naturalistic passion found minds prepared by landscapists of the Rousseau type, by the democratic passion sharpened among the intellectuals through resistance to the Second Empire, and it therefore had a formidable echo even in regions distant from France.

Proudhon, the philosopher and politician, created an aesthetic system on the basis of Courbet's experience, entitled: "Of the Principles of Art and its Social Destination" (1865). To the "irrationality of art in the eighteenth and nineteenth centuries, an irrationality which, degenerating into orgy and debauch, has ended by all but killing genius," he opposes the principle of Courbet, which states: "Art has for its object to lead us to the knowledge of ourselves, by the revelation of all our thoughts, even the most secret, all our tendencies, our virtues, our vices, our absurdities, and in this way to contribute to the development of our dignity, the perfecting of our being. It has not been given to us to feed us with chimeras, make us drunk with illusions, deceive us and lead us into evil with mirages, as the classics, the romantics and all the sectarians of a vain ideal tend to do; but to deliver us from these pernicious illusions and denounce them." "The truth is that Courbet, in his realism, is one of the most powerful idealists that we have, a painter of the most lively imagination. The idealism of Courbet is most profound; only he takes no pains to invent anything. He sees the soul through the body, of which the forms are for him a language, and every feature a sign. To sum up, Courbet, a painter critical, analytical, synthetic, humanitarian, is an expression of the time. His work coincides with the 'Positive Philosophy,' by Auguste Comte, the 'Positive Metaphysic,' by Vacherot, the 'Human Rights or Immanent Justice,' by myself (Proudhon)."

Champfleury was considered the Courbet of literature. In 1848 Baudelaire writes of him that "he dared, on his first appearance, to content himself with nature and to have in her an absolute confidence." In 1857 Champfleury published his doctrine under the title: "Realism." As far back as 1846 he had written a Salon in favour of the landscapists and Delacroix, against the eclectics, the sentimentalists and the neo-pagans. In 1848 he is already directed "toward the three masters of the contemporary French school, Delacroix, Ingres and Corot," and he adds to them a fourth, Daumier, who was then making his first appearance as a painter. The greatest merit of Champfleury for figurative art is his "History of Modern Caricature," written in 1864, which is a truthful and appropriate monograph on Daumier. He is able to understand the artistic value of caricature: "It is the property of men of genius which makes us interested in the transparency of shadows, spirited strokes of the burin, a particular turn of the crayon, an unforeseen play of light, a graphic fantasy which makes grandeur, force, style, shape, movement; the comic and the caricature live on their own foundations and do not belong to any one country or any one civilisation." Daumier "has summed up in himself the comic powers of numerous caricaturists who preceded him, and he has brought into the exercise of his art a feeling for colour which makes each of his sketches a powerful work. An engraving by Daumier can be matched against the boldest conceptions of modern art. For fire, Delacroix alone could compete with the caricaturist." That is enough to make us understand the acuteness of Champfleury and the reason why he always maintained some reserve about Courbet.

The official critic of realism was Castagnary, whose Salons, which run from 1857 to 1879, contain arguments for Millet and Courbet, and subtle appreciations of Corot and Daubigny. He was interested above all in the general thesis, to define "the true tendencies of art in our epoch," and put artistic individualities in the second place. With naturalism he associated the *indigenous,* that is, the theory of art linked with place, climate and race; and he favoured the representation of peasants in art as of a bond of union between man and nature.

As to the first romanticism of the young Delacroix was opposed a reaction personified in Ingres, so to the second romanticism, which arrived at the social realism of Courbet and the transcendental realism of Daumier, was opposed a reaction as much weaker artistically as it was stronger socially. At the Universal Exhibition of 1855 the hero was Ingres. But none of the painters who surrounded Ingres in the official world had artistic value. Hence there was dug the abyss between the painters on the one side, who were the custodians of traditions, protected by the State, exalted by the public, and despised by everybody with any sense of art; and those on the other, who were the authentic painters, the ones called the advance guard, ignored by the State, derided by the public, defended by the smallest minority, tried by every material and moral suffering, who had to await recognition and fortune until after 1890.

A typical representative of the reaction from realism was Théophile Gautier, the proclaimer of art for art's sake — that which "would say not the form for the form, but certainly the form for the beautiful, abstraction made of all foreign ideas, of all turning to the profit of any doctrine whatever, of all

direct utility." What he means by beauty is well understood
in the two volumes on "The Fine Arts in Europe," with reference to the exhibition of 1855. That beauty is the beauty of
Ingres: "It is impossible not to seat him at the summit of art,
on that throne of gold with steps of ivory where sit crowned
with laurels the glorious ones, accomplished and ripe for im-
mortality." Naturally he also praises Delacroix, but also, together with him, Gerôme and Horace Vernet. In short, the
critical direction which with so much pains had been reached
about ten years before, was now destroyed. Between the authentic spiritual life of France and the judgments of Gautier
there is no longer any relation. Sainte-Beuve in 1863 wrote
that the progress of art criticism was continuous, and its culmination reached by Charles Blanc and Théophile Gautier.
As symbols of progress he quotes various names, but not
Baudelaire nor Thoré. He prefers to admire the science of
Gautier, his universality and, above all, his art of description.
"The system of Gautier, in describing, is a system of transposi-
tion, an exact reduction, an equivalent rather than a translation.
In the same way as one reduces a symphony to the piano, he
reduces a picture to an article." I have no need to insist upon
the danger of such literary virtuosity; it dispenses with criticism, is self-complacent to the point of praising everything,
and the weaker it is in judgment, the more its virtuosity leads
to distracting one from the critical problem and taking the
relative responsibilities. With reason Delacroix wrote of Gautier: "He takes a picture, describes it in his way, makes himself
a picture which is charming, but he has not performed an act
of true criticism."

A critic who was not lacking in talent, and who began his
Salons in 1845, was Paul Mantz. Differently from Baudelaire,
Thoré, and Champfleury, he disembarked, as he wrote, from

the "land of dreams" with a dogma: "outside the laws of art, no health." And what are those laws? "Proportion, grouping, harmony." In 1847 he was, in his way, a rebel: he appreciated Corot, Rousseau and Delacroix, but not Ingres (who is an effort and not a result), nor Couture nor Vernet. In spite of the prejudice of his laws of art, his criticism was, then, sufficiently directed in 1847. After that, and up to 1891, he wrote about the Salons and occupied himself with ancient art, even with acuteness — for example, with Michelangelo and Watteau. But to open, for example, his Salon of 1889 is to feel one's self revolted. In spite of talent and continual study, forty-four years after his first Salon, instead of judging, he showers with conventional praises Roll, Zorn and Lhermitte. The prejudice of his laws of art made not only one victim, but produced that catastrophe of official French criticism and painting which lasts until now.

An event, which was the natural continuation of the abstraction made by Gautier of the problem of art from the more vital tendencies of the French mind at that time, was the launching of the fashion of the eighteenth century by the Goncourts between 1862 and 1869. It is understood that that fashion repaired an historical error of romanticism, and from then on nobody doubted any longer the absolute value of Chardin and Fragonard. But the official French taste considered it as a lucky chance to take to itself the old features of the rococo, in order to give proof of elegance, of refinement, of external cleverness, and to withdraw itself from the more pressing and human problems — less serene certainly, but alive — which nourished the authentic art of the time. To show the Goncourts' limitations of taste it is enough to recall their preference for Gavarni over Daumier. The succeeding fashion for Japanese prints, and the "artistic stylism" of the Goncourts also suggested to some authentic painters digressions displeasing to art.

A place apart must be conceded to Fromentin. Clever painter, excellent writer, an aspirant to historical culture and reflection, he also wished to write a history of criticism in order to define his ideas. In 1845 he wrote in his Salon: "Nature may be for you like an occasion to feel, dream, reflect and invent. Study processes in the masters, the truth in nature, but do not seek except in yourself the innate image of beauty and inspiration." In 1873 the subjectivity of artistic vision appears evident to him, and he asks himself if there exists a reality which is not the manner of seeing. From such premises he drew the material for "The Masters of the Past," published in 1876. The importance of the book consists precisely in the fact that the Flemish and Dutch painters of the seventeenth century are there studied for the first time in the nineteenth century with reference to a well-determined pictorial ideal, based on the experience of Delacroix, the experience of other romantic or eclectic French painters and finally on Fromentin's own. He analyses some single personalities, chiefly Rubens and Rembrandt; but he also judges them according to a pictorial ideal. He carries into the study of the art of the past the critical experience of the art of the present. His thought runs continually from the past to the present; he makes use of the present to understand the past, and of the past to limit the present. The very choice of historical theme well shows his aim: the romantics were greatly inspired in their pictorial reform by the Flemish and Dutch; Delacroix by Rubens, Rousseau by Ruysdael and Hobbema, and so on. For the first time since Winckelmann, Fromentin looks at the past with the eyes of the present. The past is thus illuminated better than by the most precise research of philologists or connoisseurs. Some of Fromentin's pages on Rubens or Rembrandt have not been surpassed.

The limitation of Fromentin's criticism consists in the restrictedness of his ideal. He had learned to paint well as a follower of Delacroix and Decamps, but he did not succed in becoming an artist in painting, and he was aware of it. His criticism remains that of disillusion; he has not the aesthetic faith of a Baudelaire or a Thoré. He does not see, like Baudelaire, that the draughtsman's form of the Ingres tradition and the chromatic form of the Delacroix tradition are irreconcilable. He believes that one can be at the same time a good draughtsman (abstract) and a good colourist, reducing in that way the problem of style and of the tradition of taste to a technical problem, according to the custom of the eclectics. With all that, he admires in the Dutch the capacity to "portray things as they are," contradicting that subjectivity of vision of which, however, he had knowledge. Therefore there filters into his criticism the academic prejudice against the new tendencies of art which were developing under his eyes. He admits that the eye of the impressionists "has very just perceptions, and particularly delicate sensations," but he does not support their detachment from drawing and traditional compositions. Confronted by the art which realised his ideal, he confines himself by distrust to the negative position.

However, within the limits of seventeenth century art, Fromentin succeeds in identifying art history and art criticism, in gathering from the pictures what is truly artistic, in explaining as nobody before him had been able to do the value of colouring — its architecture, its organisation, and the relation between colour and light; and, finally, in refusing all hierarchy of subjects in the work of art. Hence his contribution to art criticism remains one of the most valuable of the nineteenth century.

In the seventh decade of the nineteenth century the artistic scandal was the work of Manet, and the critical scandal the defence of Manet by Zola. Realism of the Courbet type had been imposed upon, and even a little accommodated to, the taste of the public, so desirous of quiet, when Manet brought forward something new, dangerous not in the social aspect but in respect to form. The realism of Courbet had, in fact, respected the traditional conception of form, which Manet would break up: no more roundness, no more gradual passages of chiaroscuro, but contrasts, broken forms, improvised touches. This was something never seen before, and it threw into fury, even more than the public, the traditional artists who felt themselves menaced in their most deeply fixed principles.

In his Salon of 1866 Zola defines his position with regard to realism: "The word *realist* means nothing to me, who declares for subordinating the real to temperament. Make true, and I applaud; but above all make individual and living, and I applaud still more." Moreover, he says: "Courbet, it appears, has passed to the enemy. Somebody must have gone to his house as an ambassador, and offered him titles and honours if he would deny his disciples." "The crowd sees in a canvas a subject which has seized it by the throat or by the heart, and asks of the artist nothing but a tear or a smile. For me a work of art is, on the contrary, a personality, an individuality. What I ask of the artist is not to give me tender visions or fearful nightmares; it is to deliver himself, heart and flesh, it is to affirm proudly a powerful and special mind, a self which seizes nature broadly in his hand and plants upright before us that which he sees there." His was not an aesthetic judgment, but "the brief in a lawsuit" against the social conventions of art and against realism itself in the name of a more intense artistic subjectivism.

"M. Manet's talent is made of simplicity and justness. Doubtless, confronted with the incredible nature of some of his colleagues he decided to interrogate reality, man to man; he refused all acquired science, all ancient experience, he would take art from the beginning, that is to say, by the exact observation of objects. He therefore put himself courageously face to face with a subject, saw this subject in broad masses, in vigourous oppositions, and painted each thing as he saw it."

All that is true only in part, and to-day it is known what assimilating ability Manet had. The true part is this, however: that Manet, though it may have been through assimilations, had reached the point of taking art from its beginning, had found his creative naturalness as every authentic artist must, and so affirmed his personality and encouraged many others to affirm theirs.

"The great scarecrow, believe me, is not realism; it is temperament. Every man who does not resemble the others becomes by that an object of distrust. As soon as the crowd do not understand they laugh. It needs a whole education to accept genius."

The "Camille" of Claude Monet "tells me a whole history of energy and truth. Ah! there is a temperament, there is a man among this crowd of eunuchs. Look at the neighbouring canvases and you will see what a pitiful appearance they make beside this window open upon nature. Here there is more than a realist, there is a delicate and strong interpreter who has been able to render each detail without falling into dullness."

As is known, Zola could not continue his Salons on account of the indignation of readers, but the scandal was made and it opened a very long period of conflict between the public

and the better artists. The Salon was reprinted and dedicated
to Zola's friend, Cézanne, who was certainly its principal inspirer. It was destined that Cézanne should become in his turn
the target of the most lively indignation of the public, and
only at the beginning of the twentieth century should be
recognised as the world master of painting. The novelty in
Zola's writing is the accentuation of the value of personality
in art — a firm, exclusive and revolutionary accentuation.

A second revolutionary action was the one-man show of
Manet outside the Universal Exhibition of 1867. It was not a
new initiative, because Courbet had already taken a similar
initiative in 1855, but it was very daring, precisely because of
its being Manet. Zola analyses his personality: the colours are
lighter than those of the other realists; the justness of the
tones has led the artist to paint in large masses; his grace is a
little crude, but attractive and truly human, as well as mundane; and, finally, the character of pure painting which belongs
to Manet is opposed to the false moral and literary pretences of
the fashionable painting. "He treats figure pictures as it is
allowed in the schools to treat still life pictures."

In the Salon of 1868 Manet has a success; Degas, Renoir,
Bazille and Monet are noted; and Castagnary can affirm that a
"radical revolution by content and form" has taken place. He
puts into relief the freedom from romanticism accomplished
by realism; understands realism still within the limits of Courbet's ideas, but is able to see in it the relations with the prevailing spirit in philosophy, morality and politics, and he wishes
for the return of public life — that is, the fall of the empire
— so that the new art may develop.

On the eve of the war, the Salon of 1870 is interpreted by
Théodore Duret, the senior critic of impressionism. Against
the limitations of realism and its photographic materiality, he

opposes the artist "who, having a personal vision of things, contrives to fix his vision on the canvas in an appropriate form, which at the same time communicates his impression. ... we do not even look at the picture in which there is nothing except for the eye: we do not look at a picture except to feel it, to receive from its aspect an impression or an emotion." The "pure painter" of Zola is thus corrected, the totality of art is called in to justify the origin of impressionism. Duret notes that Manet's drawing, unlike that of Ingres, is adapted to his vision, to his chromatic harmony, "which does not proceed from light to dark, from shadow to light, but from one tone which makes the light to another which makes the dark." He remarks before a picture by Pissarro that in spite of the banality of the motive "one feels one's self penetrated little by little by a melancholy feeling which must have been itself experienced from the aspect of the natural scene."

After the war and the Commune the public is still more averse than before from all revolutionary manifestations, even in painting, and the anger against Courbet, politically compromised, is extended to all the innovators. Hence the violence of the reaction against the impressionists' exhibitions, separated from the official Salons, in the years 1874, 1876 and 1877.

Two critics of the realistic tradition, Burty and Duranty, take up the defence of the impressionists. In 1875 the first writes that in the impressionist pictures "detail is suppressed with a decision which startles timid souls. The ensemble also expresses effects of light: oppositions of tone, silhouettes and masses by bold attacks, with little care for the approbation of the short-sighted. These are small fragments of the mirror of universal life, and the fleeting and colourful things, subtle and charming, which are reflected there, have well the right to hold one and to be celebrated."

In 1876 Duranty argues with Fromentin, and indicates thus the character of impressionistic art: their discovery "consists properly in having recognised that intense light transforms the tones, that the sun reflected by objects tends, by force of clearness, to collect in that luminous unity which fuses its seven prismatic rays in a single uncoloured glare, which is light. From intuition to intuition they have come little by little to decompose the solar gleam into its rays, into its elements, and to recompose its unity by the general harmony of the rainbow tints which they spread on their canvases." He believes that the impressionists are the primitives of a great movement of artistic renewal, and present the danger of being abused by the eclectics, which, in fact, is what happened.

The exhibition of 1877 had better success. It was for this that George Rivière founded and edited a review, "The Impressionist," and sought to determine the personalities of the various masters. "To treat a subject for the tones, and not for the subject itself — that is what distinguishes the impressionists from other painters." Joy, animation, and life of the figures are expressed in Renoir; the soul of things in Monet; science, a little ingenuous, in Degas; greatness, refinement, vast science in Cézanne; rural religiosity and epic amplitude in Pissarro; finesse and tranquillity in Sisley.

The best analysis of impressionism was, however, due to an intelligent adversary, Paul Mantz: "The impressionist is the sincere and free artist, who, breaking with the procedure of the school, with fashionable refinements, reflects in the naïvety of his heart, the absolute charm which is disengaged from nature, and simply and with the greatest possible frankness, translates the intensity of the impression experienced."

We must agree, however, that French criticism of the eighteen-eighties was not able to define the new masters, as the criticism of the eighteen-fifties had done for the romantics and realists.

In 1880 and 18881 the group of impressionists was dissolved for both material and artistic reasons, but criticism was not a-ware of it, and believed that the authentic impressionism was that after 1880.

Huysmans, who in 1876 saw the impressionists as "disor-derly," sick and mad, is converted in 1881 to Pissarro, who resolves the difficulties of daylight and *open air;* and in 1882 he expresses appreciation of Renoir and also of Monet, who, formerly held responsible for the summary and exaggerated, is now judged self-contained. That causes wonder; Monet was much more exaggerated in 1882 than in 1876, and Pissarro had indeed resolved certain technical difficulties, but to the weak-ening of his art. The truth is that Huysmans realised the error committed in 1876, but gave no reason for it, and pre-ferred to defend the very men he had formerly derided, at-tributing to them his own growth in understanding. Never-theless a flash of genius is not lacking in Huysmans when he feels the greatness of the impressionism of Cézanne. Laforgue, who writes in these years, sees justly the sincerity and the primitiveness of the impressionists, but is induced to exaggerate the technical function of Monet and Pissarro. In 1883 Monet is recognised by conservative criticism through Alfred de Lostalot, who appreciates the refined poet, the non-naturalist, and attests that he is not "anarchical" or "ignorant," like the other impressionists. In 1886 Félix Fénéon is aware of the end of impressionism, and opposes to the "arbitrariness" in the de-composition of colours peculiar to the impressionists, the "system" of Pissarro, Seurat, Signac. The language betrays him; in fact, in reference to Monet he substitutes "spontaneity" for "arbitrariness." If he had opposed "spontaneity" to "system" he would have been completely right.

In 1891 Mirbeau gives the highest praise to Pissarro, philosopher and social educator, and to Monet, tamer of the sun; and the symbolist friend of Gauguin, Aurier, who in 1890 had appreciated "the perfume, the poetry of surroundings" of the "neo-impressionist" Pissarro, in 1892 praises in the "impressionist" Monet, the mystic of the "divinity of the sun." To indicate the decadence there is only a single voice, unheard, that of George Moore, in 1893: he says many just things on Manet, Monet, Pissarro and above all on Sisley; he is astonished that Pissarro should be induced to imitate his own disciples, and to 1881 or 1882 he reports the reform of divisionism which he considers "decadent painting, scientific painting."

The first two histories of impressionism, that of Lecomte in 1892 and that of Geffroy in 1894, came out when impressionism was dead and they were not aware of it; when divisionism and symbolism had changed the creative taste of the epoch; when, to the realistic sanity of the years from 1870 to 1880, had succeeded a mystic decadency. The epoch of the struggle against the impressionists was closed; Monet, Renoir, Pissarro received the favour of the public and the two historians accepted them *en bloc*. Geffroy does not put to himself the problem of the limits within which to include impressionism, but that of the number of impressionists to deal with, and hence he regroups arbitrarily the most discordant tendencies. Both of these histories are very valuable for detailed observations upon the techniques and the characters of the artists of whom they speak, and whom they knew very well; but the mistaken arrangement of the subject hinders them from having a synthetic homogeneousness. Not very dissimilar, even if more anecdotal, is the work of Théodore Duret, the friend of Manet and of the impressionists of the early days, who in 1906 published the first edition of his "History of Impressionism." He records many things; he knows well that in 1886 impressionism was finished, but he does not draw from the fact the necessary conclusions.

Through not being able to justify impressionism with regard to the universal idea of art, criticism was not even able to understand the new artistic tendencies in art at the end of the nineteenth century. The neo-impressionism or divisionism of Seurat was interpreted by Signac in its scientific pretension and not in its artistic aspect. The symbolism of Gauguin was expounded by Gauguin himself in a confused way, though with very happy detailed observations; by Aurier with ideas taken from Hegel; by Denis with religious and decorative tendencies. Finally, the ideas of Cézanne reached the public through such distortions that they lost their true character on the way. They were pretexts for developing the taste of the abstraction of form and of geometrical composition, a taste which prevailed up to recent years. To understand this taste it is necessary to know the theory of pure visibility of which we shall speak in the next chapter.

It is necessary, then, to return to the romantico-realistic ideas of the fifth decade of the nineteenth century in order to trace the origin of a modern criticism which was entirely faithful to the art it dealt with, and which gave to that art, if not precisely a system, at least a critical representation which was conscious and truthful.

CHAPTER XI
Art Criticism and Pure Visibility

CONTEMPORARY criticism differs from that of the past in that it concentrates attention on visual symbols. The distant origins of these symbols are best understood if one recalls the distinction made by Lucian which is given in Chapter II. With reference to Zeuxis' *Centaur*, Lucian said that he wished to speak only of the terrifying and savage appearance of the centaur and the sensuous appearance of the centauress, leaving to others—artists and connoisseurs—the task of speaking of the correctness of the drawing and colouring, the effects of the modelling and shading, and so forth. Thus, Lucian saw two types of phenomena: one concerned with psychological expression, the other with the artist's vision. It is the task of criticism to overcome this dualism by understanding how psychological expression is turned into painting and how the vision of the artist expresses what he feels. It is impossible, however, to arrive at a synthesis without a knowledge of the thesis and antithesis. Quite naturally, critics have always been occupied and preoccupied in studying the emotional and visual phenomena. They did not have to invent a special science for the former, since it has always existed and is called psychology.

But where is the critic to find the science needed to grasp the phenomenology of vision? Neither physics nor geometry would do since they deal with colour and form in a very different manner from that of painters and sculptors. The science of artistic vision, therefore, had to be a body of generalized knowledge derived from the observation of form and colour as used by artists. In any work of art form and colour are the art in that they are imbued with the individual feeling of the artist. But, when the forms or compositions of two different person-

267

alities are compared, that emotional emphasis that makes them art is abstracted. What remains is the physical symbol of a reality that, like all realities, is made up of both spiritual and physical components. Just because it is a symbol, composition, even when it is abstracted from the work of art that it informs, is charged with historical connotations. Hence, besides being a material thing, it is also an expression of taste and a link between the creative individuality of the artist and the historical development.

For example, there are certain similarities in the way Raphael and Michelangelo use composition. This common attribute is called closed composition. It has also been noted that Titian and Tintoretto use a very similar type of composition but that it is very different from that used by Raphael and Michelangelo. That similarity in the work of Titian and Tintoretto is what is called open composition or open form. Here, then, two types of composition have been isolated—open and closed composition. The reason for such a formulation of types is that they serve the same purpose as psychological types. When Byron's poetry is called melancholy or Lamartine's tender, two psychological characteristics are given that do not inform the poets' art but that help to describe their personality. In the same way, when it is said that Raphael is linear and Titian pictorial, this is not a judgment of their art but identifies two usual tendencies that describe their personalities. The experience of melancholy and tenderness, like the experience of the linear and the pictorial, is thus an experience of classes, systems, schemata, and symbols that is indispensable to the process of coming to understand the individuality of any work of art. The intuitive relation between the universal idea of art and a specific work is immediate. It is the task of history to represent that relation in its intuitive perception but through a body of concepts which, in fact, are the symbols or schemata, and represent the analytical moment of intuitive perception, that is, the moment the viewer exercises taste. The transition from the universal to the particular work of art by means of symbols or schemata is, therefore, within the logical scheme of things.

However, it is essential not to confuse art with the viewer's taste, and therefore never to make a visual symbol the yard-stick for critical judgment. For example, we know from Xeno-crates that a distinction between contour and modelling was common in the third century. Parrhasios excelled in the contours of the figures but was not as adept at modelling as Nikias, who showed relief by means of light and shade. We also know that the transition from contour to modelling was considered progress. This was a mistake. We should free ourselves of the idea of progress. What remains is that Parrhasios could find perfection in the line of the contour and Nikias in the shading of the modelling. Although the personalities of Parrhasios and Nikias were too complex to be summed up by the terms contour and modelling, there can be no doubt that for Xenocrates contour and modelling served as thumbnail descriptions of the two artists. It was a way of showing their personalities.

What has been said of symbols that are related to specific individuals can also be applied to periods in art. In the twelfth century Theophilus said that painting consisted of the composition and blending of colours; in the fourteenth century Cennino Cennini stated that it consists of drawing and colour; in the fifteenth century Alberti sees the element of painting in the outline and the composition of planes, reducing the function of colour to that of chiaroscuro. Now take a twelfth-century Byzantine mosaic, a fourteenth-century Tuscan painting with a gold background, and a fresco by Masaccio. With the guidance of Theophilus, Cennini, and Alberti respectively, the chromatic ideals of the Byzantine mosaic, the balance between line and colour in the fourteenth-century painting, and the severe emphasis on plastic form in the fresco become readily understandable. Without a knowledge of the three treatises, the criterion of progress in the imitation of nature still found in some manuals of art history might have been applied, using the following reasoning: The Byzantine mosaic belongs to the barbaric Middle Ages when knowledge of form had been lost and only the splendour of colour was considered important; but Giotto rediscovered the art of natural form, though it remained somewhat rigid until Masaccio learned to make figures that were set squarely on the ground and of which it can be said that they are alive as well as painted.

Though the absurdity of such a treatment is obvious today, it was not so at the beginning of the century. Criticism has made real progress since then because it acquired a knowledge of the visual symbols that reveal the different ways in which artists or groups of artists conceive of style and the various idioms they use. In respect to artistic judgment, however, symbols have had simultaneously a negative and a positive function. Because they are abstract in form, symbols belong to psychology and do not have a judgment value. Aristotle said that line is essential to art; colour, incidental. But just because line and colour are two symbols and not art itself, they have the same value, and any preference is arbitrary and depends on individual taste rather than reason. Any symbol can occur in both masterpieces and poor works.

At the same time, since criticism had always used symbols to justify judgment, the fact that we have now put all the symbols on the same level in relation to art, has liberated the judgment of art from abstraction. We do not demand colour from Michelangelo but understand that his art is consummated in form; we no longer censure Rembrandt for his dark tonalities but understand that his luminous idiom requires them. In this sense of liberation, the use of visual symbols has been useful in giving historic consistency to art criticism.

The use of visual symbols is related to the historico-philological method of art history. A work of art is broken down into its elements of taste for much the same reasons that an historical text is broken down into its sources. Once the subject matter, the moral, religious, philosophical, or political principles, and the techniques have been isolated, the visual symbols, too, are found. Hence, visual symbols used since antiquity have in some measure been purified and systematized. For example, according to Mengs, if a young man was to become a painter, he had to learn: 1) drawing, 2) chiaroscuro, 3) colour, 4) harmony, 5) composition, 6) grace, and 7) the proportions of the human body. A comparison of these symbols with those of Wölfflin—the linear and the pictorial, open and closed form, etc.—shows at first glance that Mengs' symbols are homogeneous while Wölfflin's are heterogeneous. As long as drawing has not become the linear and colour not the pictorial, they remain techniques for imitating nature as well as visual symbols that define art historically. In composition, Mengs included the subject and such attributes of the figures as expression, contrast of the members, propriety, quality, and age. To Wölfflin composition may be on the surface or in depth. Among his symbols Mengs included grace, which is certainly one of the most desirable states of mind for achieving art, but is not a concept that the painter can hold up as a standard for his art. He may at times paint gracefully, but he cannot paint grace, and all he obtains, if he studies grace in order to paint it, is affectation. Thus, in something over a century, the visual symbols were purified and systematized in that emotional elements, and in general, all psychological elements, like the technical elements, were strictly separated from the visual symbols.

Certain artistic tendencies and certain aesthetic theories favored the creation of symbols.

In reaction to the unrestrained Romantic effusion toward the Divine and the Romantic intuition of reality, Hans von Marées (1837–1887), impelled by a desire for form, rediscovered visual standards. In Italy, the wish to return to the classic awoke in him, but he did not become a Neo-Classicist since his attitude toward the classical consisted of a moral need for restraint, reflection, and concentration. He was influential in the development of taste, inspired Conrad Fiedler and Adolf von Hildebrand, and initiated the formalism that was to become popular later. Unfortunately, his creative ability did not equal his taste; his colours were dead, and the plasticity of his forms had something abstract about them.

For the original theories of the criticism of pure visibility it is necessary to go back to the distinction Kant made between free beauty and dependent beauty. Free beauty is beauty that in itself has no intrinsic meaning, such as Greek frets or the foliate ornament on frames and carpets. Dependent beauty is the beauty of a woman, a horse, or a building, all of which presuppose the concept of an aim which determines what the object is and, therefore, the ideal of its perfection. Idealistic aesthetics, and especially Hegel's, recognized only dependent beauty and thought of artistic form as the perceptible manifestation of the idea.

However, in his argument against idealistic philosophy, Herbart, faithful to Kant in admitting that the "thing itself" was unknowable, reduced all knowledge to form and all beauty to form free from sentiment. He thus established an abstract formalism that is in opposition to the doctrine of content in idealistic aesthetics. The distinction between the arts assumed a new importance for him, in that the value of the individual work of art depends on the purity of the art to which it belongs. According to him, confusion between the arts is contrary to the artistic, and a knowledge of beauty requires a double abstract: 1) of sentiment, and 2) of the identity of the art. In fact, Herbart fulminated against those who consider music a kind of painting, painting a kind of poetry, poetry supreme sculpture, and sculpture a kind of aesthetic philosophy.

Robert Zimmermann, a follower of Herbart, had a marked influence on the criticism of pure visibility. In his work on aesthetics (1865), he reassigned the study of the content of imagination to psychology and retained the images of imagination for aesthetics. Aesthetics cannot create systems of knowledge, such as logic, but can only supply models for judgment. These models are symbols conceived as works of art reduced to their simplest expression. He distinguished a primary group of works of art whose representational manner is material or tactile. To this group belong representations of line, surface, and volume. A second group consists of works whose representational methods depend on the perceptions. These are representations of chiaroscuro and colour. Poetry belongs to a third group that represents thought.

Herbartian criticism annihilates the theoretical justifications of abstract formalism, but this criticism has already been set forth and need not be repeated here. What is more important is to point out here that Zimmermann's system of pure visibility is different from the system of poetics that is related to the sphere of thought.

Though it may seem strange at first glance, the psychological discovery of *Einfühlung* (empathy), which Basch interpreted to mean "symbolic sympathy," is another road that leads to pure visibility. Herder already stressed the concept of *Einfühlung*, but in the sense of visual form it was only defined by Robert Vischer in 1872. Vischer thought of sentiment as a spiritual activity that assumes external form as symbols of its existence because of the sympathy it feels for them, because of the analogy between its own intimate feelings and relations with the external, and because of a pantheistic desire to unite with the world. It was clear to him that the content of a work of art is not its material theme but the artist himself and his spiritual life. However, the analysis of the work of art is made by means of emotional symbols. In response to a vertical line the spirit rises, a horizontal line gives a sense of breadth, and in response to a jagged line there is a more lively sense of movement than to a straight line. It is just because we identify ourselves with the elements of the composition that we can study the elements of art per se. According to Volkelt, the sentiments aroused by these elements are "objective" sentiments, and *Einfühlung* would then be the union of the objective sentiments with the intuition of the aesthetic elements. In 1908 Worringer (in *Abstraction and Empathy*) proceeded otherwise. Starting with Lipps' system of "*Einfühlung*." This defines abstraction as the "integration of *Einfühlung*." This leads to pantheism—abstraction as a transcendental conception of the world. This is so because it effectuates the transition from *Einfühlung* to the myths of form and colour abstracted from the work of art.

The theory of pure visibility was the work of Conrad Fiedler (1841–1895). He started with the Kantian distinction between a subjective perception that determines the feeling of pleasure or displeasure and an objective perception that is the representation of a thing. To Fiedler, objective perception is the proper sphere of art so that vision and representation, intuition and expression become identified with the work of art. The essential character of art leads to the concept of "productive contemplation" which, in turn, relates art to the problem of cognition, excludes sentiment from art, and deduces art to knowledge of form, to pure visibility. This is a way of returning to Kant, but it is a variant of Kantian thought created by Herbart, and, in fact, Fiedler, in the name of aesthetic realism, is opposed to aesthetic idealism. Furthermore, like Herbart, Fiedler not only refuses to recognize the problem of beauty but also that of art in general and says that there are only specific arts. He intended to concern himself only with the visual arts, but he is the founder of the "science of art" as distinct from aesthetics.

Comparing the senses of sight and touch, Fiedler noted that touch does not have its idiosyncratic expression, so that we have to resort to the concepts of hardness, softness, roughness, and so on, to represent it. In contrast, for sight there are activities that are an immediate outgrowth of visual sensation, for instance, gesturing, drawing, painting, modelling. These activities do not require the mediation of thought. For this reason painting, sculpture, and architecture have their own laws which are not the laws of nature but of visibility. Nature as understood by science can never become the object of artistic representation. The manner of considering objects, as fragmentary for science as for art, is what distinguishes nature seen as art from nature described by science. The artistic manner is that of representation and of form, and it is subject to certain conditions which are the laws of knowledge as visibility. Laws cannot be imposed on artistic activity, and we have to understand how it conforms to the laws of its own manner of seeing. In order to understand

Rembrandt's manner of painting with obscure shadows, it is necessary to clarify the formal significance of his style.

The history of art should be a history of that special knowledge that is obtained through art and not an imaginary representation of art, for example, as the expression of the spirit of the times or of peoples, or a pedantic, petty history of the philological kind. In refuting the kind of history that is limited to a search for origins and historical connections, Fiedler pointed out that the significant artistic personality, the true genius, appears unexpectedly and is more often the beginning of a new era than the end of an old one. It is the essence of the genius that he makes men see the world with new eyes. He does not have forerunners but only imitators.

A painter's ideal world is not nature improved by the rules but a way of understanding and representing nature that has its roots deep in the individual. For this reason it is a mistake to admire the evolution of art from primitive ornament to the masterpieces of the great eras; art does not progress, it jumps. The value of artistic rules lies in the artistic production of those who made them, not in their being obeyed by those to whom they were bequeathed. If technique is treated as something learned, style takes the place of art. Raphael, Michelangelo, Correggio, Leonardo, Titian, each in his unique way created his own artistic universe, though it is impossible to say that one is better than another. In contrast, Canova and David, Carstens and Cornelius did not express such artistic truths, for theirs was an anti-artistic era.

Fiedler recorded these and other cogent insights in a fragmentary manner as aphorisms. His book on architecture is his only attempt to develop a consistent history of art. He felt that architecture achieved the stature of true art only during two periods, the Greek and the Romanesque. His thesis is based on the idea of an essence of architecture and he rejects the study of architecture as a manifestation of peoples and periods. The essence of architecture would thus be a progress from the formless to the formed. The formless, that is, the material of art, is the original practical demand for enclosed and covered space. Form is not a pre-existing fact that must be impressed on the material, for it has no existence outside the material, and it is the most coherent expression possible of the original practical need (in this respect Fiedler agreed with Semper). The Greek stone temple has its origins in a wooden structure and is the highest architectural expression of those formal elements that originally expressed the practical requirements of wood construction. This is the reason why the Greeks achieved architectural perfection. After them, architecture sank to the level of not very successful attempts. The Gothic displayed marvels of structural ability but is not a coherent development and does not fulfill a functional requirement. The Romanesque style, with its enclosed spaces covered by vaults, is much superior to it. Here the shell is unified; there is no question of a vault punctuated by supports but of a vault that rises from the very ground through the solid walls. Typically, the Romanesque style abandons columns for piers. These piers are in reality pieces of wall left between interstices and their most perfect expression is the clustered pier because it is a direct continuation of the ribbed vault. The Romanesque style is echoed in Brunelleschi's and Michelangelo's domes; the latter completely frees itself of all ties with materiality to become pure form.

This strict treatment is based on the principle that in architecture, as in other fields, a wealth of discoveries and ideas makes it disjointed rather than stimulating it, when it is not governed by the rigid laws of internal development. Clearly, this principle suffers from the excessive intellectualizing that Utitz and others have observed in all Fiedler's work. Human imagination is actually much freer than the rigid laws of internal development admit. The value of Fiedler's criticism, however, does not lie in its restrictiveness but in its interpretation of Greek and Romanesque architecture.

Adolf von Hildebrand (1847–1921) was a close friend of Fiedler and von Marées in Rome. His book, *Das Problem der Form in der bildenden Kunst* (1893), was widely acclaimed. Though Hildebrand limited and degraded Fiedler's ideas and displayed a tendency toward academic art, he did examine more directly the consequences of his friend's theories of judgment as applied to sculpture. He saw the symbolic distinction between a distant and a close-up view, the first being synthetic, that is, the artist's vision, the second being analytic, that is an empirical vision. Since the distant view is a vision of surfaces, any representation in depth, to be artistic, has to be referred continually to the projection plane; that is, more than anything, vision in depth is a suggestion within the limits of a vision in terms of surfaces. This kind of vision is used to express the artistic need for unity of surfaces. Michelangelo used it; Cellini did not. Similarly, as it is in part the form of natural existence, only the form of the effect corresponds to the artistic vision. And yet, light and shade have a more powerful effect than plastic form. Each object should be immersed in space and the value of the object depends on the impression of unity of space, seen as an enclosed volume. In art, movement as such cannot be shown but is indicated by means of a stationary body in the pose of a movement because functional values are not artistic if they are not rendered within the spatial unity. Canova thought of a monument as architecture to which plastic figures are added; this is a mistake since the whole would have to have an architectural framework if the relief is to seem to be composed in depth rather than stuck on the wall. Another error is exemplified by the ancient group known as the Farnese Bull in which the plastic parts are held together by the action alone and not by a close spatial unity. In modern art the stylistic demands of spatial unity have been completely forgotten, whereas the Greek sculptors and Michelangelo observed them. In brief, Hildebrand had set out to determine the characteristics of artistic vision as opposed to sensuous imitation of nature and, within the limits of historical interpretation and polemical reaction, he undoubtedly succeeded.

Fiedler and Hildebrand based their judgments on a lively experience of Greek and Italian Renaissance art as well as on the ideas mentioned above. According to them, nothing outside these two periods achieved perfection. Fiedler's attempt to apply to the Romanesque church the criteria particular to the Greek temple is timid and unsure. Anyone can refute his refusal to consider Gothic architecture art since anyone can recognize the perfect, coherent, and free realization of a high human imagination in the cathedrals of Chartres and Reims. In the same way, while admiring Hildebrand's idea of the artistic representation of movement as a stationary body in the pose of movement to explain the artistic value of certain poses in Greek and Renaissance reliefs, it has to be noted that this idea is not a norm, as Hildebrand thought, but only one method of interpretation that is useful for certain works of art but not for others. In fact, the representation of the figure as perpetual motion of light and shade, typical of Titian, Rembrandt, and Daumier, must also take its rightful place among the perfections of art.

Therefore, if the theory of pure visibility was to achieve the full measure of its possibilities in the judgment of art, it had to renounce its ability to set standards and recognise that its application to history had to be relative.

The most important contributions on this score were made by Aloïs Riegl (1858–1905). It is not known whether he had any direct intellectual contact with Fiedler, but they shared the formalism of the school of Herbart (Riegl had been a student of Zimmermann) as well as the liveliest interest in the materialistic interpretations of Semper, and, finally, the reaction against the purely philological method and against Taine's art historical theories. Riegl does not have the Kantian strictness of Fiedler, although he strongly felt the need to overcome positivisitic ideas; and he also had a much more extensive knowledge of works of art.

Convinced that the history of art should be universal history, he battled against the two leading traditional prejudices in art history. The first is the hieratic distinction that continued to be made, and, in fact, is still being made, between the fine arts, which applies to the representation of man and what concerns him, and the applied or minor arts, which refers to decoration only. In 1893, in his *Stilfragen, Grundlegungen zu einer Geschichte der Ornamentik,* he published a history of ornament from Egypt through Islam.

The artistic production of certain periods was, and often still is, disparaged, among them imperial Roman and Baroque art which were judged according to the standards established for Greek and Renaissance art. In 1901 Riegl published *Die spätrömische Kunstindustrie nach den Funden in Oesterreich-Ungarn* (Late Roman industrial arts) and wrote *Die Entstehung der Barockkunst in Rom* (The Origins of Baroque Art in Rome) which was published posthumously in 1907. It was his aim to rediscover the characteristics and determine the manner of seeing and feeling in the art of these periods, which were not decadent but only different from those that preceded them since they created a new art even though they did this through uncertainty, error, and deviation.

The principle with which Riegl justified both his historic interest and his aesthetic judgment is *Kunstwollen* (will for art). He did not give it a theoretical definition but applied it as the antithesis of that aspect of the arts that is merely the technical ability to reproduce nature. Having determined that form changes through the ages, he asked himself what the force was that transformed them. Semper and his followers had qualified style by aim, materials, and techniques without taking the creative spirit into account. Riegl criticised this solution and proposed instead *Kunstwollen* as idealistic affirmation. The work of art is dead if it is detached from the spiritual creative process; it is necessary to trace it back to the origins of its creation. *Kunstwollen* is therefore not the synthesis of the aims of art of any given period but is its tendency, its aesthetic impulse, its germination; in other words, a dynamic value, a true force. It is the principle of style and must be distinguished from the external characteristics of a style. Riegl also asked himself whether the possible directions of the *Kunstwollen*, that is, its categories, could be established *a priori*, and decided that it was possible to do so in the Herbartian tradition of the tactile and the optic in the vision of the thing in itself and of it in space, in the objective and the subjective. Thus, by showing that each work of art is at the same time a representation of nature and a stylization of it, he refuted the opposition between naturalism and idealism. He made a mistake, however, in believing that his *a priori* categories could also be systems for orientation *a posteriori*. He was aware that in art the individual is the only reality and that a school or group is merely a name, but he also believed that the spirit changes during its development, even in its basic elements. For this reason, Riegl lost sight of the eternality of the human spirit, and his theories are more accurate in the idealism that propelled him to free himself of the historical and positivistic preconceptions of his time than in the organism itself as an aesthetic system.

In his *Stilfragen*, Riegl still submitted to the positivistic prejudice that complex phenomena can be known by isolating their simple elements. In this way he isolated certain ornamental types from prehistoric, Egyptian, Mesopotamian, Phoenician, Persian, Greek, Roman, Byzantine, and Islamic monuments and studied their development. These are the geometrical style, the symmetrical style in which motifs are repeated on both sides of a central element, and foliate motifs (the lotus, acanthus, palmette, rinceaux) in all their aspects, seen in front and profile view, as well as all their combinations and harmonies. It was his aim to discover the structural principle of each ornamental motif and also to trace the development of ornamentation from Greek through Islamic art. Thus he was concerned with a history of the sources and of the development of ornamental motifs abstracted from the historic reality which is the individual work of art on which they appear, an error Riegl was not to commit in his later works.

In his last book, on the industrial arts of the Late Roman period, he effectively outlined the history of art of that period in architecture, sculpture, and painting, as well as in ornament, and presented a general picture of the *Kunstwollen* of the period. He also related artistic forms to social, religious, and scientific conditions of the period, and has even touched upon the history of criticism in regard to the aesthetics of St. Augustine. However, the author is not dealing with an external complex, for his attention is focused on the individual work of art and the *Kunstwollen*, or, better, its visual patterns served him to trace the principles according to which each individual work was created. In this sense the *Kunstwollen* becomes the effective consciousness of the creating artist, historically recreated.

For example, Riegl's analysis of the so-called sarcophagus of Alexander Severus in the Capitoline Museum, Rome, is as follows: The background of the relief is visible only as a narrow strip which the heads touch instead of the uninterrupted surface of earlier examples. Below this strip there no longer is any background since the figures appear in two ranks with only the heads of the rear rank visible. The figures in the front are carved in such high relief that there are deep shadows in the spaces between them and they seem to move freely in space. This characteristic seems all the more pronounced in comparison to other contemporary or nearly contemporary sarcophagi in which the figures are attached to a background surface. The tendency toward full spatial isolation finds its fullest expression in these works. However, the permanence afforded by the background even when it is limited to a narrow strip induces the artist to give his contours a precision that is not usual with the figure isolated in space. In the sarcophagus of Alexander Severus classical precision gives way to a brilliant approach to light and shadow even though the many shadows betray remnants of a tactile conception. As this style becomes more coherent the figures become more optic and there is a greater simplification in the outlines.

A value judgment does not enter into this analysis. In fact, adherence to the optical style, which is an abstraction, is not necessary for the work to be artistic. Its necessity to the work of art depends on the personality of its author and not on any abstraction. In this compromise between the tactile and the optic the artist may have found perfect form or a poor one. The importance of Riegl's analysis lies in having determined the character of this compromise, that is, not only what the relation of this sarcophagus is to the dual term tactile-optic, but also to the development of artistic vision during antiquity. What is evaluated in the work of art is the creative process of the artist, and one could reconstruct this process better than Riegl, although his analysis is clearly incomplete since the artistic vision referred to corresponds to a particular way of feeling that should have been elucidated. It is, therefore, incomplete, but as far as it goes, indisputable.

Riegl would not have been able to achieve this if he had not clearly experienced the formal compromises that occurred in antiquity and which he re-established through a direct analysis of the work of art. Their main points can be summed up as follows: In Egyptian reliefs the tactile surface is so important that the figures are related to the background plane without any consideration for depth. The Greeks gave the figure freedom in space, and this resulted in the centralization of the composition, foreshortening, and shadows. Their innovation is limited to three-dimensional, enclosed space but does not include unlimited, open space. They were interested in the individual form within space but not in space as such. The composition of the figures continued to be conceived in relation to the background plane, in height and breadth but not in depth, until the Hellenistic period. At this time the figure began to be conceived in relation not to the background plane but to three-dimensional space. A further step was taken during the early part of the Roman Empire when an optical compromise was permitted to replace the tactile (here Riegl profits from Wickhoff's observations) in consequence of which the relief becomes lower and the shadows are reduced. The scene takes on the appearance of a distant view. During the middle of the Imperial age an overlapping of figures, the disappearance of the background surface, and sharp contrasts of light and dark in place of the earlier chiaroscuro and transitional passages may be noted. During the Late Empire, symptoms of a return to the past as well as hints of the future appear. The latter consist mainly of an ability to express in the figure new ways of feeling (Christianity) and a new isolation in three-dimensional space. However, as the result of the compromise with the optic, details of a tactile nature were sacrificed and profiles again introduced, much as profiles had been common in the Ancient Near East.

To return once again to the Alexander Severus sarcophagus, its analysis would not have been possible without all the visual symbols of antiquity that have been given summarily above, and the sarcophagus would have been interpreted according to criteria foreign to it that would have given rise to ambiguities.

Riegl analyzed the Baroque art of Rome by means of similar symbols, that is, according to the consistency or inconsistency of symbols, not in order to judge by means of the symbols but to liberate the judgment from the academic prejudices derived from the formalism of Greece and the Italian Renaissance.

Heinrich Wölfflin (1864–1945) is far more famous than Riegl and is now considered the leading discoverer of the symbols of pure visibility. He was much more acutely aware of the need for a history of culture and of psychological traditions in art, for Burckhardt had taught him cultural history and Hildebrand the history of vision. However, he juxtaposed the various historical methods so that they became confused and remained incomplete. His thought was more highly refined than Riegl's but less creative. Most important, his taste was limited to Renaissance and Baroque art and he did not have the comprehensive universality that is Riegl's advantage. For example, Wölfflin had no understanding of primitive art and in discussing it speaks of its rigidity, incoherence, and lack of unity.

His two books *Renaissance und Barock* (1888) and *Die*

klassische Kunst (1899; *Classic Art*, 1952) are rich in commentary on psychology, cultural history, and pure visibility. His *Kunstgeschichtliche Grundbegriffe* (1915; *Principles of Art History*, 1932) is much more coherent and certainly superior to the two earlier volumes in its discussion of problems of development of style in modern art. Its fundamental concepts are the five symbols of pure visibility whose discussion takes up the whole book.

Each symbol consists of two antithetical terms.

1) The development from the linear to the pictorial. Wölfflin begins with a definition of line as the guide of the eye and proceeds to the gradual depreciation of the line. More generally, linear refers to the conception of objects in the tactile sense of contours and surfaces, while pictorial means the rejection of palpable design and the preference for a purely visual appearance. In the first case the emphasis is on the precise limits of the object; in the second it is on its indeterminate and changing appearance. Seeing objects in terms of plasticity and contours isolates them; when seen pictorially, they blend. The interest of the former concentrates on the individual, corporeal object, as though it had a palpable and solid value; the interest of the latter is identified with total visibility as though it were an uncertain appearance.

2) The development from plane to recession. In classic art, that is, art of the High Renaissance, all the parts of the composition are brought to the surface plane whereas in Baroque art the emphasis is on overlapping. Plane is an element of line and extension in one plane is the form of maximum clarity. The depreciation of contours is accompanied by the depreciation of surfaces so that the eye establishes objects mainly in terms of whether they move forward or backward. This is not a qualitative difference because the vision of recession does not have any

relation to the greater or lesser ability to represent space. It is a fundamentally different way of seeing. Hence, the "surface" or "plane" style is not the style of primitive art but appears for the first time at a moment when foreshortening and perspective have been completely mastered.

3) The development from closed to open form. Although every work of art should be a self-contained unit since otherwise it is inadequate, this requirement was interpreted very differently in the sixteenth century than in the seventeenth. As compared to the loose form chosen by the Baroque, classic design may be considered as closed form. This is not a matter of a simple reversal because the relaxing of the rules and the weakening of the constructive strength brought into being an essentially new manner of representing which must be included among the fundamental forms of representation.

4) The development from multiplicity to unity. In classic systems of co-ordination the individual parts always maintain some independence no matter how much they may be a part of the whole. There is not the fragmentation of primitive art, for the part is in harmony with the whole without having sacrificed its individual character. The spectator is thus presented with an articulation, a transition from member to member; and this corresponds to a very different state from that of a totality such as the seventeenth century initiated and demanded. Both styles have unity (as opposed to the pre-classic period which did not understand this idea in its true sense), but in the former it is achieved through harmony of free parts whereas in the latter it is through a union of all the parts in a single theme, or, to put it another way, all the parts are completely subordinated to the principal element.

5) The development from absolute to relative clarity of the object. This contrast is comparatively close to that of the linear-

pictorial, absolute clarity being the representation of the thing as it is, taken singly and accessible to plastic sensation, and relative clarity being the representation of the thing as it appears, seen in its totality and especially in its non-plastic qualities. It should also be stressed that in the classic period an ideal of perfect clarity was cultivated which in the fifteenth century was only barely suspected and in the seventeenth was voluntarily abandoned. Not that Baroque art had become confused—confusion is always unpleasing and not artistic—but the clarity of the motif was no longer considered the prime aim of the representation. Form no longer had to be displayed in its completeness, and it was enough if it appeared in its essentials. Composition, light, and colour no longer had the simple purpose of clarifying form but are imbued with a life of their own. As a general form of representation, relative clarity is introduced at that moment in the history of art at which the essential assumes a perfectly new appearance. In this respect, too, when the Baroque departs from the ideals of Dürer and Raphael, it does not make a qualitative difference but indicates an orientation toward the world that is very different.

These five symbols may be considered, as Wölfflin himself did, as five views of the same phenomena. The linear or plastic evinces a natural relation to the tight spatial distribution of the surface composition as well as to contructivist or closed form, to individuality of the separate parts, and to absolute clarity. On the other hand, relative clarity of form may be related to emphasis on unity to the detriment of the parts, to non-structural fluidity within the confines of the surface, and to pictorial-impressionistic compromises; despite superficial appearances, the style in depth also belongs to this second family since it is based on certain appearances that have significance for the eye but not for the tactile sense. Here, then, it is possible to reduce these five symbols to the double term tactile-optic used by Riegl (which he had inherited from Herbart through Zimmermann).

In later years, criticism of his symbols caused Wölfflin to make some revisions. He more cautiously avoids a sharp distinction between form and content, saying that in each new visual style a new world is crystallized. Not only does one see differently, one also sees different things. The reason it is not possible simply to speak of a new expression is that we are here dealing with developments that, though they can occur only within the realm of the visual process, actually belong to the history of the mind; they remain inexplicable without the internal factor of the continuous influence of image on image, form on form. Here Wölfflin did not take into account that the origin of each work of art lies in life and not in a preceding work of art, for he went on to say that when Franz Hals and Velazquez replaced Holbein's rigid design with a vibrant brush stroke one might believe that it is the result of a new vision of man which no longer saw the essential quality in the static aspect but in movement. The same change occurs in still-lifes where one cannot speak of real movement. Still-lifes, however, also have a sense of movement, not in the objects themselves, to be sure, but in the play of light and shadow for which they served the seventeenth-century artist as pretext. Similarly, Wölfflin is less sure in the historic development of his symbols, that is, that open form necessarily has to follow closed form. And, in fact, history demonstrates that the changes of taste do not depend on logic and that as often open form was transformed into closed form. This point is made explicit by the example of modern art.

Today, the symbols of pure visibility are generally employed by art historians and critics. Many have even multiplied them, which is an advantage since it is their purpose to prepare the approach to the work of art. Indeed, it would be a paradoxical ideal to find a symbol for each work of art.

Their use sometimes gives rise to ambiguous kinds of art history, as for example, the history of abstract symbols intended as a history of origins, or art history "without names" because it is intended as a history of modes of seeing. This type of history ignores the function of the artist's personality in the work of art, which Fiedler had shown to be important. The history of visual symbols must be limited to supplying a history of only one aspect of taste. It can thus be conveniently integrated with the cultural history of the type developed by Burckhardt and Dvořàk and discussed in the previous chapter.

CHAPTER XII
Modern Art

THE HISTORIC link between the pure visibility of Von Marées and Fiedler and the origins of abstraction in French art may perhaps be seen in Laforgue, who has already been mentioned. In any case, by 1880, with the crisis of Impressionism, there arose the need for a doctrine of form and the tendency toward abstract art.

Cézanne, the divisionist Seurat, and the symbolist Gauguin are considered the precursors of abstract art in France. About 1890 Maurice Denis began his definition of neo-traditionalism with the well-known words: Se rappeler qu'un tableau—avant d'être un cheval de bataille, une femme nue, ou une quelconque anecdote—est essentiellement une surface plane recouverte de couleurs en un certain ordre assemblées. (It should be remembered that before representing a war horse, a nude, or whatever episode, a painting is essentially a flat surface covered with colours arranged in a given order.)

Two great revolutions occurred in painting between 1905 and 1910—Fauvism and Cubism. Though at first they seemed destined to be short-lived, they did last some time and today's painting would not exist without them.

In respect to social conditions, the two revolutions were the result of the instability, malaise, and search for radicalism that have characterised our age since the early years of the century.

In respect to philosophy, they were a revolt against reason and a triumph of Bergsonian intuition.

In respect to morality, they represented a desire for truth at any price, in opposition to all conventions without, however, producing new principles.

Finally, in respect to culture, they emphasized the crisis of humanism and the conviction that a new order could be constructed without reference to the old and even in opposition to it. The natural sciences contributed to the new intellectual orientation because the great new hypotheses suggested that reality might be more than the senses and reason could apprehend and might be discovered by the imagination. Some mysteries had been unveiled by scientific discoveries and others were being studied so that everyone, painters first among them, believed they could unveil more of them.

Ever since the Renaissance artists have taken one of two stands toward science. Either they profited from it by assigning to art a rational basis, or they revolted against it in the name of the rights of the imagination. The Fauves took this second position. In contrast, the Cubists claimed to substitute art for science, or at least to create a science of their own. Such a goal required a theory. Cézanne, Seurat, Gauguin, and Van Gogh had also felt the need of a theory, whereas the Fauves had no such preoccupations and their aesthetics were vague and undefined. It was because they were armed with a theory that the Cubists had more of an impact than the Fauves.

However, the Fauves and Cubists were not diametrically opposed, and by 1919 Apollinaire could assert that the work of the Fauves between 1906 and 1908 was a preamble to Cubism. In fact, both the Fauves and the Cubists refused to rely on emotions produced by a response to appearances, stating that they wanted to supplant the sensationalism of the Impressionists and that they wanted to make contact with a truer and more profound reality. Out of this grows the denial of traditional culture, which impedes such a contact through the apparatus of its conventions, and the profound suspicion of historical values. In fact, they attempted to bypass history by turning to non-historical cultures, as exemplified by Gauguin's Tahitian sojourn and Rimbaud's African adventure. Hence, in visual representation both the Fauves and the Cubists rejected conventional perspective and the classical ideal of plastic form. Instead they turned to a painting consisting of flat areas of colour, which means, to the absolute value and expressive immediacy of colour.

Picasso, especially during his first Cubist period, was strongly influenced by African art, whereas Braque, the other leader of Cubism, was formed chiefly by Fauvism.

It is true that in its second phase Cubism, especially as represented by such French artists as Metzinger, Delaunay, and Léger, formulated a historical credo that loudly proclaimed its adherence to the machine age. This mystique of the machine age seems to be in sharp contrast to the Fauves, but it may also be seen as another means of avoiding history and projecting oneself into the future, just as the exaltation of African art was a way of projecting oneself into an immemorial past, away from history and into pre-history.

Analytical Cubism, however, represented requirements of critical thought that took form through a close re-examination of Cézanne's painting as against the expressive immediacy of Fauvism.

At the same time, the Cubists could not avoid another requirement rooted in modern art which is also another aspect of the need for the absolute. This is the expression of religious feelings, which were so forcefully asserted by Rouault and which paved the way for Expressionism. Thus, the successive phases of Picasso's style can be explained by this need to satisfy complex and contradictory demands.

Finally, if it is true that reality is not the same as appearance, nature, or history, it is also true that appearance, nature, and history comprise our experience and only through an analysis of them is it possible to reach the intuition of reality that transcends them. Thus, Cubism, in spite of its initial program, is a revision of tradition and a new attempt to discover the proportional and mathematical laws that are supposed to rule and regulate nature. It is analysis meant to restore the deeper and most primary values to the visual idiom.

However, when these revolutionary artists turned their attention to the works of art in the museums, they discovered to their amazement that almost all the great masters of the past could be considered Cubists from one point of view—to the extent that they had perceived and expressed the lasting structural values of reality.

Though painting has set the style in the twentieth century, as so often in the past, sculpture has made great advances toward realising the new vision of the world supplied it by painting. Since the basis of this vision is the relation of the object represented to everything around it, rather than its isolation, which was characteristic of classical sculpture, modern sculpture had to break with its traditions and has accepted the principle of abstract form from Cubist painting.

Up to the beginning of this century taste in architecture did not keep up with the rapid changes in painting and sculpture, and the forms of the Renaissance and Baroque were repeated in an ever more mechanical manner. Once it did occur, however, the revolt against tradition was more violent in architecture than in the other arts. Destruction having been more complete, reconstruction, understandably, was slower and more hesitant. Furthermore, the resultant works of art are fewer, even though the reform of architectural concepts has had a much greater social importance and is much more far reaching. The principles of the new taste are based on the correspondence between form and function and on the organic interrelations of the forms.

A Cubist painter, Albert Gleizes, endeavored to discover in the forms of old art, and especially in Romanesque and Gothic works, a basic law of rhythm that has validity as a fundamental perception of reality. Once it is granted that the history of art has to have a scientific method based on positive laws, it becomes understandable how one would come to re-evaluate the classical idea of form, or how one would come directly to integrate Cubism into the historical continuity in that it "studies volume in its mechanism, and restores to perspective the multiplicity of its points of view." Though different in method, this process does not differ substantially in its results from that of the theories of pure visibility presented by Riegl and Wölfflin. After having deprived classical form of its historical justification, the recognition of an absolute, theoretical, or metaphysical (i.e., non historical) value of classical form re-emerges just where one might legitimately expect a radically anti-classical stand.

Another theoretical Cubist painter, André Lhote, looked on the work of art with a more vivid participation and with a greater figurative interest. His evaluation of Ingres is strange, to say the least. To Lhote, Ingres was not the pure Classicist and strict, Raphaelesque purist whom Romantic criticism considered the antithesis of Delacroix. On the contrary, he said that "ce nu (la *Grande Odalisque*) possède, aux yeaux des censeurs professionnels, entre autres tares, deux vertèbres de trop et un sein déraisonnablement placé sous le bras: voici profanée l'anatomie, cette science sacrée, cette clef de voûte du temple de l'Académisme décadent" (professional censurers have found imperfections in this nude [the *Grande Odalisque*], among others, two vertebrae too many and the misplacement of a breast beneath the arm. This is a desecration of anatomy, that sacred science, that keystone to the temple of decadent academic art). He continued that Ingres is most profoundly

HISTORY OF ART CRITICISM

moved by nature so that "il n'y a plus de véité anatomique, si cette vérité est en opposition avec la sensation que lui donne le corps qu'il a devant les yeux. Cette courbe adorable du dos, si déliée, si souple, si longue, il l'allongera encore, malgré lui, pour mieux rendre apparent à autrui le trouble qu'elle lui inspire. Il déformera, il entrera en contradiction avec ce que son esprit sait pour exprimer ce que son coeur vient d'apprendre" (there can no longer be an anatomical truth if this truth is in opposition to the sensations aroused in him by the body before his eyes. This adorable curve of the back, so flowing, so supple, so long—he elongates it further in spite of himself in order to convey more clearly to others how disquieting he found her. He distorts and contradicts what his mind knows in order to express what his heart has just realized). In the *Jupiter and Thetis*, Thetis' arm stretching toward the head of Jupiter is not an arm "tel qu'il est en réalité, avec ses angles, et le fouillis de ses beines et de ses muscles, c'est une forme inventée, une chose chaude et sinueuse faite pour caresser et envelopper sensuellement" (as it is in reality, with angles and a jumble of veins and muscles but an invented form, a hot and sinuous thing made to caress and embrace sensually). Hence the dualism, the contrast, and interaction of sensuality and reason that impell Ingres to express a reality beyond nature. A process is here outlined that leads from Ingres through the Impressionists and Cézanne to Cubism. The tradition of Impressionism, at first misunderstood and condemned as part of the Romantic tradition, in Cézanne's hands became something of immediate significance because he used it to create "something solid and lasting like the art in museums." Sensation again takes first place; without a deep commitment to his own sensations, Cézanne could never have come to the "pouvoir de lire à travers les objets" (ability to read through the objects). Without it "l'univers pour lui n'eut des limites matérielles" (the universe would have material limits). Instead, "les phénomènes devinrent transparents, et laissèrent voir leurs sources" (the phenomena became transparent and revealed their sources) A classical value once again became the ideal of art but now it was achieved by means of a new sensibility.

In Cubism, the ascendency of sensation as a guide in judging both old and modern masters is evinced in J. W. Power's writings on pictorial construction and in his geometrical analyses of works by Raphael, Duccio, Rubens, and Juan Gris. All his energies are still concentrated on solving the Cubist "dualism" which here, however, is expressed in purely geometric terms: the concept of surface (or plane) and the concept of depth (or volume). In actuality, this dualism is resolved in critical observation since, obviously, surface cannot be excluded in favor of depth or volume in favor of plane. This attitude also reveals the ambiguity inherent in wanting to express the ideal of originality and formal newness without irremediably impairing tradition, and in a reality that strives to fulfill itself without wholly negating the value of natural appearances and of emotions.

This is the contribution of Juan Gris, the Spanish painter who together with Picasso and Braque was one of the early Cubists. Gris's ideas on art have been recorded by D. H. Kahnweiler in a close analysis of the master's work. Juan Gris, he says, may be compared to Picasso in much the same way as Raphael may be compared to Michelangelo. Gris and Raphael are measured, static, classical, and have an ardent purity; Picasso and Michelangelo are tumultuous, romantic, and violently expressive. Yet Juan Gris gave emotional values first place, and replied to Braque's statement that he loves the rule that corrects the emotion that he himself preferred to have emotions correct the rules. Thus, rule precedes emotion as the noumenon precedes the phenomenon, and it is within the intuitive rhythm that experience is submerged, revitalising it. However, Gris wished to distinguish his own, synthetic, Cubism from analytical Cubism: "Je commence par organiser mon tableau, puis je qualifie les objets. Il s'agit de la création d'objets nouveaux ne pouvant se comparer à aucun objet de la réalité. C'est précisément ce qui distingue le cubisme synthétique du cubisme analytique. Ces objets nouveaux, du coup, échappent à la déformation. Mon violon, étant une création, n'a plus à craindre la comparison." (I begin by organising my picture, and then I define the objects. It is a matter of creating new objects that cannot be compared to objects existing in reality. It is precisely this that distinguishes Synthetic Cubism from Analytical Cubism. These new objects escape distortion. My violin [in *Violin and Engraving*], being itself a creation, no longer has to fear comparison.) That is, in Juan Gris the tendency to distort is the ex- reason Juan Gris's painting realizes the conceptual value that Apollinaire assigned to it, since by "conceptual" he meant an art that realises ideas immediately instead of translating them into parables or metaphors—Medieval rather than Renaissance art. We must therefore conclude that though Cubism on the one hand resolved itself into pure emotion or colour sensations, giving rise to a decorative formula that rapidly spread everywhere, it on the other hand led back, along indirect routes, to statements by Ruskin and William Morris on the value of medieval art as a collective or social art, matrix of objects, and of a spirituality inherent in the progress of work.

If the work of art is no longer an intellectual representation of nature but a fact of reality, that is, if it is a creation that is artistically valid as an "object" in itself and not for what it represents, then the activity of the artist is essentially the technical process of the craftsman. The artist neither creates nor invents but obeys a profound law of reality and can discover within himself this law to the extent that he divests himself of everything in him that is conventional and that is a sentimental or emotive habit.

The formal limits of analytical Cubism were proclaimed, though confusedly, by the Italian Futurists of whom the most outstanding were the sculptor Umberto Boccioni, the painter Carlo Carrà, and the architect Antonio Sant' Elia. Boccioni expressed the most original ideas, and they are epitomized in the concepts of simultaneity and plastic dynamism. Boccioni as well as Carrà criticized Cubism for being static and dealing with objects and insisted that Futurism was an art that no longer revolved around objects but around a state of mind. Nonetheless, these artists were more preoccupied with their purely Italian heritage than with the European traditions of Impressionism. They spoke of synthesis, yet not of a synthesis of the elements of vision, but of the synthesis of empirical facts. When Boccioni said that a moving horse is not a stationary horse that is moving but a completely different thing, he was substituting the idea of movement for the idea of horse, that is, one physical fact for another. However, the concept of simultaneity, instead of becoming a synthesis, only too readily deteriorated into the concept of speed. From this stems the much abused myth of the machine age, the actual rather than stylistic anti-traditionalism, and the rapid deterioration of aesthetic controversy into mere political arguments.

Another Italian painter, Gino Severini, worked in Paris for a long time and was in contact with the Cubists; his writings are concerned with research into the fundamental laws of proportions of the structural norms of forms that have been obscured since the Renaissance. Here the antithesis is no longer between Middle Ages and Renaissance, as it had been for Wackenroder and Ruskin, the Nazarenes and the Pre-Raphaelites but between an art that is truth and an art that is illusion, an art that rests on the ancient wisdom of tradition and an art that turns to invention and dramatic effect. Art "is nothing but science humanised," and the cause of decline in art is separation from science; nor should theory ever be separated from practice and experience. The artist's purpose is to "reconstruct the universe according to the very laws that govern it." But such a "reconstruction" neither makes sense nor has a purpose unless it repeats the process and act of creation. Thus, with the aid of the neo-scholastic aesthetics of Jacques Maritain, the religious element again enters into the theory of modern art, and unfortunately it no longer has Van Gogh's rigor and moral force, but has become a principle of authority that presides over artistic activity. It is at this point that the artistic movement that began with Cubism is transformed into a useless neo-primitivism, or worse, neo-classicism—the inevitable reaction to the most important characteristic Futurism shared with Cubism, that is, anti-traditionalism.

Amédée Ozenfant and some other critics have insisted that a distinction has to be made between true Cubism, which was already dead by 1914, and the movements and trends that appear in European art after the First World War. This stand, which seems so full of historical wisdom at first glance, is much less persuasive when one recalls that the leaders of these movements were the same artists who had participated in early Cubism. In the final analysis, the history of art is first and foremost a history of artists and cannot be relegated to a logical working-out of premises. There is another cogent argument: Cubism has created a visual language that rapidly replaced the naturalistic idiom that, in all its varied forms, had been the language of painting and sculpture until then. In fact, all the most valid pronouncements of modern art since Cubism have been based on its formal neo-naturalism, that is, on the principle of non-representational or non-figurative form, or to put it another way, on form-reality and not form-image. Cubism may thus be considered as the genus and the successive movements as species. In his *From Cubism to Surrealism in French Literature* Georges Lemaître divided the development of Cubism into four branches.

1) Scientific Cubism is the original form of the movement. It is justified mainly as a reflection and elaboration of Cézanne's innovations, and focuses on the discovery of a pure reality beyond the illusions of the senses.

2) Orphic Cubism goes beyond the analytical process of scientific Cubism and strives toward a mystic communion of universal consciousness, that is, the synthetic expression of the "whole psychic content of the world."

3) Physical Cubism, in spite of the misleading name, went a step further toward abstraction. In order to communicate with "the purely spiritual, unencumbered by material implications," they wished to create out of themselves the physical objects to which a painter must have recourse to express his message. While the early Cubists still made use of fragments of natural forms, though combined in ways dictated by their inner selves, only forms stemming from the depths of their internal consciousness, unrelated to any visual experience, are admissible to the Physical Cubists.

4) Instinctive Cubism is related to the Bergsonian proposition that the instinct, too, is a way to transcendental insight, and this is the first formulation of Surrealist automatism.

Though Lemaître was discussing literature rather than the visual arts, his arguments apply equally to both. Indeed, by denying the value of form as representation and assigning the value of art to the purely creative act, the Cubists broke down the barriers between the various art forms. Art became the message of a hidden and more real world but one beyond the reach of reason—a pure state of being. Surrealism thus becomes a necessary development of the Cubist premises and is the poetic conquest of their scientific formulation. In fact, the most valid critical statements on Surrealism were made by poets. The earliest poetic expression of Surrealism is found in Jarry and in Apollinaire who had been the herald of Cubism and Futurism before the war. The word "Surrealism" first appeared in the sub-title of Apollinaire's comedy *Les Mammelles de Tirésias*, written in 1917. The next year, in his manifesto, *L'Esprit nouveau*, he reiterated the idea that it is the artist's task to "exalter le vie sous quelque forme qu'elle se presente" (exalt life in whatever form it may present itself).

Marcel Proust was more explicit when he said, "La grandeur de l'art véritable . . . c'était de retrouver, de ressaisir, de nous faire connaître cette réalité loin de laquelle nous vivons, de laquelle nous nous écartons de plus en plus au fur et à mesure que prend plus d'épaisseur et d'imperméabilité la connaissance conventionelle que nous lui substituons, cette réalité que nous risquerions fort de mourir sans l'avoir connue, et qui est tout simplement notre vie, la vraie vie, la vie enfin découverte et éclaircie, la seule vie par conséquent réellement vécue, cette vie qui, en un sens, habite à chaque instant chez tous les hommes, aussi bien que chez l'artiste. Mais ils ne la voient pas, parce qu'ils cherchent pas à l'éclaircir. Et ainsi leur passé est encombré d'innombrables clichés qui restent inutiles, parce que l'intelligence ne les a pas développés." (The greatness of true art . . .

was to rediscover, to grasp again, to make us know this reality far from the one in which we live, from which we are separated further and further as the conventional knowledge which we have substituted for it assumes greater thickness and invulnerability. We are in danger of dying before we have experienced this reality that is simply our life, the real life, life finally revealed and made clear, and consequently the only life that is really lived; this life, which, in a sense, lives every instant in every man, as well as in the artist. But they do not see it because they do not look for enlightenment. And so their past is encumbered with innumerable clichés that remain useless because undeveloped by intelligence.) Poetry, like painting, is life, and like the act of living it is not subject to critical judgment. Du Bos felt that the function of the critic could not be separated from that of the creative artist, and Paul Valéry more than once voiced the same opinion. As a result, criticism tended to be reshaped into artistic action, and the critic became the *artifex additus artifici.*

The leading Surrealist critics were André Breton, Louis Aragon, Paul Eluard, Jean Cocteau, and Jean Paul Sartre. They derived their principles from the theories of the irrational of Bergson, Freud, and Existentialism. In the First Surrealist Manifesto (1924) Breton defined the movement as "automatisme psychique pur par lequel on se propose d'exprimer soit verbalement, soit par écrit, soit de toute autre manière, le fonctionement réel de la pensée. Dictée de la pensée, en l'absence de tout controle exercé par la raison, en dehors de toute préoccupation esthétique ou morale" (pure psychic automatism, by which it is intended to express, verbally, in writing or by other means, the real process of thought. It is thought's dictation, all exercise of reason and every esthetic or moral preoccupation being absent). It was actually by showing the close relation that links these two poles, the real and the imaginary, that Breton hoped to redefine the distinction between the subjective and the objective and to establish a link between the long unconnected worlds of waking and sleeping, of exterior and interior reality, of reason and madness, of the calm of consciousness and love, of life and revolution.

This is the final crisis in figurative art. To discover within oneself a positive reason to protest against all conventions meant to participate in a general revolutionary process. A work of art is valid to the extent that it participates in and furthers that total revision of values. It is already a criterion for judgment and, therefore, the principle of the critical system for non-figurative works. Picasso, "qui trompe sans cesse l'apparence avec la realité" (who is unceasingly deceiving appearance with reality), accepts it, and Braque, "qui aime la règle qui corrige l'émotion" (who loves the rule that corrects the emotion), disclaims it because it is just this rule which must be sacrificed first. Criticism is thus no longer criticism of the representation because the value of art lies beyond the representation in an active principle that guarantees that the sign survives the thing signified. Instead, it lies in the recognition of this survival, or in the eternal nowness and activity of the sign long after the object has been destroyed. In fact, Breton tends to turn from the purely theoretical or controversial discourse to a criticism committed to ascertaining the validity of the work of art in its immediacy or in its internal revolutionary force. In this way Breton restricts the short period during which De Chirico's painting was truly Surrealistic and states that the fact that Chagall's contribution was not appreciated was a serious gap in movements (Dada and Surrealism) directed at effecting a fusion of poetry and the visual arts. Finally, Breton was able to transcend the limits of historical Surrealism when he recognized both a passive and an active moment in automatism without distinguishing between them. "La découverte essentielle du Surréalism est, en effet que, sans intention préconçue, la plume qui court pour écrire ou le crayon qui court pour dessiner, file une substance infiniment précieuse dont tout n'est peut-être pas matière d'échange mais qui, du moins, apparaît chargé de tout ce que le poète ou le peintre recèle alors d'émotionnel." (The fundamental discovery of Surrealism is, in fact, that the pen writing automatically and the pencil drawing automatically, without preconceived aim, spin out an infinitely precious substance all of which may not be gold but which at least seems to radiate the brilliance that the poet or painter draws from his emotions.)

Or, again, "Une oeuvre ne peut être tenue pour surréaliste qu'autant que l'artiste s'est efforcé d'atteindre le champ psychophysique total (dont le champ de conscience n'est qu'une faible partie). Freud a montré qu'à cette profondeur abyssale règnent l'absence de contradiction, la mobilité des invertissements émotifs dus au refoulement, l'intemporalité et le remplacement de la réalité extérieure par la réalité psychique, soumise au seul principe du plaisir. L'automatisme conduit à cette région en droite ligne. L'autre route qui s'est offerte au Surréalisme pour y parvenir, la fixation dite 'en trompe-l'oeil' (et c'est là sa faiblesse) des images de rêve, s'est avérée à l'expérience beaucoup moins sûre et même abondant en risque d'égarement." (A work of art can only be called Surrealist when the artist has striven to reach the total psychophysical area [of which the conscious is only a small part]. Freud has shown that this deep abyss is governed by an absence of contradiction, by a facility of emotive reversals caused by repressions, by timelessness, and by the substitution for exterior reality of a psychic reality ruled only by the pleasure principle. Automatism is the direct road to that region. The other possible way that Surrealism can reach it is by recording dream images with deceptive precision [and this is weakness] which is a much less certain way of confirming experience and is riddled with pit-falls.) This is the basis for his positive judgment of Yves Tanguy, in whose work he tried to recognise a poetic principle, and for his negative judgment of Dali, whose expressive technique he saw as retrogressive (a return to Meissonier) and whose style he saw as academic.

Thus, Breton arrived at the interesting judgment that abstract art had found its most convincing form in sculpture which is free of any psychoanalytical ambiguities. "D'extérieur qu'il était, cet objet traverse, en se niant de plus en plus dans son aspect, les deux grandes crises du cubisme et du futurisme (Archipenko, Lipchitz, Laurens, Boccioni, Duchamp, Villon), au sortir desquelles il est amené à se mesurer dans le constructivisme avec l'objet mathématique tout récemment apparu, d'une élégance infaillible, bouleversante. Dès lors il ne lui restera plus qu'à renaître de ses cendres, en faisant appel pour cela aux puissances accrues de l'automatisme (Arp), aux pures joies de l'équilibre (Calder), aux jeux nécessaires, dialectiques, du plein et du vide (Moore)." (Though it was outside them, this object passed through the two great crises in Cubism and Futurism, more and more repudiating the existence of its appearance [Archipenko, Lipchitz, Laurens, Boccioni, Duchamp, and Villon] and on emerging from them it had come to measure itself in constructivism with the mathematical object that had only just appeared clothed in infallible, staggering elegance. After that it had only to be reborn from its ashes by appealing to the powers accrued to automatism [Arp], or to the pure joys of balance [Calder], or to the requisite dialectical play between mass and void [Moore]).

It is not appropriate to dwell on too subtle interpretations or literary reconstructions of the visual arts, especially of paintings by Picasso and De Chirico, as Cocteau did, or on the chiefly theoretical, polemical, and moralistic contentions, as Aragon did who ascribed to modern art, and especially to Surrealism, the power to exorcize the Christian and historical character of our world. The orientation of European art since then evidently rejected the vaguely social and revolutionary assumptions of Surrealism.

The French painters who formulated their program in 1941 thought of themselves as concrete abstractionists who had a new historical awareness and referred to themselves as young painters in the French tradition. They rejected the subjection to pure form and wanted to rediscover the spirit beneath the letter of the law that had produced them and to reassert the value of a tradition that is continuously growing. This is not a circuitous or reactionary movement but the restitution of the content of experience and of an active function to consciousness, whereas the preceding artistic currents had preferred to relate consciousness to the periphery and to experiment with mechanical processes. Therefore, the new movements are a projection to the world, often with intense and at times with dramatic social awareness, of the ideal experience of Cubist, Surrealist, and abstract art.

Two exhibitions called the attention of English and American critics and public to the new artistic trends in contemporary art. One was at the Grafton Galleries in London in 1910, the other was the Armory Show in New York, Boston, and Chicago in 1913. His connection with the London exhibition was to cost Roger Fry (1866–1934) much of his influence with conservative elements, but made him the idol and guide of the new generation of artists.

In 1912 Roger Fry propounded the ideals of the new painters. "Now, these artists do not seek to give what can, after all, be but a pale reflex of actual appearance, but to arouse the conviction of a new and definite reality. They do not seek to imitate form, but to create form; not to imitate life, but to find an equivalent for life. . . . The logical extreme of such a method would undoubtedly be the attempt to give up all resemblance to natural form, and to create a purely abstract language of form—a visual music; and the . . . works of Picasso show this clearly enough."

Roger Fry clearly saw that the origins of this new type of "created" form were to be found in Cézanne, and by 1917 he planned to clarify Cézanne's work and position. This he did in a monograph published in 1927. Without knowing Cubism, Fry might not have understood the "abstract" element in Cézanne's work, but because of it, he emphasized it. Certainly this awareness of abstraction permitted him to place his final interpretation of the artist on a new basis. In discussing a landscape, he wrote, "The actual objects presented to the artist's vision are first deprived of all those specific characters by which we ordinarily apprehend their concrete existence—they are reduced to pure elements of space and volume. In this abstract world these elements are perfectly coordinated and organised by the artist's sensual intelligence, they attain logical consistency. These abstractions are then brought back into the concrete world of real things, not by giving them back their specific peculiarities, but by expressing them in an incessantly varying and shifting texture."

This attitude toward understanding the formal creative process of a work of art, which he applied to Giotto and Fra Bartolommeo, to Rembrandt and Chinese art with the same success as to modern art, constitutes the importance of Fry's criticism.

His close adherence to the work of art, which differentiates him from German scholars such as Wölfflin, stems from his direct experience of contemporary art, art in the process of becoming.

Many times, implicitly and twice expressly, Fry attempted to formulate the theory that would justify his judgment. By far his best effort is his first essay in *Transformations*, "Some Questions in Esthetics." Using the device of a discussion with Richards (whose *Principles of Criticism* had been published a few years earlier), he studied the psychological and formalistic aspects of the works of art in order to understand their relationship. What is best in his essay, however, is the analysis of his examples where his sure taste dominates, and not theories that lack the necessary philosophical background.

It was Sir Herbert Read who specifically set out to formulate the theory of contemporary art (*Art Now, an Introduction to the Theory of Modern Painting and Sculpture*, London, 1933). Read had read more extensively than Fry on art theory but his unshakable prejudice against any *a priori* philosophy led him into ambiguities and contradictions. For example, he considered Vico's theories empirical because he interprets empirically and rejected Croce's theory without perceiving that the absorbtion of the concept of the beautiful into the concept of art, one of the most important achievements of Croce's aesthetics, is essential to an understanding of contemporary art. He is also mortified at not being able to find a justification in modern psychology for the concept that art is a perceptual and intellectual activity tending to formulate absolute and ideal types, an idea on which Read feels the value of contemporary art is based. After having discussed, though in fact inadequately, the theories of Semper, Fiedler, and others, he sets forth justifications that are often odd or mistaken, such as when he assimilates the integral vision of Matisse to what Francesco De Sanctis said of Dante, or again, when he uses Plato's statements in the *Philebus* on the absolute beauty of geometric figures to justify abstract art, which he would not have done if he had not confused concept of beauty with the concept of art.

Thus, Read's search for a relation between contemporary art and modern aesthetics is erratic, and he does not find one because he does not know the history of aesthetics well enough. However, this does not detract from other aspects of his work. His direct experience of contemporary art allows him to explain the symbolic character of Matisse's work, the value of abstract art, as well as the value of subjective idealism. He concludes that by art he understands the "capacity to allow the personality to express itself in the craftsmanship: some mysterious equivalence between thought and action. The act of putting pencil to paper, brush to canvas, becomes an act of what Croce has called lyrical intuition, and in that act, in that instant, the personality, and indeed, the spirituality of the artist is revealed." This is taste, even though Read does not formulate it with precision and does not always keep it in mind when speaking of certain artistic tendencies, for example, German Expressionism. His theoretical unsureness becomes historical unsureness when he considers contemporary art a complete break with the past, whereas it should always be the task of the historian to see evolution, even in revolution.

The sculptor Henry Moore, using the premises of historical Surrealism and abstraction as his point of departure, achieved a clear concept of the value of form: "Sculpture fully in the round has no points of view alike. The desire for a form completely realized is connected with assymetry." "All art is an abstraction to some degree: in sculpture the material alone forces one away from pure representation and towards abstraction." The work of art must have "a vitality of its own. . . independent of the object it may represent." From the beginning the artist should have "the solid shape, as it were, inside his head —he thinks of it, whatever its size, as if he were holding it completely enclosed in the hollow of his hand." Because he visualizes his work in this way, "he realizes its volume, as the space that shape displaces in the air." That part of the artist's working process that is conscious must resolve conflicts, organise memories, and prevent him "from trying to walk in two directions at the same time." But form must be felt as pure, solid form, not as description or reminiscences. For this reason form is outside of history and is pure presence. It becomes apparent that a complex form cannot be defined this way since it has to be assembled in a composite process. In contrast to the composite or constructed form, the elementary form is organic, to borrow a definition from Frank Lloyd Wright's architectural theories. Form that is called abstract, however, is organic and shaped according to internal laws assembled from reality, that is, it is concrete and profoundly realistic. This theory of abstract form as absolute reality supercedes the ambiguities of Cubist and Surrealist theories and their dialectical predicament of being caught in a continuous contrast with representational form. Form as the absolute presence is not realized with immediacy in the Impressionist sense but is form that realizes the spirit in its immediacy. Hence, abstract form has been re-absorbed into the theory of empirical experience of the Impressionists, and European art has rediscovered the road reuniting it with its traditions, and through this justifies itself. It is no accident that abstract sculptors once again, like the Impressionists, considered the outdoors the proper setting for their work.

Contemporary art was not accepted by most American critics

or any considerable part of the American public for some years after the Armory show, nor did it find a place in the museums. In the United States, however, new forms are generally more readily accepted and cause less controversy because the traditions of aesthetic thought are not as diffused or as deeply rooted as in Europe.

Alfred H. Barr, Jr., for many years director of the Museum of Modern Art, did much toward making abstract and Surrealist art accepted and, in his writings, he classified the various currents and cross-currents with great clarity and precision. His justifications, however, are somewhat oversimplified. He said that abstract art "is based upon the assumption that a work of art, a painting, for example, is worth looking at primarily because it presents a composition or organisation of color, line, light and shade. Resemblance to natural objects, while it does not necessarily destroy these aesthetic values, may easily adulterate their purity. Therefore, since resemblance to nature is at best superfluous and at worse distracting, it might as well be eliminated." More simply still, Barr asserted that the interest in Surrealism lies in man's profound and persistent need for what is irrational, spontaneous, marvelous, and enigmatical and for what belongs to the world of dreams.

Questions on the worth of this type of art are ignored. In general, contemporary painting and sculpture exist; this is accepted as a fact. They are then analysed and classified. James Thrall Soby in two of his books on art, *After Picasso* and *The Early Chirico*, displayed this same attitude toward the fact of Art. Nonetheless, one should emphasise that Barr's, and even more Soby's, analyses are frequently highly sensitive and perceptive and critical justifications are implicit if never verbalised.

W. R. Valentiner revealed the same agnosticism on what is aesthetic theory but accompanied by an extensive experience of art, in his attempt to explain the origins of modern sculpture. He stressed the analogies that can be drawn between Prehistoric, Romanesque, and Gothic sculpture and the work of the modern sculptors. He also emphasised the value of light in achieving a plastic effect and the resultant importance of planes, that is, clear-cut surfaces. A related problem is that of the differences inherent in reliefs and sculpture in the round. An example of the latter is the equestrian statue, originally attached to a wall supplying a background plane, which lost in artistic value when it was set up in the center of a square so that it appeared in unlimited space. The need for a background plane is one of the abstract plastic values of the relation to reality. Furthermore, in modern art, as in Prehistoric and medieval, the plastic image is not isolated from the world as it is in classical sculpture, but institutes a relationship between itself and the entire universe, which is mirrored in it by means of light.

Valentiner thus illuminated the character of modern sculpture by studying its origins. Because of his aesthetic agnosticism, however, he lost the distinction between a work that is perfectly realised as art and one that has a purely programmatic interest. The fault lies in the criticism.

There is considerable interest in art theory in the United States, and an extensive literature on aesthetics and the principles of criticism has appeared. Here as elsewhere, a meeting of aesthetics and connoisseurship is missing. What is distinctive of American writers on aesthetics is their tendency to refer their theories more to modern art and less to the art of the past. The first to cite Cézanne, Matisse, and other contemporaries as examples was Dewey, in *Art as Experience,* and other writers have followed suit.

Stephen C. Pepper's *The Basis of Criticism in the Arts* (1945) is more recent and probably the most able attempt to adjust aesthetic thought to the requirements of contemporary criticism. Pepper, too, belongs to the pragmatic tradition and asserts the empirical character of his work. However, by working with alternative philosophical systems of others, he in his own way created a historical rather than empirical work in which he attempted to draw an eclectic deduction from the theories discussed.

According to Pepper, there are four valid hypotheses, or theories, on the nature of art:

1) Mechanistic criticism defines the field of aesthetics as objective pleasure, as proposed by George Santayana in *The Sense of Beauty*.

2) Contextualistic criticism, which is pragmatic, sees "the aesthetic field as the voluntary vivid intuitions of a quality and the more vivid the experience, and the more extensive and rich its quality, the greater its aesthetic value."

3) Organistic criticism, which is idealistic, considers the work of art as a highly integrated whole that stands per se and of which the intuition of quality is only a fragment. This definition was derived from Bernard Bosanquet, *Three Lectures on Aesthetics*.

4) Formistic criticism deals with perceptions "satisfying in themselves to the normal man." The aesthetic value is represented by a norm and conformity to the norm implicit in the work of art, and also conformity to the genre or style, and finally to the culture of which it is an expression.

The ideal of catharsis is also related to satisfying normalcy. This critique is one of the oldest and reaches back as far as Plato and Aristotle.

All four types of criticism can operate together and throw light on different aspects of the same work of art, and the eclectic conclusion reached by Pepper is that "an experience of beauty is one vivid in quality, highly organised, and a source of immediate enjoyment for a normal mind, *or* an objective beauty is a normal perceptual integration of feelings highly pleasant, and vivid in quality."

The art thus defined may belong to the past or to the present but Pepper has modern art in mind, and there are many references to such artists as Picasso. A certain similarity may be seen in Pepper's eclecticism and the pretence to classicism, objectivity, and integral organisation in Cubist painting.

Modern architecture has produced fewer masterpieces than painting, but it has been the object of a tremendous ideological movement. The introduction of cement and steel construction and the great advances in engineering revolutionised traditional building methods about the middle of the last century. It is not difficult to realise that the Crystal Palace·built in London for the Great Exhibition and the Eiffel Tower in Paris, if not works of art, certainly are important affirmations of constructional honesty and seriousness in comparison with the eclectic and incoherent combining of historical styles then usual in public buildings.

At this time the Industrial Revolution produced two new problems: the crisis in handicrafts and the adjustments required by the tremendous population increases in the cities. In England Ruskin and William Morris held industry responsible for the destruction of traditions of craftsmanship and the rapid progress toward a new barbarity and supported a return to the handicraft community by arguments and direct action. The ability of German industry, starting from the same premises as Ruskin and Morris, to maintain or improve the quality of production was a considerable aid to social progress. Instead of mass producing crude reproductions of the artisan's work, however, industry, in turn, had to create new types and forms that were the natural expression of the processes of mechanised industry. Whereas Ruskin felt that architecture was essentially ornamental, Adolf Loos felt the opposite and became the exponent of a simplified, unornamented architecture, expressing only its practical functions. Yet it is evident that Ruskin and Morris in their way and Loos in his moved toward the same end: that is, they insisted on the unity of structure and decoration, whether the decoration was reabsorbed in the structure or the reverse. For both, the common enemy was academic architecture imitating a historical style or combining several.

Antonio Sant'Elia published his Manifesto of Futurist Architecture in Italy in 1914. He, too, proclaimed the need for unity of structure and decoration and extolled the possibilities inherent in the new methods of construction for the use of space and saw space as the dimension of the feverish life of the machine age. However, he also wanted the product or synthesis of these ideas to have beauty. Since Sant' Elia died young during World War I and left only a few designs illustrating his concept of the ideal machine-age city, it is impossible to ascertain by what artistic processes and through what formal values this beauty was to be realised. To modern architects Sant'Elia's work, which is not devoid of idealistic reasoning, is a call to arms not to forsake artistic goals and not to confuse utilitarianism with what is actually only an awareness of a historical actuality.

Argument would probably have been confined to practical and social utility if the visual experience of Cubism had not transformed it into stylistic terms. Credit for having realised that the problem of architecture is above everything visual must go to Le Corbusier, a Swiss architect working in France. He stated that architecture is a matter of surfaces, masses, and voids. However, in order to inform surface, mass, and void with pure and absolute values, it is necessary to discard the spatial or perspective conventions that determine the value of each element in relation to a preconceived image of space. Consequently, it becomes necessary to consider form only in relation to itself, and to its own function so that it is the logical solution of a solidly founded problem. The problem is naturally a practical one, but to find its formal expression and its rational forms, the empirical data governing execution have to be reduced to a system. Le Corbusier intends his argument to be a social argument but he bases it on a mistaken premise, that of reducing a factual situation to an abstract scheme, which necessarily obscures its historical awareness. He attempts to realise his reform of architectural taste within a framework of social reform but when he thinks in utopian terms of an ideal civilization—the machine civilization—instead of seeing it within the historical progression of society he makes the same mistake as the Cubists. Le Corbusier, like the Cubist theorists, is inclined to see new evidence for an architectural rationality whenever he can find absolute formal values in ancient monuments. Without being aware of it, he then goes on to reassert the old myth of formal clarity in Classical art as compared to the romanticism of the north and then postulates the superiority of Mediterranean cultures. Unconsciously, his tendency toward a social or international architecture, though free from traditional schemes, is finally caught in a universalism based on the ascendancy of Western intellectualism.

The idea of an international style in architecture and industrial design proposed by Walter Gropius (born 1883) is much more significant. Gropius was a German architect whose earliest activities were interrupted by World War I. The horrors of war and the misery of the post-war years turned his thoughts toward the possibilities of an architecture that would be a new force for civilisation and would help to bridge the abyss between reality and ideal. His European work covers only the short period of the Weimar Republic, for with Hitler's rise to power came persecution and emigration to the United States where he has continued his work. Gropius' moral basis is more profound than Le Corbusier's, for he sees architecture not as the image but rather as the instrument of a better (but not perfect) society. Architecture is not the goal of progress but an agent that influences the collective consciousness and furthers the process of progress. In this social proposition it is possible to sense an echo of Morris' humanitarianism and of his espousal of an art no longer separated from morality, politics, and religion. And, in fact, through his teachers, Behrens and Van de Velde, Gropius had close ties with the movement for a social art based on industrial production, which takes Morris' position as a starting point and goes on to found the *Deutsche Werkbund*, the first art school geared to the industrial production of quality furniture and furnishings based strictly on function. Furthermore, from 1910 on, Gropius was strongly influenced by the writings of Frank Lloyd Wright, whom Ashbee had made known in Europe and who, by way of his teachers, Louis Sullivan and H. H. Richardson, also descended from Morris.

The writings of Gropius are few, concise, and couched in almost ostentatiously technical and economic terms. The two basic concepts, rationality and standardisation, are the same two that are repeatedly discussed by Le Corbusier. Gropius, however, sees the module less as a rational than as a pure form, the image of a perfection that the mechanised process can reproduce impersonally and with absolute precision. In this great importance given the mechanical process as a perfect method of expression, the Cubists' diffidence and opposition to sensibility, emotionalism, and the uncertainties of nature emphasised by the Impressionists are easily recognisable. One need only recall the Cubist medium of *collage*. Another idea held in common is that abstract form is seen as concrete excellence in that it is not related to a representation of life but to life itself; it is not the catharsis but the action. In fact, this theory of architecture contains the development and provides the explanation of the concept of art as a value that is no longer merely theoretical but also ethical and social. To put it more precisely, it is ethical and theoretical at the same time, since if the spirit does not find expression outside the act, it is also an act of knowledge, and the traditional barriers between ethics and aesthetics must fall, just as the barriers between the visual arts and literature were levelled.

The critical value not immediately evident in Gropius' terse theories becomes clear when he declares that this theory is inseparable from a pragmatic movement: just as his theory is actually a codification of a completed experience (and here we have the outgrowth of an historical requirement unknown to Le Corbusier and contrary to his mythical concept of modern civilization), so it naturally becomes a didactic principle, or, in a higher sense, a pedagogy of art. The Bauhaus, as the school of Arts and Crafts at Weimar was called after Gropius reorganised it in 1919 and which some years later was moved to Dessau, was much more than an art school. It was a meeting place for artists from many countries—Kandinsky from Russia, Klee from Switzerland, Moholy-Nagy from Hungary—united by a common interest in the new art that recognised the positive expression of unification through an international social consciousness, that is, the direct expression of the historical reality of a democratic and socialistic Europe. The social revolution of the Expressionists and the destructive anarchy of the Dadaists were thus also reabsorbed in a new and concrete view of history.

Frank Lloyd Wright (born 1864) has produced architectural masterpieces that are also masterpieces of poetry. His extensive writings have no clarity or theoretical discipline whatsoever but are rich in that impulse that propels the architect to attack the structure with the same effort, the same participation, and the same immediacy as the painter attacks the canvas or the sculptor the block of stone.

It has already been mentioned that Wright learned Ruskin's and Morris' principles through Richardson and Sullivan. Furthermore, a Middle Westerner and a devotee of the poetry of Walt Whitman, he cordially disliked Europe with its classical and Catholic tradition. He never tired of admonishing Americans to beware of European influence, the industrial myth of the machine civilization and of its art, which is an intellectual construction and does not participate in fundamental organic laws.

These laws are not the abstract laws of space but the laws governing the natural growth of things. Thus, they are not laws of form but laws of matter. He teaches that the student should begin by studying the nature of the materials and learn to see them. He will then come to know brick as brick, wood as wood, cement, glass, metals, each as it is and for itself. Though this may sound strange, it requires a great deal of concentration of the imagination. Each material calls for a different treatment and has possibilities for use that are particular to its nature. A design appropriate to one material is not right for another because of the ideal of simplicity as organic plasticity.

To Wright the design or plan is the abstraction of natural elements in purely geometric terms. Here, geometric form is not meant as an expression of space according to Euclidean geometry but as pure, mental abstraction, the conscious step toward the highest values of organic form found in reality that occurs in the creative mind. This is no longer the machine-age civilisation, the mechanical Moloch, but civilisation as moment or as supreme form, or more precisely, as the reality of the moment. Thus, reality is no longer expressed in nullifying consciousness, as it was by the Surrealists, but is given a new value. This explains why in connection with Frank Lloyd Wright, E. Persico, an Italian writer, mentioned Cézanne, the painter to whom modern art since the Surrealist phase had turned again in order to clarify one of its own traditions from which it could no longer remain apart.

This also explains how Wright, working from these foundations, arrived at a clearer formulation not only of the relation between function and beauty in architectural form, but also of the relation between architecture and city planning. While Le Corbusier still thought of city planning in terms of an ideal city (*la ville radieuse*) and Gropius as a basically social problem, Wright saw it as a problem of the human personality and activity in direct relation with nature, or as a problem of the realisation of individual freedom as continuous and organic creativity. With Wright's ideas and works, the theory of modern architecture throws off the bonds of its battle against tradition by which it had been imprisoned in Europe. Understandably, after so much argumentative discussion, the need for a history of the new architecture became apparent. Such a history had to sum up and justify in relation to a constant, ideal goal the many one-sided attempts at explaining the growth of this architecture in terms of discoveries in structural methods, of the development of form, or of social and political change. It became evident that a history of architecture could not be reconstructed without taking into account the history of modern taste and that technical, social, or political considerations could find positive rather than polemical expression only by making form concrete. These are the conclusions reached by Nikolaus Pevsner for architecture and by Lewis Mumford for city planning.

CHAPTER XIII
The Critical History of Art

SCHOLARS, archaeologists, historians of technique, iconography and culture, connoisseurs, journalistic critics and the critics of pure visibility, all continue to write upon art. All bring their contribution to the truth. But a renewal of art history cannot derive from the sum of all these one-sided viewpoints, but from a new consciousness of the problem of art, which positivism allowed to decline but which has returned, more alive than ever, to make itself felt since the beginning of our century. It seems, indeed, evident to everyone that, if to write the history of politics it is necessary to have an idea of what politics is, to write the history of art it is necessary to know what art is. Whence derives that identity of art history and criticism spoken of in the first chapter.

Therefore we have tried to choose and expound some typical judgments for each epoch and to put them in relation with the art judged, on the one hand, and with the principles of judgment, on the other. However, the treatment has a strong disproportion: four chapters, in fact, have been devoted to the criticism from the third century B.C. to the eighteenth century A.D., while six chapters have been devoted to the criticism of only a little more than a century and a half. The justification for such disproportion is found in the fact that aesthetics as autonomous science, was born in the middle of the eighteenth century, while the principles of artistic judgment, even if they always existed, did not have their scientific organisation before the middle of the eighteenth century. Before then the principles of judgment, even if they had some seed of truth, were erratic, because they confused aesthetic judgment either with logical or with moral judgment, or allowed it to disappear in mystical soarings, or, finally made it trivial in technical empiricism. We have seen, however, that critics previous to the middle of the eighteenth century were able to find the way to judgments, not only just, but even fine and illuminating even for our century, so well-pervaded with aesthetics. Not without a certain sorrow we have confirmed that the enormous production of art history peculiar to the nineteenth century was not accompanied by a vigourous judgment capable of real aesthetic results, or even equal to some judgments previous to the rise of aesthetics as a science. On the contrary, some art historians rebelled against aesthetics, not in order to construct a new system (in that case rebellion would have meant progress), but to deny aesthetics and re-nounce judgment on art, and boast of not wishing to judge. Yet from their observations they have drawn empirical schemes, good for description, incapable of judging, and with those schemes they have created a science of art which they wished to oppose to aesthetics. Some even among the better recent art historians, with the aim of finding principles of judg-ment, have turned to aesthetic heresies and arrived at good concrete judgments, through an attempt at adjustment be-tween principles and intuitions, a very great effort and one never completely realised.

One might suppose either that aesthetics had mistaken the way and therefore become an obstacle rather than a help to artistic judgment, or else that the art historians had ignored or misunderstood the truth of aesthetics. As was said before, judgment on art is a relation between the idea of art, which depends upon aesthetics, and the intuition of the work of art. If the fault were not in the idea it might be sought in the intuition. Could it be possible that art historians of the nineteenth century had less capacity of critical intuition than a Vasari or a Boschini, a De Piles or a Diderot?

Let us examine separately these possibilities. Anyone who knows the history of aesthetics knows very well that, in spite of all deviations, it offers a fundamental and unquestionable critical nucleus. If not by a point, it could be represented by a line from Baumgarten to Croce. The autonomy of art has been recognised and made to consist in a spiritual activity, an activity creative and not imitative, distinct from logical activity. To logical activity belongs the rational activity, as to aesthetics belongs the imaginative or intuitive activity. If the rational activity proceeds by demonstration, the imaginative activity proceeds by representation: whence the theoretical identity of intuition and expression. Artistic expression is not of concepts, since the formulation of concepts is the work of logic, but of sentiments — practical feeling, desire and will. Outside artistic activity beauty does not exist, because nothing exists outside spiritual activity. What is called beauty, when it is not an object of the senses, is only the perfection of art. Since the category of the beautiful does not exist, all the other categories of the laws of art, of kinds, of types fall to the ground; and the only reality of art is in the personality of the artist, as it is manifested in his works of art. There exist the individuality of the artist and the universal idea of art: between the individual and the universal there are no intermediate verities. There are only practical schemes, which may be useful for reaching the idea of art in universality, or the judgment of art in individuality. And the idea and the judgment must be identified, since the macrocosm is all in the microcosm; in other words, the individual artist is only one aspect, only a moment of universal art.

If we arrive at this central nucleus of aesthetics we cannot but see that art historians ought to profit from it. They study a painter or a sculptor, know what they must look for, not without but within the art of the master — the character of his art, his coherency, his beauty; they have only to follow his imagination, reconstruct it, and finally confirm in it the value of art. For standards they have to-day all the schemes imaginable, whether psychological or figurative; they have only to individualise them, to admit them only in so far as they fit as an integral part into the personality.

It is not, therefore, the fault of aesthetics, if the judgments on art are not satisfactory to-day. Is it the fault of ignorance or misunderstanding on the part of art historians? In many cases, yes; perhaps in the greater number. But there is no doubt than even those who have a theoretical consciousness of aesthetics succeed with difficulty in directing themselves in the judgment of art.

It only remains, then, to find out if the defect consists in the intuitive experience of art. Here is necessary a summary review of the critical intuitions expounded in the preceding chapters.

Recall Xenocrates. He judged according to an intellectualistic conception of art or according to the technical practice. But he also judged according to the experience of Lysippos and Apelles: he succeeded, therefore, in understanding that a line must reveal what it conceals, that the extreme of art is to represent man as he appears, not as he is; and that perfection of art is not identified with perfection of material execution, but may exist in the unfinished. Neither his aesthetics nor his technique, but only his intuitive experience could suggest to him these truths.

In order to meet the spiritual needs that were more intense

as they neared the triumph of Christianity, Dio Chrysostom perceived that Phidias represented a "body in which we recognise with every certainty the presence of mind," and Seneca must have looked at a figure that was not Greek, but Roman of his time, to conclude that "virtue has no need of ornament" — in order to free art from the preoccupation of the beautiful.

Witelo certainly had to learn from Plotinus and St. Augustine that "artificial things seem more beautiful than natural things"; but without having felt the beauty of a Gothic sculpture, he could never have written that almond-shaped eyes are more beautiful than round. Nor, without the splendour of mosaics could Isidorus of Seville have written that "beauty is something added to edifices for ornament." On the other hand, without his own peculiar poetry and the painting of Giotto, Dante would not have affirmed that rhetorical style is beautiful when, from outside, a work appears unadorned, and within truly embellished. Boccaccio, looking at Giotto, realised that he had found again the art which pleases the intellect of the learned, while for many centuries it had delighted the eyes of the ignorant. Villani, considering the painting of Giotto and his followers, understood the value of physical realism and the expression of the passions; and Cennini felt the creative value of imagination, combated eclecticism, and distinguished between the design, which is a spiritual conception, and that which is material. Similarly, looking at fourteenth century painting, Ghiberti did not repeat the mistake of Greek and Roman criticism, which had confused technical with artistic progress, but rather saw in Giotto the discoverer and, at the same time, the perfectioner of the new art.

The aesthetic of Alberti is intellectual in the sense that art may be the mathematical representation of reality, or else mystical, in the search for grace. But his inspirers were Masac-

cio, Brunelleschi and Donatello; and Alberti theorised, not geometrical perspective, but the ideal human form, the artistic
form which his inspirers had imagined. Leonardo spoke in the
name of his own art, and, though venerating science, he theorised beauty through that pictorial gradation which he adored
in nature at sunset, and which he realised in his painting, which
is all sensibility and not at all scientific reason.

Nor in the sensualism of Venetian critics of the sixteenth
century there is enough to suggest their theory of the unfinished as vivacity of touch, of tone; as the synthesis of form and
colour; as spontaneity, and so on: it was not their elementary and crude aesthetic ideas which guided them, but the
intuitive experience of the art of Titian and Tintoretto.
The same inspiration remained vital at Venice for nearly two
centuries, up to the time of Boschini, who was little cultured,
but was, however, able to see justly; and up to Zanetti.

The intuitive factor has special outlet in the judgments of
Vasari. His historical interest, more developed than that of his
predecessors, enables him to indicate approximately who were
the greatest masters of the fourteenth and fifteenth centuries,
judgments which later criticism has in great part ratified. As
to his principal inspirers, Michelangelo and Raphael, not only
does Vasari succeed in explaining their character, but even in
understanding the harm produced on the personality of Raphael by the influence of Michelangelo, showing thus that he
perceives the value of personality in art. And even in the art
contemporary to him, in which he was both judge and partici-
pant, Vasari sometimes succeeds in indicating and appreciating the new Venetian and Lombard tendencies, different from
his own.

In the seventeenth century, with the work of Bellori, the
critical waters began to be troubled. Yet Bellori had knowledge

of Raphael and the antique statues. But that knowledge is very little intuitive experience of art and very largely theory of the "Idea" of the beauty and the prejudice of the imitation of the antique. Moreover, mid-way between Bellori and Raphael there were the Carracci, which is to say, the theory of eclecticism, of the choice of the "merits" of different artists in order to construct perfect art upon them. Theory, then — and a theory in contrast with what was more alive in the art of seventeenth century — is interposed between Bellori and the critical intuition of art. Besides, the "Idea," of Platonic origin, is manifested in a standard of choice from nature, a choice connected with a social prejudice. From all that derives the misdirection of Bellori, who praised Domenichino much more than Caravaggio or Rubens. And to praise Poussin, he was not able to do other than recount the scenes represented.

The artistic principles of Poussin, which were much worse than his art, were similar to those of Bellori; and it is no wonder that they, taken to France and forming the foundation of the French Academy, should have led to an abstract rationalism, confused with social habits; to a stiffening into hierarchies of kinds, to an overvaluation of the theme treated, as compared with the mode of treatment. All that was called in Italy "splendid manner," and in France *"grand goût."*

The polemics between admirers of Poussin and of Rubens, the quarrel of the ancients and moderns, and above all the critical personality of De Piles, succeeded in liberating taste from critical intellectualism, from the hierarchy of kinds, and from the tyranny of the antique. How vital was that reaction is proved by its coincidence with the revival of French painting and taste in the eighteenth century, reaching its climax in Watteau.

This live current of criticism continued with Dubos, who

was able to distinguish pictorial composition from allegorical, which he called poetical; with Diderot, who felt the value in art of moral seriousness, who identified artistic correctness with the coherency of nature, and maintained the freedom of art with respect to rules, with an impetus precursory of romantic criticism; and finally with Reynolds, who insisted upon the affinity of taste and genius, rejected the rules of art and denied eclecticism.

In the meantime the judgment of the senses, of mediaeval memory; the idea of the pictorial, of Boschini and De Piles; the sensism of Dubos and the English aesthetes, all found their philosophical systematisation in the idea of irrationality and primitivism of art by Vico, in that of "sensitive knowledge" by Baumgarten. For a moment justness of critical judgment and clearness of the aesthetic idea coincided for the first time in history. But precisely in that moment the reaction against baroque excesses and the relativity of taste went on to the pretence of philosophical painting and to the eclecticism of Mengs; and also to that first abjuring of contemporary art, to that myth of the unique and unreachable perfection of Greek art, which was impersonated in Winckelmann and took the name of neo-classicism. The aesthetic ideas of Winckelmann were reactionary, belonging to the tradition from Bellori to Mengs, based upon the neo-Platonic Idea. His intuition of art was limited, not only because he did not feel the art of his time, but also because he knew Greek art only through Roman copies; in other words, through academic schemes. But in addition to this he had a very lively historical sense, and therefore he found a nexus between works of art with greater certainty and precision than his predecessors; thus he offered a type of genetic history that was new. Being deficient in the intuition of art, of its individuality, its irrationality, he made, in fact, the history of schemes and types, not of art, under the guise of art history.

Therefore he identified the idea of art, not with Greek art, as he would have wished, but with neo-classical schemes; and at the same time he destroyed faith in the creative freedom of modern art. Neither the cult of antique during the Renaissance, nor the classicism of Bellori had gone so far: Alberti or Vasari knew that the true classics were the moderns, and Bellori loved Poussin. For the critical intuition of contemporary art, Winckelmann substituted the dead schemes of a past art. Since he had an exceptional influence upon the aesthetics and art history of the nineteenth century, he was one of the greatest obstacles to the direction of art criticism.

The romantic movement, with the discovery of the primitives and the Middle Ages, freed minds from neo-classicism. It is necessary to make it quite clear that, at least in the figurative arts, there has never been a contrast between classics and romantics, but only between neo-classics and romantics. Nevertheless the romantic movement suffered the most disastrous of the results of neo-classicism: detachment from contemporary art. If Gothic architecture is understood, a relation is seen between it and the a-classicism of Shakespeare; and the personality of Shakespeare helped to an understanding of Rembrandt. On the other hand, the new sense of history prevented the adhering to the idea of art as a gift to humanity of a Greek epoch; and already Herder objected that art is the apparition of God in the becoming of history, and Wackenroder said some admirable words on artistic intuition, against eclecticism and academic or social rules, for the humility of the critic, for the appreciation of art beyond the limits of time and place. Frederick Schlegel destroyed the myth of the Carracci. Ruskin, better than anyone, understood Gothic art and that of the Italian primitives, because he was able to see in them the relations with sensibility, religion and morality, against the pretence of perfection, against choice from nature; and he drew from these ideas some unquestionable truths on the limits of antique art and Italian Renaissance. All that was obtained chiefly by means of happy intuitions, because Ruskin's aesthetic reasoning was very weak. But distance from contemporary art led Ruskin to disparage Constable and to fall into the snares of the Pre-Raphaelites; just as it led Frederick Schlegel to appreciate the Nazarenes.

But the greatest effect of the detachment from contemporary art was felt in aesthetics, and particularly in that of Hegel, who would overcome the contrast between classic and romantic. Through having added to aesthetics a general history of art, his influence has been great both on later aesthetics and on art criticism. Well, Hegel accepted from Winckelmann the idea of unreachable perfection in Greek sculpture, and believed that in that perfection was fully realised his conception of art as the sensible appearance of the idea. Hence the triad of the symbolic-classical-romantic, in which the symbolic is an advance in art, without the sensible appearance being complete; and the classic — that is, Greek art — is the perfect equilibrium of sensible appearance and idea; and the romantic, or Christian art, is a prevailing of the idea, with the consequent departure from art and approach to science. Logically, then, Hegel drew from such systematisation the sentence of death upon art in the modern age. And that in spite of the acuteness of his intuitions on the primitives, and above all on Dutch painting. Nevertheless, the authority of Winckelmann, though based on elements extraneous to the idealistic philosophy, was sufficient to make the aesthetics of Hegel misleading for criticism. The consequences were the appreciation of the so-called painters of ideas in the nineteenth century, worth nothing as artistic values; the anti-historical formulation of an abstract ideal for every artistic period; the consideration of art as a document of the life of peoples — in short, various deviations from the criticism of art.

The work of the historico-philologists, of the archaeologists and connoisseurs, promoted by idealism, while it accentuated the detachment from art in general, was not concerned with contemporary art. Indeed, contemporary art could be treated without that philological labour which was the chief interest of the nineteenth century historians; and the habit of being occupied with ancient art suggested a certain dignified indifference to that which was happening around them. Worse still, with rare exceptions, the historians who spoke of contemporary art championed false artists, who, through being more or less clever imitators of the ancients, did not at all represent the ideals of their own time, but offered those same schemes which the historians had the habit of finding in the art of antiquity.

Neither the iconographical studies nor the histories of culture could be interested in contemporary art; nor could even the studies of technique, because contemporary technique is of obvious knowledge. Therefore the advantages occasioned to art history by the work of the philologists, archaeologists and connoisseurs are those of scepticism in aesthetic judgment, the non-rationalisation of genius, the immense amplification of knowledge — all that which did not directly favour critical intuition.

The criticism of pure visibility was in origin classicising, on account of the ideas of Herbart, the taste of Fiedler and the artistic tendencies of Hildebrand. But Woelfflin, also starting from classicism, succeeded later in understanding through his schemes certain aspects of baroque art in an unprejudiced way; and Riegl above all by his universalism, was able to understand the value of Roman art as distinct from Greek, the value of baroque architecture and of some decorative arts. Finally, Fry believed he could extract from Cézanne artistic principles with which to interpret the art of the past.

With rare exceptions, neither the writers on aesthetics, nor those on art history of the nineteenth century, had, then, that direct experience of figurative art, in so far as it was art, without which criticism is not made, and which the writers up to but excluding Winckelmann had based on contemporary art. The treatment of this in the nineteenth century was left to journalists, to the reporters of exhibitions. Fortunately this form of criticism was invented in France in the eighteenth century and made illustrious by the name of Diderot; also in France, during the nineteenth century, some great artistic personalities were not wanting. Therefore, in France, the country in which aesthetics has had the least cultivation and even art history has not shown great results, there was during the nineteenth century an extraordinary flourishing of artistic criticism, directed, much more than by aesthetic ideas, by life lived with the artists and by happy intuitions. The capacity which some among the French artists had of formulating their critical judgments (Delacroix above all); the brotherhood between the painters and certain great writers (Stendhal, Baudelaire and Zola); the identification of the artistic with the political and social struggles — all these gave to French criticism extraordinary adherence to artistic phenomena. Art was no longer the motive of rhetorical disquisitions, nor of learned academic studies; it was a spiritual life lived in common by artists and critics. On the other hand, the academic tradition, being stronger in France than elsewhere, differed from them without compromises, digging an abyss between itself and the creative artists. Every new motive of art assumed then the character of revolution, and from every revolution arose an interpretative myth, which was a provisory systematisation of standards of judgment.

Some of these myths were, for example: that of landscape, for valuing the landscapists of 1830 who did not find appreciation in the face of the academic tradition; or romanticism, for appreciating Delacroix; or realism, for Courbet; or caricature, for Daumier; or impressionism, for some of the painters between 1870 and 1880. Nor was there lacking the ample and comprehensive reflection of Baudelaire, who overcame the contrast of form and colour, indicating the formal possibilities of colour, and distinguished the *finished* from the *made*, and *certainty* from *chic*, and affirmed the universality of art against Winckelmann. Thoré represented well the pantheistic ideal of modern art — its social character, its indifference to kinds; and promoted the return of art to origins — not, it is understood, to the historical but to the psychological origins. The aesthetic of Zola was very elementary and reduced itself to the *temperament* of the artist; but it sufficed for understanding at their beginning, and for defending, some among the greatest modern artists — for example, Manet. It sufficed, because the intuitions of Zola and his friends were directed with a perspicacity unknown to Hegel.

The proof of the value of experience of contemporary art, always in dealing with the art of the past, is furnished by Fromentin, whose "Masters of Other Times" is a masterpiece apart in the historiographical production of the nineteenth century. Fromentin occupied himself with Flemish and Dutch arts, finding the relation between them and the living art of France in his time. He judged the past in the name of Delacroix and himself; looked objectively, without prejudices, and judged according to his own artistic ideal. At the same time, he profited by his experience of the art of the past to discuss his own contemporaries, using it to direct his judgment upon the present. But it was the present that interested him, and his very intense interest in that life of art which is art in the making, took the place of clear aesthetic ideas.

Knowledge, then, of the history of criticism throws light on the problem which we set ourselves. The reason why, in spite of the great progress of aesthetics present day art history reached its critical level with such difficulty, lies not only in a defect of the philosophical culture but also in the defect of intuitive experience of art.

The opinion that in the nineteenth century there was not an art so great as in the preceding centuries is a stupid one, good enough only for him who does not wish to understand. At least eight painters of the nineteenth century were of supreme greatness: Goya, Corot, Daumier, Manet, Renoir, Cézanne, Seurat, Van Gogh. These are enough to give us assurance that art is not dead; that our aspirations, our ideals of yesterday have found their perfect pictorial expression. And they direct us to what is produced of authentic art at the present time.

It is evident that so long as we refer to information of sources, without controlling them, without re-living them, without transforming them in our thought, without having reduced them to present life, there is no history but only chronicle. For the same reason, without having re-lived ancient art through the present day artistic ideal, without having transformed it into present day artistic life, one can make chronicles of art but not art history.

The critical experience of present day art is then the necessary condition for the history of art; here is the truth springing up both from the history of art criticism, delineated up to now, and from the fundamental principle of the theory of history.

Why had aesthetics neglected this truth, when it was occupied in the methodology of art criticism? Aesthetics came out together with neo-classicism, and the taste of the neoclassical period has conditioned the ideas on art in modern aesthetics. The paradox of the death of art in the modern era has nothing to do with the definition of art given by Hegel as the sensible appearance of the idea, but derives from the influence of Winckelmann upon the formation of Hegel's taste. He could not therefore have an intuitive experience of the art of his time, because he believed that it was dead, and nourished a blind faith in the perfection of Greek sculpture, unreached and unreachable.

There is no idea, and therefore no definition of art, however universal it may be, that does not imply a complete judgment of works of art, that is not excited by the desire to understand and judge determinated groups of works of art. Whence it is deduced that in books of aesthetics there necessarily emerge together aesthetic ideas and critical judgments. certainly connected, but not in a way so inseparable that the value of the aesthetic idea bears necessarily the value of critical judgment. Aesthetics may depart from a critical judgment, which is limited and passing, and reach an idea which may be eternal.

Kant, for example, clarified the universality and the undemonstrability of the judgment of taste, and therefore the absurdity of rules of art; and this idea has the aspect of eternal aesthetic truth. But he also wrote that in all the figurative arts the essential is the design, while colours are added to make attractive and be limited by the form. Now, is this an eternal aesthetic truth or a preference of taste, true in one case, false in another, a judgment not absolute but relative to certain phenomena historically determined? Anyone familiar with the history of art knows that the affirmation of Kant on design and colour is true for the Raphael of the "School of Athens," and false for the Raphael of the "Mass of Bolsena"; true for Michelangelo and false for Titian. Then the affirmation is no longer an objective truth, philosophical and universal, but is the subjective preference of the sensibility of the individual, Kant.

Similarly, when Hegel affirms that art is the representation of the ideal and not of nature, nobody can contradict it; but when he affirms that painting, to express feeling and passion, has at its disposition only the face and the attitudes of the body, anybody who has had experience of art refuses to believe him. In fact, every authentic painter expresses his own feeling and his own passion by means of forms and colours and not by means of the face and the attitudes of the body; without taking into account that landscape is art precisely because it expresses the feeling of its author, without either faces or human bodies. The two affirmations of Hegel move, then, on two different planes, the first being a universal aesthetic truth, the second being an error derived from a residue of naturalistic taste dispersed in the idealistic philosophy.

Again, when Croce affirms that art is the expression of feelings rather than of concepts, every critic is grateful to him for having distinguished thus between art and science. But when he states that "the present problem of aesthetics is the restoration and defence of classicism against romanticism," various objections arise. First of all, there has never been a struggle between classicism and romanticism, but only between neo-classicism and romanticism. In fact, the present defence of classicism ends in the restoration of neo-classicism. Besides, the present problem of aesthetics cannot be the struggle against romanticism; that is the task of the politics of taste, not of aesthetics. Croce is rightly the enemy, both aesthetically and morally, of futurism. But from being an enemy of futurism to dreaming of a classical restoration – that is a long way. There exists a modern art which has nothing to do either with futurism or with classicism, which nevertheless is a perfect art, as, for example, Baudelaire already saw. The two affirmations of Croce referred to above also move on two different planes, the first being a philosophical truth and the second a questionable practical exhortation.

Therefore, to the question which we formulated of why modern aesthetics, with regard to the methodology of art criticism, had neglected even to indicate the imperative necessity for the critic of an intuitive experience of present day art, we can now reply: because present day art has not, in fact, entered into the formation of the taste of the writers on aesthetics, and because they have not been able to keep sufficiently distinct the aesthetic truths from the manifestations of a personal taste.

Intuitive experience of art is not the artist's intuition, because it is not productive, and it is not even criticism, because it does not comprehend the idea of art with which one judges. What is it then? It is the sensible stage of criticism, the individual direction, still too personal to have the right to universality; in a word, it is *taste*. The history of criticism teaches that the critic has need of a present taste to direct his judgment even upon past art. But there is another exigency which seems opposed and which is only integrative: that he should also have intuitive experience of art in the past. To re-live in the present the art of the past we must not falsify it, we must not interpret it according to our desires and ideas, but according to the desires and ideas of past art. The understanding of a work of art becomes objective in analysis as the taste of its author. The mistake of Vasari was not that of having the taste of the followers of Michelangelo, but, when he spoke of Giotto, of not distinguishing the taste of Michelangelo from that of Giotto. Through having believed in the perfection of Lysippos, Xenocrates expressed some of his best judgments, but through not having distinguished the perfection of Lysippos from that of Phidias, Xenocrates committed a critical error.

It is necessary, then, to define that, if art is absolute and eternal, tastes are relative. All tastes are of equal value with respect to art. In such a way are avoided arbitrary preferences, the institution of models with which to judge, the concepts of progress and decline — in short, all the misunderstandings of the personality of the artist. Nor does the necessity of present taste hinder in the critic the recognition of different tastes. On the contrary, the more the critic knows the present taste, the more he is aware of its limits, and therefore the more he recognises what is outside those limits. If he is habituated to recognising whence art arises in present taste, he will easily find where art dwells in the antique taste. The opposition of the eternity of art and the relativity of tastes is necessary to the identification of aesthetic and historical judgment, to the end of achieving the critical history of art.

It remains to indicate how the knowledge of taste is obtained. Intuition of art in a work of art and analysis of the constituent elements are naturally the first and essential conditions. But the control of the personal intuition and the personal analysis, and therefore the guarantee of their objectivity, is obtained only with the history of criticism. In the words of the artist upon his own ideal, in his own technique, in the judgment of contemporaries, in the interpretation of posterity, every taste defines the essential elements of its own nature, and constitutes a stage for the development of criticism. And in taste are included all the scientific, religious, moral and utilitarian motives which the artist has held in the moment of his creation and to which he has given the form. The demand of the history of culture justifies itself thus and is transformed: no longer detached from the work of art, since it deals with the taste of art, the history of culture is made one with the history of art. It has departed from intuition of the work of art by a journey through all the domains of the mind; and it returns to the intuition of the work of art and of the personality of the artist, enriched with a complete humanity.

At this point a comparison with what happens in the history of poetry is opportune. We know that the history of poetry and the history of literature are distinguished, not by their extrinsic characters, as would be verse and prose, but by their intrinsic value, poetry having a universal and eternal value, while literature has a value relative to places and times — that is, to the civilisation to which it belongs. Poetry is a synthesis of the individual and the universal, of the finite and the infinite; and literature is individual and finite only. Because it is relative, individual and finite, literature has its function as an institution and a convention, as compared with the poetical freedom which is peculiar to genius. The so-called histories of poetry and literature are always histories of literature, except in the moments, rare enough, when they come into contact with authentic poetry, which produces ecstasy, makes all the rest forgotten, and takes us and transports us into an enchanted castle. But, the enchantment ended, we perceive that that moment of poetry is only a happy parenthesis in the everyday labour, and to that we return as one returns to life after a dream. Literature expresses therefore the sentimental, moral or intellectual tendencies, which have not yet found and never will find their complete poetical form, and represents that analytical moment of poetry which is the material of its history.

A parallel distinction to that between poetry and literature has been wanting until now in the history of the figurative arts. Nobody, however, ventures to maintain that all the paintings, sculpture, and architecture which form the subject of history are perfect and absolute art — that is to say, poetry. Indeed, in the figurative arts, as in literature and music, perfect and absolute art is the rare exception. And all the rest — what is it? There is, it is quite agreed, the ugly, the negation of art. But very many paintings, sculptures and works of architecture, though they are not perfect and absolute art, are not purely negative works, completely deprived of all value; on the contrary, they are, as we say, *interesting*. They are not to be measured by the standard of absolute art, by which they would be annihilated, but by a different standard. They are the historical documents of the sentiments, of the will, and of the ideas of the respective civilisations, and they present the so-called *illustrative* values; or they are works which prepare the practical conditions for the birth of the masterpiece — that is to say, the works of *forerunners;* or they are works which continue the style of one among the great masters, and interpret it, make it accessible and familiar to the public — that is, they are the works of *pupils* and *followers*. It is not, of course, denied that among the works of illustrators, forerunners or followers one finds now and then perfect art. But as a rule their result is practical rather than artistic; it is precisely that of illustration, preparation or interpretation. They make possible the every-day life of painting, sculpture and architecture, in expectation of the heroic moment. The history of art is occupied with every-day life, though on the alert to recognise the "masterpiece."

How, then, can we describe this every-day life, this figurative activity parallel to literary activity, this civilisation which has art for its aim, but is identified with it only in rare moments? The so-called "styles" have in common with this every-day life the character of historical relativity, but are distinguished from it by being abstractions rather than historical realities, and are, at most, abstract aspects of those realities. Recall then the function which at the beginning of this book we assigned to taste, as the analytical moment of the work of art, as a bridge between the creation of genius and the historical development; and you will understand how the distinction between poetry and literature corresponds to the distinction between art and taste in the figurative arts.

In the long review thus far completed, the qualifications which have accompanied the judgments on art present the character of determinations of taste. The reader will remember, for example, the condemnation of the gold background and the demand for a perspective background, which led to the blue sky. Since with the gold background, as with the perspective background, are created both masterpieces of absolute art and mediocre works, neither the one background nor the other is a demand of art, but of taste. In the limits of taste it may be understood that the perspective background belongs to a civilisation which pays more attention to the physical world, and in which the rational control is more alive. Similarly, the habit of painting landscapes is formed only when the pride of man in respect to nature is diminished, and human sympathy for so-called inanimate things is made more intense; yet both the separation of the human figure from surroundings, and the humanisation of things have given rise to masterpieces and to mediocre or imperfect works, and the one and the other mode of seeing and feeling belong therefore to the history of taste.

Since history is history not only of heroic moments, but also of every-day life, without which the heroic moments would neither be possible nor understood, the history of art is, always has been, and, so far as can be foreseen, always will be a *history of taste*. As taste tends to become art, and justifies itself in so far as it is a possibility for art, so the history of art analyses and describes taste with the aim of recognising the moment in which taste is identified with art by force of genius. That is the moment in which the history of art is identified with critical judgment.

To attain then its supreme goal, which is that of recognising when a painting or a sculpture or a work in architecture is perfect and absolute art, the history of art must fulfill two demands. One is the intuitive consciousness of art in the making — that is to say, contemporary art; and the other is the distinction of the absolute and the relative, the eternal and the momentary, the value which transcends history and the reality which is subject to it; in short, art and taste. Only he who possesses the most perfected taste which his civilisation allows, can understand the tastes of past civilisations or remote regions; and discern, whether around him or in the past, the absoluteness of art and the relativity of tastes. This is the condition necessary for art history to overcome its every-day phase of erudition, aestheticism or the "science of art," and become truly the critical history of art.

If the present book brings a contribution to this end the aim of the author has been achieved.

CHAPTER XIV
Conclusion

THE ROAD followed in this study is a long one and it was travelled too fast. However, it seems to me that we can come to optimistic conclusions about the progress art historical criticism has made during the last century and a half. It is true that the union of art criticism and art history that is so necessary has not yet been achieved, but history and criticism each have acquired greater depth. What now remains is the problem of bringing them closer to each other.

French nineteenth-century criticism, with Baudelaire as its most outstanding exponent, showed that artistic sensibility, that is, the participating in the experience of the artist, is the necessary well-spring of critical perception. These critics created a new and more vital awareness of contemporary art and they apprehended art in the process of becoming, that is, by reconstructing the artist's personality. They could not have achieved so much without the ideas of idealistic aesthetics; but had they not participated in the experience of the artist, had they not been so impassioned in their feelings, these aesthetic ideas could not have born fruit. The importance of this interaction is demonstrated by the aesthetic judgments of Hegel and the art historians of his time. In fact, students of aesthetics and art history are better acquainted with the works of the past than with contemporary art, for they are never, or almost never, able to grasp art in the process of becoming. Too often, they consider the activity that surrounds them merely decadent or a denial of art, and this prevents them from understanding eternal human creativity. A sympathy for past cultures can be rational but it cannot identify with the passion for art. Moreover, such sympathies often lead the critic to judge the art of

347

his own time by the standards of the past and therefore to mis-
understand that which is original and authentic in contemporary work, or worse yet, to confuse the imitating of traditional
schemes with creativity—servile ability with the freedom of
art. Furthermore, this attitude may also mean that the art
of the past, too, is not understood, since it is not seen in terms of
its creativity, which give it an immediacy that makes it lasting,
but in terms of its cultural schemes which, because they belong
to taste and not to art, constitute the conditional and transient
aspects that have no lasting worth. Neither the present nor the
past can be understood in this way.

It is the experience of contemporary art that teaches us to see
the art of the past and not the reverse, because this experience
sums up and justifies in itself the experience of the art of the
past. This truth is as valid for art as it is for philosophy; all the
history of civilization lives in today's thought. It is impossible
to come to know Greek taste if one is not able to find one's way
in contemporary taste. This is confirmed by Winckelmann and
Hegel who, just because they based the interpretation of all art
on the absolute pre-eminence of Greek art, ended by misunderstanding both Greek and contemporary art. All later attempts to make the concept of the Classic into a measure of
excellence to be applied to the art of all other periods also failed
and created a cultural hedonism that may well seem attractive,
but is devoid of authentic feeling for art.

The person confronting a contemporary work of art does not
have recourse to established, well-defined criteria and authoritative tradition. He must also exercise critical acumen in select-
ing and rejecting by re-creating the flow of creative imagination and by discovering the intellectual combinations, as well
as the tricks that are meant to pass for art. The ability practiced

in evaluating the past is then revealed for what it is, empty virtuosity devoid of spiritual content.

Inevitably, the critic shows partiality in what he selects or rejects. Out of this arises the impassioned (or political, as Baudelaire said) character of every living critic. Only that passion that judges according to abstract principles and not out of the spontaneous love of the creative act should be avoided. Detachment, natural to the scientist, is not suitable to the art critic since he moves within the human world of man's passions and fantasies. Nor does the critic's partiality hinder him from observing something from many sides and even, theoretically at least, from all sides. He is partial to the ever-lasting creativity that is reborn every day and at every instant with the work of art. If he has acquired that force that makes a work art, he will be able to recognize it in any work, irrespective of the taste in which it was executed. Baudelaire understood the creativity of Delacroix and of Daumier but he could also recognize the moment of art in so different an artist as Ingres. Using this same critical basis, others have been able to understand Phidias and Raphael.

Since the artist's soul is not expressed by means of forms and colours but in forms and colours, twentieth-century criticism has emphasized the study of the methods used in the treatment of form and colour. If at times this study has degenerated to a mere appreciation of abstract form, forgetting the unity of form and motif, and at other times distracted criticism from the artist's personality, as, for example, in the case of Riegl and Wölfflin, the progress in the knowledge of form and colour is still evident. In a way paralleling modern art, criticism has been able to exclude those values that art owed only to the association without experience of reality, when the experience has not passed through and been completely transformed into values of form and colour.

The creativity of form and colour is the unique harmony on which to judge art, but creativity is not, and cannot be isolated from life. Painting is a profession, but in order to become art even painting must reach beyond the confines of a profession and take up the whole of the artist's existence. Hence, the moral and religious demands of a work of art, which do not consist of the pretext that art teaches morals and religion (in which case it would be rhetoric and not art), but in the requirement that the artist's attitude toward his own creativity be informed by moral seriousness and by aspirations toward the infinite and the universal. Ruskin taught this and his teachings should not be forgotten by modern criticism.

When it is said of a work of art that it transcends its own times, one means that its creativity belongs to all mankind, to whoever feels and imagines irrespective of time or place. And yet, imagination is not exhausted in creativity but participates in the life of its own times by either adhering to or rebelling against it. Art, however, transcends history while participating in it. Thus it is impossible critically to see an artist's creativity without a complete knowledge of his historical environment. Two factors contribute to this knowledge: the method of formulating human ideals employed by Hegel and cultural history of the type formulated by Burckhardt and Dvořàk.

The critical history of art differs from traditional art history in the greater emphasis placed on its critical function and in the pre-eminence given to critical activity. Its central concern is the personality of the artist, which is distinct from the personality of the man because it encompasses the moment at which man's creative imagination is realized in form and colour. The intellectual, moral, religious, social, and all other human activities that constitute history surround this core and serve to explain its nature, but have value only as a function of this center. Hence, the essential principle of the critical history of art may be stated as follows: the history of art is a function of the criticism of art.

If a knowledge of the historical development of art criticism can induce anyone to accept this principle, this book will have achieved its aim.

BIBLIOGRAPHY

BIBLIOGRAPHY

CHAPTER I

FOR the philosophical principles of art and history used in this and the following chapters, consult: —

Kant, Kritik der Urtheilskraft; *Hegel*, Aesthetik;

Croce, Estetica, Problemi di estetica, Nuovi saggi di estetica, Teoria e storia della storiografia, La critica e la storia delle arti figurative, La poesia; *Windelband*, Geschichte der Philosophie, (8th ed., 1919); *De Ruggiero*, Storia della filosofia, 8 vols;

B. Bosanquet, A History of Aesthetic (2nd ed. 1904);

Menendez y Pelayo, Historia de las ideas estéticas en España (3rd ed: Madrid 1909 and following);

Robert Zimmermann, Geschichte der Aesthetic als philosophischer Wissenschaft; Vienna 1858; *E. Utitz*, Geschichte der Aesthetik, Berlin, 1932; *H. Tietze*, Die Methode der Kunstgeschichte; Leipzig 1913;

R. Hedicke, Methodenlehre der Kunstgeschichte, Strassburg, 1924.

The quotations on "taste" are taken from: —

Baldinucci, Vocabolario toscano dell 'arte del disegno, 1681, p. 72;

De Piles, Cours de peinture par principes, 1st ed. 1708, Amsterdam ed. 1766, p. 142;

Mengs, Riflessioni sulla bellezza e sul gusto della pittura, 1st ed. Zurich, 1762, Rome ed. 1787, Part II, p. 16.

For Baudelaire, consult Chapter X.

To the ideas expressed in this chapter, and already in part published by me in "Art et Esthétique" vol. 1, No. 1, 1934, and in "Bulletin de l'Office International des Instituts d'Archéologie et d'Histoire de l'Art," No. 4, July 1935, have replied in support or contradiction Messrs. W. Deonna, A. Philip McMahon, E. Schaub-Koch, Ch. Lalo, Victor Basch, in the same "Bulletin," nos. 5, 6, 7.

BIBLIOGRAPHY

CHAPTER II

General works: —

E. Müller, Geschichte der Theorie der Kunst bei der Alten, (Breslau, 1834-37);

J. A. Overbeck, Schriftquellen zur Geschichte der bildenen Kunste, (Leipzig, 1868);

Bénard, L'Esthétique d'Aristotle (Paris 1887);

Julius Walter, Die Geschichte der Aesthetik im Altertum (Leipzig 1893);

Ed. Bertrand, Etudes sur la peinture et la critique dans l'antiquité (Paris, 1893);

H. S. Jones, Select passages from ancient writers illustrative of the history of Greek sculpture (London 1895);

A. Reinach, Textes grecs et latins relatifs à l'histoire de la peinture ancienne (Paris 1921);

Aristotle, La poetica, ed. Rostagni, Torino, 1928, IV, 10-15;

E. Bignami, La poetica di Aristotele, (Firenze 1932).

On Xenocrates: —

The Elder Pliny's Chapters on the History of Art, translated by *K. Jex-Blake*, with commentary and historical introduction by E. Sellers, London 1896 (the quotation of passages — XXXIV, 56; XXXV, 76, 68, 131, 126, 97, 79, 128, 98, 74, 145, 50 — is taken from this translation);

A. Kalkmann, Die Quellen der Kunstgeschichte des Plinius, Berlin 1898.

Cicero, De oratore, III, 7.

Quintilian, Institutionis oratoriae, Liber XII, 10.

Dio Chrysostom, De dei cognitione, Oratio XII.

Philostratos, Imagines, Vita Apollonii Tyanoei, vi, 19 and II, 22.

Vitruvius, De architectura, VII, v, 3-4; VII, v, 7. Consult

BIBLIOGRAPHY

Jolles, Vitruvs Aesthetik, Freiburg i. B. 1906.

Lucian, Imagines; Prolaliai; Zeuxis, 3-8.

Horace, De arte poetica.

Plutarch, Quomodo adolescens poetas audire debeat, III and I, 40.

Seneca, Epistulae ad Lucilium.

Dionysius of Halikarnassos, De antiquis oratoribus, 1. De Isaeo, 4.

CHAPTER III

For this and for the succeeding chapters up to the 6th, consult *Julius Schlosser*, Die Kunstliteratur, Wien 1924. Also consult *L. Venturi*, Il gusto dei primitivi, Bologna 1926.

On the aesthetic of Plotinus, besides the histories of philosophy of Bosanquet, Croce, Zimmermann, already quoted, consult *E. Panofsky*, Idea, Leipzig, 1924; on the aesthetic of St. Augustine:
K. Swoboda, L'esthétique de Saint Augustin et ses sources, Brno 1933; on the aesthetic of St. Thomas consult *Adolf Dyroff*, Ueber die Entwicklung u. den Wert der Aesthetik des Thomas von Aquino, Archiv fur systematische Philosophie and Soziologie, XXXIII 1929. On the mediaeval recipes, consult *Mrs. Merrifield*, Original Treatises dating from the XIIth to XVIIIth Centuries on the Arts of Painting (2 vols, London 1849); *Achille Pellizzari*, I trattati attorno le arti figurative in Italia (Naples 1915); *G. Loumier*, Les traditions techniques de la peinture médiévale (Paris 1920)
Theophilus Presbyter, Schedula diversarum artium (Vienna 1874), Quellenschriften fur Kunstgeschichte, VII; *D. V. Thompson*. "Liber de coloribus illuminatorum," Speculum, July 1926; "The Schedula of Theophilus Presbyter," Speculum, April 1932; The "De Clarea of the so-called "Anonymus

Bernensis," Technical Studies, 1, July and October 1932 (and *G. Hamilton*); De arte illuminandi, transl. from the Latin, New Haven 1933; Artificial Vermilion in the Middle Ages, Technical Studies 2, October 1933; De coloribus, naturalia exscripta et collecta, from Erfurt, Stadtbücherei, Technical Studies, 3, January 1935; Medieval Color-making: "Tractatus qualiter quilibet artificialis color fieri possit" Isis 1935; "The liber magistri Petri de Sancto Andemaro de coloribus faciendis" Technical Studies, 4, July 1935. *R. P. Johnson*, The "Compositiones ad tingenda" Technical Studies 3, 1935; *Denys*, Le guide de la peinture, manuel d'iconographie chrétienne par *Didron*, Paris 1845.

On Witelo consult *E. Tea*, L'Arte XXX, 1927, p. 3-30; *Pauli Silentiarii*, Descriptio ecclesiae sanctae Sophiae, Patrologia graeca, 86 bis. Consult *J. P. Richter*, Quellenbuch der Byzantinischen Kunstgeschichte, Wien 1897.

On St. Bernard, consult *J. Schlosser*, Quellenbuch zur Kunstgeschichte des Abendländischen Mittelalters, Wien 1896.

On the criticism of Dante, Petrarch, Boccaccio, Filippo Villani, Cennini, consult *Lionello Venturi*, La critica d'arte in Italia durante i secoli XIV et XV (L'Arte XX, 1917), La critica d'arte e Francesco Petrarca (L'Arte XXV, 1922), La critica d'arte alla fine del trecento (L'Arte XXVIII, 1925)

Cennino Cennini, Il libro dell'arte, Firenze, 1859, and New Haven 1932.

CHAPTER IV

Consult *Lionello Venturi*, La critique d'art en Italie à l'époque de la Renaissance, Gazette des Beaux-Arts, June 1922, July 1923 January and May 1924, and Quaderni Critici, Rieti 1928; *G. von Schlosser*, Sull'antica storiografia italiana dell'arte Palermo, 1932; *K. Borinski*, Die Antike in Poetik und Kunsttheorie, Leipzig, 1914; *K. Birch-Hirschfeld*, Die Lehre von der Malerei im Cinquecento, Rom, 1912.

Lorenzo Ghiberti, Commentarii, ed Schlosser, Berlin 1912. *L. Venturi*, Lorenzo Ghiberti, in "Pretesti di critica," Milan 1929.

Leon Battista Alberti, La pittura, Lanciano, 1911; De re asolificatoria, Florence 1485. On his criticism consult *G. Vesco*, in L'Arte XXII, 1919; *J. Behn, L. B. A.* als Kunstphilosoph, Strassburg 1911; *W. Flemming*, Die Begründung der modernen Aesthetik und Kunstwissenschaft durch L. B. A., Berlin 1916; P. H. Michel, La pensée de L. B. A., Paris 1930.

Leonardo da Vinci, Trattato della pittura, ed. Ludwig, Wien 1882; idem, Lanciano, 1914; consult *J. P. Richter*. The literary works of Leonardo, London, 1883; *L. Venturi*, La critica e l'arte di L. da V., Bologna 1919.

Michelangelo, Lettere, ed. Milanesi, Firenze, 1875; Poésie, ed. Frey Berlin 1897; *Francisco de Hollanda*, Tractado de pintura antigua, 1538, ed. Pellizzari, Napoli 1914.

Albert Dürer, Proportionlehre, Nürenberg 1528. Consult *Panofsky*, Dürer's Kunsttheorie, Berlin 1915.

Pietro Aretino — Lettere, Paris, 1609. Consult *K. Vossler*, P. A's künstlerishes Bekenntnis, Neue Heidelberger Jarbücher, 1900;

S. Ortolani, La origini della critica d'arte a Venezia, L'Arte, XXVI, 1923.

Paolo Pino, Dialogo di pittura, Venezia 1548.

Ludovico Dolce, Dialogo della Pittura intitolato l'Aretino, Venezia 1557.

Giorgio Vasari, Opere, ed. Milanesi, Firenzi, 1878/85, 9 vols.; *K. Frey*, Der literarische Nachlass G. V's, München. 1929/30. 2 vols. Consult *W. v. Obernitz*, V's Allgemeine Kunstanschaungen, Strassburg, 1897; *W. Kallab*, Vasaristudien, Wien

1908; *C. L. Ragghianti*, Il valore dell'opera di G. V., Rendiconti Accademia dei Lincei, Roma, 1934.

Sebastiano Serlio, Dell'architettura, Venezia, 1566. Consult *G. Argan*, S. S. L'Arte, xxxv 1932.

Andrea Palladio, Quattro libri dell'architettura, Venezia, 1570.

Paolo Lomazzo, Trattato dell'arte della pittura, Milano, 1584, Idea del tempio della pittura, Milano 1590.

For the concept of Mannerism, consult *E. Panofsky*, Idea, Leipzig, 1924.

CHAPTER V

For the conception of the baroque, consult: —

H. Woelfflin, Kunstgeschichtliche Grundbegriffe, München 1915;

A. Riegl, Die Entstehung der Barockkunst in Rom, Wien 1907;

B. Croce, Storia della età barocca in Italia, Bari, 1929;

For the relations with the Counter Reformation: —

W. Weisbach, Der Barock als Kunst der Gegenreformation, Berlin 1921;

E. Mâle, L'art religieux après le Concile de Trente, Paris 1932;

G. Paleotti, Discorso intorno le immagini sacre e profane, Bologna, 1582.

J. B. Dubos, Relexions critiques sur la Poésie et la Peinture, Paris 1719, II, 313;

Gio. Pietro Bellori, Le vite de' pittori scultori ed architetti moderni, Roma 1672. Consult *G. von Schlosser*, Sull'antica storiografia italiana dell'arte, Palermo, 1932.

On the Carracci, consult: *C. L. Ragghianti*, I Carracci e la critica d'arte nell'età barocca, La Critica, vol. xxxi, 1933.

G. B. Passeri, Vite de' pittori, scultori ed architetti che hanno lavorato in Roma, morti dal 1641 fino al 1673, Roma 1772. Critical edition by J. Hess, Leipzig u. Wien 1934.

BIBLIOGRAPHY

F. Baldinucci, Notizie de' professori del disegno da Cimabue in qua, Firenze 1681-1728.

F. Scannelli, Il microsmo della pittura, Cesena 1657.

L. Scaramuccia, Le finezze dei pennelli italian, Pavia 1674.

N. Poussin, an extract from his treatise on painting was published by Bellori, Lives quoted p. 288 and following. Consult also Lettres de P., Paris 1929.

On French criticism of the period, consult: — *A. Fontaine*, Les doctrines d'art en France de Poussin à Diderot, Paris 1909.

R. Fréart de Chambray, Idée de la perfection de la peinture, Le Mans, 1662.

Chantelou, Journal du voyage du Cavalier Bernini en France, Gazette des Beaux-Arts, 1877 and following.

A. Félibien, Entretiens sur les vies et les ouvrages des plus excellens peintres, anciens et modernes, Paris 1666-88;

M. Boschini, La carta del navegar pittoresco, Venezia, 1660; Le ricche minere della pittura veneziana, Venezia 1674. Consult *L. Lopresti*, M. B., L'Arte XXII (1919).

On the polemic between the *Poussinists* and the *Rubenists* and on the "quarrel of the ancients and the moderns," consult: — *Fontaine* (already quoted).

R. De Piles, Abrégé de la vie des peintres, Paris 1699; Cours de peinture par principes, Paris 1708. Consult *L. Mirot*, Roger De Piles, Paris 1924.

CHAPTER VI

On the aesthetics of the XVIIIth century, consult: —

Croce, Estetica (quoted chapter 1); La Critica, Jan. 1933 and July 1934;

E. Cassirer, Die Philosophie der Aufklärung, Tübingen, 1932;

BIBLIOGRAPHY

Shaftesbury, Characteristics of men, manners, opinions, times, 1709-11;

Vico, Scienza Nuova, 1725 and 1730;

Baumgarten, Aesthetica, 1750 and 1758.

On the form of the criticism and history of art: —

Fontaine, Doctrines (quoted);

Dresdner, Die Kunstkritik, München, 1915;

Schlosser, Kunstliteratur (quoted);

Rocheblave, L'art et le goût en France, Paris, 1923.

La Font de Saint Yenne, Réflexions sur la peinture, Paris 1746; Réflexions sur quelques causes de l' état présent de la peinture en France, Paris 1747 and 1752.

Caylus, Nouveaux sujets de peinture et sculpture, Paris 1755.

Cochin, Recueil de quelques pièces concernant les arts, Paris 1757 (Consult Rocheblave, C. Paris 1926.)

Diderot, Oeuvres Complètes (T. X. XII: Salons 1759-1781, Sur l'origine et la nature du beau, Essai sur le peinture).

Ciocchi, La pittura in Parnaso, Firenze, 1725.

Zanetti, Della pittura veneziana, Venezia, 1771.

Lanzi, Storia pittorica dell'Italia, Bassano, 1789.

On Lodoli, consult: — *Memmo*, Elementi d'architettura lodoliana, Rome, 1786;

Milizia, Vite de' piu celebri architetti, Rome, 1768; Dell'arte di vedere nelle belle arti del disegno, Venezia, 1781; Opere, Bologna, 1826.

Richardson, An Essay on the Theory of Painting, London, 1715; The Connoisseur, London, 1719.

Hogarth, The Analysis of Beauty, London 1753.

U. Price, Essay on the Picturesque, 1794; *R. Payne Knight*, Dialogue on the Distinct Characters of the Picturesque and

Beautiful, 1801; Analytical Enquiry into the Principles of *Taste*, 1805. Consult: *C. Hussey*, The Picturesque, London & New York, 1927; *J. Steegmann*, The Rule of Taste from George I to George IV, London 1936.

Reynolds, Discourses, London 1771, Fry ed. 1905; Literary Works, London 1794-97; The Letters of Sir Joshua Reynolds, ed. by F. W. Hilles, 1929.

On neo-classicism: — *L. Hautecoeur*, Rome et la Renaissance de l'antiquité, Paris, 1912.

Mengs, Gedanken über die Schönheit hund den Geschmack in der Malerei, Zürich, 1762; Works, London 1796.

Winckelmann, Gedanken über die Nachahmung der grieschischen Werke in der Malerei u. Bildhauerkunst, Dresden u. Leipzig 1755; Werke, 1808-1825.

On Mengs and Winckelmann, consult: —

Waetzoldt, Deutsche Kunsthistoriker, Leipzig, 1921, vol. 1;

Heidrich, Beiträgen zur Geschichte und Methoden der Kunstgeschichte, Basel, 1917;

C. Justi, Winckelmann und seine Zeitgenossen, Leipzig, 1866-72;

V. G. Simkhovitch, Approaches to history, V, in Political Science Quarterly, 1934, vol. 49, pages 44-83.

Lessing, Laokoon, Berlin, 1766; English ed. London 1836.

CHAPTER VII

General works: —

L. Venturi, Il gusto dei primitivi, Bologna, 1926;

K. Clark, The Gothic Revival, London, 1928;

W. Waetzold, Deutsche Kunsthistoriker, Leipzig, 1921, vol. 1;

C. G. Heise, Overbeck u. s. Kreis, München, 1928;

BIBLIOGRAPHY

A. Raczynski, Histoire de l'art moderne en Allegmagne, Paris 1836/39;

W. H. Hunt, Pre-Raphaelitism and the Pre-Raphaelite Brotherhood, London 1905, 2 vols.

H. Walpole, Anecdotes of Painting in England, Strawberry Hill, 1762-1771.

R. Hurd, Letters on Chivalry and Romance, 1762; Works, London, 1777, 10 vols.

C. L. von Hagedorn, Betrachtungen über die Malerei, Leipzig, 1762.

J. J. Heinse, Breife aus der Düsseldorfer Gemäldegalerie 1776 and 1777.

J. H. Fuseli, Lectures on Painting, London 1830, (1st ed. 1801).

Hamann, Leser und Kunstrichter nach perspektivischem Unebenmasse, 1762.

Herder, Kritische Wälder, 1769.

W. Goethe, Von deutscher Baukunst, 1773, (Werke, D. N. L., 26).

W. H. Wackenroder, Herzensergiessungen eines kunstliebenden Klosterbruders, Berlin, 1797, Leipzig (ed. Warzel), 1921. Consult: *B. Tecchi*, Wackenroder, Firenze, 1927.

F. Schlegel, Ansichten und Ideen von der christlichen Kunst, Sammtliche Werke, Band 6.

G. Lami, Dissertazione aggiunta al trattato di Leonardo da Vinci, Firenze, 1792.

P. Frisi, Saggio sopra l'architettura gotica, Livorno, 1766.

G. Della Valle, Lettere Sanesi, Roma, 1785.

L. Cicognara, Storia della scultura, 1813-18.

A. Bianchini, Del purismo nelle arti, Roma, 1843.

J. B. Seroux d'Agincourt, Histoire de l'art par les monuments, depuis sa décadence au ivieme siècle jusqu'à son renouvellement au xviième, Paris, 1823. Consult: *M. Lamy*, La découverte des primitifs italiens au xixiéme siècle, in Revue de l'art ancien et moderne, 1921, I and II.

Artaud de Montor, Considérations sur l'état de la peinture en Italie, dans les quatre siècles qui on précédé celui de Raphael (Paris 1808.)

Paillot de Montabert, Traité complet de la peinture, Paris 1829.

Rio, De l'art chrétien, 1836 and following. Epilogue à l'art chrétien, Paris 1872.

Viollet-le-Duc: consult *P. Gout*, V. L. D. Paris 1914.

W. Y. Ottley, The Italian school of design, London 1823. Consult: *T. Borenius*, The Rediscovery of the Primitives, in the Quarterly Review, April, 1923.

Lord Lindsay, Sketches of the History of Christian Art, 1847.

A. W. Pugin, Contrasts, 1836; True Principles of Christian Architecture, 1841.

J. Ruskin, Works, Library edition, 39 vols. Consult:—

W. G. Collingwood, The life and work of J. R., Cambridge 1893;

E. T. Cook, The life of John Ruskin, London 1911;

J. Milsand, L'esthétique anglaise, Paris, 1864;

De La Sizeranne, Ruskin et la religion de la beauté, Paris 1899.

CHAPTER VIII

For the idealistic aesthetic, besides the works quoted in the bibliography of Chapter I, consult: —

M. Schasler, Kritische Geschichte der Aesthetik, Berlin 1872;

E. v. Hartmann, Die deutsche Aesthetik seit Kant, Leipzig, 1886;

W. Waetzoldt, Deutsche Kunsthistoriker, Leipzig, 1921 & 1924 2 vols.;

Mustoxidi, Histoire de l'esthétique francaise, Paris, 1920;

BIBLIOGRAPHY

On the end of art, consult: — B. *Bosanquet*, Croce's Aesthetic, in Proceedings of the British Academy, vol. IX, 1914; *B. Croce*, La "fine dell'arte" nel sistema hegeliano, in Ultimi Saggi, Bari, 1935.

Kant, Kritik der Urtheilskraft. Consult:—
O. *Schlapp*, Kant's Lehre von Genie und die Entstehung der Kritik der Urtheilskraft, Gottingen, 1901;
V. *Basch*, Essai critique sur l'esthétique de Kant, Paris, 1927.

Herder, Kritische Wälder, Werke, III, 2. Consult:—
Croce, La teorie del giudizio estetico come giudizio storico, in Ultimi Saggi, Bari, 1935.
Schiller, Briefe über die aesthetische Erziehung der Menschheit, and Uber naive und sentimentale Dichtung, Werke, 11 and 12.
W. v. *Humboldt*, Uber männliche und weibliche Form, Uber Goethes Herrmann und Dorothea, Sammtliche Werke, I and IV.

Goethe, Aufsätze über bildende Kunst, Winckelmann (1805), Italienische Reise: Werke, Deutsche National Literatur, B. 30, 27, 21.

A. W. *Schlegel*, Vorlesungen über schöne Literatur und Kunst, Berlin 1801/2; Heilbronn, 1884.
F. *Schlegel*, Ansichten und Ideen von der christlichen Kunst, Sammtliche Werke, B. 6.
Schelling, System des transcendentalen Idealismus, Philosophie der Kunst, Uber das Verhältniss der bildenden Künste zu der Natur, Werke, B. 3, 5, 7.
Hegel, Vorlesungen über die Aesthetik, Werke, B. 10. Consult *Croce*, Saggio sullo Hegel, Bari, 1913.

BIBLIOGRAPHY

On the problem of the ugly in Art, consult: —
E. v. Hartmann, Die Deutsche Aesthetik seit Kant (already quoted)

Idealistic criticism: —
Hotho, Vorstudien für Leben und Kunst, 1835;
Schnaase, Geschichte der bild. Künste, 1843-1864;
Guizot, Etudes sur les beaux-arts en général, 1851;
Rio, De l'art chrétien, 1836, 2 ed. 1861-67;
E. J. Delécluze, Louis David, son école et son temps, Paris 1855;
P-Selvatico, Storia estetico-critica delle arti del disegno, Venezia 1852-56.

CHAPTER IX

On history and the philological method: —
B. Croce, Teoria e storia della storiografia, 3d ed., Bari, 1927;
Fueter, Geschichte der neueren Historiographie, München & Berlin 1911;
C. B. Stark, Systematik und Geschichte der Archaeologie der Kunst, Leipzig, 1880;
Déonna, L'archéologie, sa valeur, ses méthodes, Paris 1913;
Brutails, L'archéologie du moyen-âge et ses méthodes, Paris 1900;

G. E. Rizzo, Storia dell'arte greca, 1913, Prolegomeni;
W. Waetzoldt, Deutsche Kunsthistoriker, Leipzig, 1921-24.

On the sources of Pliny, consult: —
The Elder Pliny's Chapters on the History of Art, with historical Introduction, by *E. Sellers,* London 1896;
A. Kalkmann, Die Quellen der Kunstgeschichte des Plinius, Berlin, 1898.

BIBLIOGRAPHY

On the sources of Vasari, consult: —
W. Kallab, Vasaristudien, Wien & Leipzig, 1908;
Schlosser, Die Kunstliteratur (quoted)

Manuals and encyclopaedias: —
C. O. Müller, Handbuch der Archaeologie der Kunst, 1830;
Pauly-Wissowa, Real Encyclopaedie, beginning from 1894;
Kraus, Real-Enzyklopadie der christlichen Alterthümer, 1882-86;
Thieme a. Becker, Allgemeines Lexicon der bildenden Künstler, 1907 and following;
F. Kugler, Handbuch der Kunstgeschichte, 1842;
Springer, Handbuch der Kunstgeschichte, 1855;
Ch. Blanc, Grammaire des arts du dessin, Paris, 1880;
Histoire de l'art publiée sous la direction d'André Michel, Paris 1905 and following;
Handbuch der Kunstwissenschaft begründet von Fritz Bürger, Berlin.

Writings on technique or on art under the technical aspect: —
Chevreul, Loi du contraste simultané des couleurs, Paris 1838;
Helmholtz et Brucke, Principes scientifiques des beaux-arts, 2d ed., Paris 1881;
Choisy, Histoire de l'architecture, 1899;
Dehio & Bezold. Kirchliche Baukunst des Abendlandes, 1884-99;
Courajod, Leçons professées a l'école du Louvre, Paris, 1901;
E. Loewy, La scultura greca, 1911;
G. Semper, Der Stil in den technischen und tektonisken Künsten, 2nd ed n. München, 1878-79.

Writings of an iconographical tendency: —
A. Conze, Heroen und Götter Gestalten in Griechischen Kunst, 1875;

BIBLIOGRAPHY

J. Overbeck, Griechische Kunstmythologie, 1871-89;
De Rossi, Roma sotterranea, 3 vols., 1864-77;
Garrucci, La storia dell'arte cristiana nei primi otto secoli della chiesa, 6 vols., 1873-81;
Wilpert, Die Malereien der Katakomben Roms, 1904;
Kondakoff, Histoire de l'art byzantin, 1886-91;
Strzygowski, Orient oder Rom, Leipzig 1901;
Ch. Diehl, Manuel d'art byzantin, Paris 1910;
Millet, Monuments byzantins de Mistra, Paris 1910.

Writings on the history of art as the history of civilisation: —
G. Perrot and Ch. Chipiez, Histoire de l'art dans l'antiquité, 1892-1914;
E. A. Gardner, A Handbook of Greek Sculpture, 1915;
M. Collignon, Histoire de la sculpture grecque, 1892 & 1897;
W. Klein, Geschichte der griechischen Kunst, 1904-07;
H. Thode, Franz von Assisi und die Anfänge der Kunst der Renaissance in Italien, 1885; Michelangelo und das Ende der Renaissance, 1902-12;
Stendhal, Histoire de la peinture en Italie, 1817;
H. Taine, Philosophie de l'art, 1881;
E. Müntz, Histoire de l'art pendant la Renaissance, 1889-95;
J. Burckhardt, Der Cicerone, 1855; Die Kultur der Renaissance in Italien, 1860; Geschichte der Renaissance in Italien, 1867;
H. Grimm, Michelangelo, 1860-63; Das Leben Raphaels, 1872;
C. Justi, Winckelmann u. seine Zeitgenossen, 1866-72; Diego Velazquez und sein Jahrhundert, 1888.

Writings of connoisseurs: —
C. F. v. Rumohr, Italienische Forshungen, 1827-31 (ed. with introduction by Schlosser, 1920);
J. D. Passavant, Raphael, 1839-58;

BIBLIOGRAPHY

Waagen, Treasures of Art in Great Britain, 1854-57;

H. Brunn, Geschichte der griechischen Künstler, 1853-59; *Crowe & Cavalcaselle*, The History of Flemish Painting, 1857; A New History of Painting in Italy, 1864-66; History of Painting in North Italy, 1871; Raphael, 1882-85; Life and Times of Titian, 1881 (Italian edition: 1877);

G. Morelli (Lermolieff), Kunstkritische Studien über italienische Malerei 1890-93;

Adolfo Venturi, Storia dell'arte italiana, 1901-36;

W. Bode, Florentiner Bildhauer der Renaissance, 1902;

A. Furtwängler, Meisterwerke der griechischen Plastik, 1893; *F. Wickhoff*, Römische Kunst, 1912;

Max J. Friedländer, Die altniederländische Malerei, 1924 and following, 11 vols;

Hofstede de Groot, Beschreibendes und Kritisches Verzeichnis der Werke der Holländischen Maler des XVII Jahrhunderts, 1907 and following;

B. Berenson, The Italian Painters of the Renaissance, Italian Pictures of the Renaissance, 1932; The drawings of the Florentine Painters, 1903;

A. Kingsley Porter, Lombard architecture, 1917; Romanesque sculpture of the Pilgrimage Roads, 10 vols; Beyond Architecture, 1918.

CHAPTER X

General works: —

P. Petroz, L'art et la critique en France depuis 1822, Paris 1875; *Bougot*, Essai sur la critique d'art, Paris (without date, but after 1875);

Rene Janssens, Les maîtres de la critique d'art, 1935; *L. Rosenthal*. Du romantisme au realisme, 1914;

BIBLIOGRAPHY

M. Pittaluga, E. Fromentin e le origini de la moderna critica d'arte, L'Arte, 1917/18;

M. Tourneux, Salons et expositions d'art à Paris 1919.

E. J. Delécluze, Louis David, son école et son temps, Paris 1855, Souvenirs de soixante années, 1862;

Stendhal, Salons de 1824 and 1827, in Mélanges d'art, 1932;

A. Thiers, Salon de 1822, ou collection des articles insérés au Constitutionnel, Maradan, 1822; Salon de 1824, Le Constitutionnel 25 août — ler decembre (On Thiers' criticism of art, consult: Gazette des Beaux-Arts 1873, I, p. 295 and following);

L. Vitet, Etudes sur les Beaux-Arts, 1847;

E. Delacroix, Oeuvres littéraires, ed. by E. Faure, 1923; Journal, ed. by Joubin, 1932; Correspondance, ed. by Burty 1880; (Consult: *M. Tourneaux*, E. Delacroix devant ses contemporaines, 1886);

G. Planche, Etudes sur l'école française (1831-52), Paris 1855; Portraites d'artistes, 1853;

Ch. Lenormant, Les artistes contemporains, Salons de 1831 & 1833, Paris 1833;

G. Laviron et B. Galbacio, Le Salon de 1833, Paris 1833;

G. Laviron, Le Salon de 1834, Paris 1834;

L. Peisse, Salon de 1831 and 1834, in the National; Salons de 1841 and 1843, in the Revue des Deux Mondes;

Ingres, Notes et pensées, Lettres, in H. Delaborde, Ingres, 1870, p. 93 and following;

Ch. Baudelaire, L'art romantique, Curiosités esthétiques, 1868; Variétés critiques, ed by E. Faure, 1924 (Consult: A. Ferran, L'esthétique de Baudelaire, 1933);

T. Thoré, Le Salon de 1845, 1846, 1847, Alliance des Arts 1845/7; Salon de W. Bürger 1861/8, Paris 1870 (Consult: *Sensier*, Souvenirs de Th. Rousseau, 1872);

Courbet, Manifestes, 1855 & 1861, in Léger, Courbet, 1929

BIBLIOGRAPHY

(Consult: *Max Buchon*, Recueil de dissertations sur le réalisme Neuchatel 1856; Riat, Courbet, 1906);

Proudhon, Du principe de l'art et de sa destination sociale, 1865;

Champfleury, Salons 1846-51, Paris 1894; Le realisme, Paris 1857, Histoire de la caricature moderne, Paris, 1865 (Consult: P. *Martino*, Le roman réaliste, 1913;

Castagnary, Salons 1857-79, Paris 1892 (Consult: *Gustave Larromet*, L'Art réaliste et la critique, Revue des deux Mondes, Dec. 15, 1892 and March 1, 1893);

Th. Gautier, Les Beaux-Arts en Europe, 1855; Guide de l'amateur du musée du Louvre, 1882; (Consult: *Sainte-Beuve*, Nouveaux lundis, VI, 1866, p. 315 and following;

A. Cassagne, La theorie de l'art pour l'art en France chez les derniers Romantiques et les premiers Parnassiens, 1906);

P. Mantz, Salon de 1847, Paris 1847; Salon de 1889, Paris, without date;

E. & J. de Goncourt, Salon de 1852 et La Peinture a l'exposition de 1855, in Etudes d'art 1893; Journal; some passages of Manette Salomon (1867); L'art du XVIII siècle, 3rd ed. 1880 (Consult P-*Sabatier*, L'esthétique des Goncourt, 1920);

E. Fromentin, Maîtres d'autrefois, 1876; Correspondance et fragments inédits, Lettres de jeunesse. (Consult: L. *Gonse*, Eugène Fromentin, 1880; G. *Beaume*, Fromentin, 1911);

E. Zola, Mes Haines, 1866 (Consult: *Rewald*, Cézanne et Zola, 1936);

Th. Duret, Critique d'avant garde, 1885; Les peintres impressionistes, 1906;

Ph. Burty, Préface à la vente du 24 mars 1875, Hotel Drouot; *Duranty*, La nouvelle peinture, 1876;

G. Rivière, L'exposition des impressionnistes, in L'Impressionniste, 6, 14, 21 april 1877;

BIBLIOGRAPHY

Huysmans, L'art moderne, 1883;

J. *Laforgue*, L'impressionnisme, in Mélanges posthumes;

G. *Moore*, Modern Painting, 1893;

G. *Lecomte*, L'art impressionniste, 1892;

G. *Geffroy*, Histoire de l'impressionnisme in "La vie artistique" in 8 vols. (vol. 3, 1894);

F. *Fénéon*, Les impressionnistes en 1886, Paris 1886;

G. A. *Aurier*, Oeuvres posthumes, Paris 1893;

P. *Signac*, D'Eugène Delacroix au néo-impressionnisme, 1899.

CHAPTER XI

On the science of art, consult: —

Max Dessoir, Aesthetik und allgemeine Kunstwissenschaft, 1906;

Zeitschrift für Aesthetik und allgemeine Kunstwissenschaft, 1906 and following;

E. *Utitz*, Grundlegung der allgemeinem Kunstwissenschaft, 1914, Geschichte der Aesthetik, 1932;

W. *Worringer*, Abstraktion und Einfühlung, 1908;

H. *Tietze*, Die Methode der Kunstgeschichte, 1913;

Bites-Palevitch, Essai sur les tendances critiques et scientifiques de l'esthétique allemande contemporaine, 1926;

Earl of Listowel, A Critical History of Modern Aesthetics, 1933.

On pure visibility, Einfühlung, pure art, and so on, consult:

Croce, La critica e la storia delle arti figurative, 1934, and Ultimi Saggi, 1935.

Herbart, Einleitung zur allgemeinen praktischen Philosophie, 1808; Lehrbuch zur Einleitung in die Philosophie, 1813.

R. *Zimmermann*, Geschichte der Aesthetik, 1858; Allgemeine Aesthetik als Formwissenschaft, 1865.

BIBLIOGRAPHY

Robert Vischer, Drei Schriften zum Aesthetischen Form-problem, 1872-90, republished Halle 1927.

Conrad Fiedler, Schriften über Kunst, 1913-14. Consult: *H. Konnerth*, Die Kunsttheorie Conrad Fiedlers, 1909.

A. Hildebrand, Das Problem der Form in der bildenden Kunst, 1893; Gesammelte Aufsätze, 1909.

Alois Riegl, Stilfragen, 1893; Die spätrömische Kunstindustrie nach den Funden in Osterreich-Ungarn, 1901; Die Entstehung der Barockkunst in Rom, 1908; Gesammelte Aufsätze 1929. (Consult: *H. Sedlmayr*, Die Quintessenz der Lehren Riegls, Einleitung in Gesammelte Aufsätze, quoted; *J. V. Schlosser*, Die Wiener Schule der Kunstgeschichte, 1934).

Heinrich Woelfflin, Renaissance und Barock, 1888; Die klassische Kunst, 1898; Kunstgeschichtliche Grundbegriffe, 1915, Italien und das deutsche Formgefühl, 1931; Kunstgeschichtliche Grundbegriffe, Eine Revision, in Logos, XXII, 1933; Consult: *F. Landsberger*, H. W. 1924; *L. Venturi*, Gli schemi del Woelfflin, in Pretesti di Critica, 1929; Hanna Lévy, H. W., Sa theorie, ses prédécesseurs, Paris 1936.

E. Panofsky, Uber das Verhältnis der Kunstgeschichte zur Kunsttheorie, Zeitschrift für Aesthetik und Allgemeine Kunstwissenschaft, XVIII, 1925, p. 129.

Consult also: —

A. Schmarsow, Grundbegriffe der Kunstwissenschaft, 1905; *O. Wulff*, Grundlinien und Kritische Erörtungen sur Prinzipienlehre der bildenden Kunst, 1917; *H. Cornelius*, Elementargesetze der bildenden Kunst, 1908; *L. Coellen*, Der Stil in der bildenden Kunst, 1921.

Roger Fry, Vision and Design, 1920; Transformations, 1926; Consult: *G. Price-Jones*, Le condizioni attuali della critica d'arte in Inghilterra; Roger Fry e la critica Inglese contemporanea, in L' Arte, 1934 & 35.

Bibliography

On the criticism and theory of cubism and its derivatives, consult: —

A. Gleizes et Jean Metzinger, Du cubisme, 1912;

G. Apollinaire, Les peintres cubistes, 1913;

Boccioni, Pittura scultura futurista, 1914;

A. Gleizes, Du cubisme et des moyens de le comprendre, 1920, Vers une conscience plastique, la forme et l'histoire, 1932;

Ozenfant, Art, 1927-28;

Ozenfant et Jeanneret, La peinture moderne, without date;

G. Severini, Du cubisme au classicisme, 1921;

A. Lhote, La Peinture, 1933;

C. Einstein, Die Kunst des 20. Jahrhunderts, 1931

CHAPTER XII

Sources of abstract art: —

M. Denis, Théories (1890-1910), Paris, 1912; 4th ed., 1920; Journal (1884-1943), 3 vols., Paris, 1957.

S. Barazzetti, Maurice Denis, Paris, 1945.

G. A. Aurier, Oeuvres Posthumes, Paris, 1913.

L. Venturi, Premesse teoriche dell'arte moderna, Rome, 1951, reprinted in "Saggi di Critica," Rome, 1956, pp. 307-331.

Theories of modern art. General works: —

A. Salmon, L'art vivant, Paris, 1920.

A. Ozenfant-Ch. E. Jeanneret, La peinture moderne, Paris, 1925.

A. Ozenfant, Art, Paris, 1928.

H. Focillon, La peinture aux XIXe et XXe siècles, du réalism à nos jours, Paris, 1928; La vie des formes, Paris, 1934 (Eng. Trans. C. B. Hogan and G. Kubler, New Haven, 1942; 2nd enlarged ed., New York, 1948).

L. Justi, Von Conrinth bis Klee, Berlin, 1931.

C. *Einstein*, Die Kunst des 20. Jahrhunderts ("Propyläen Kunstgeschichte," Vol. XVI), Berlin, 1926.

R. *Huyghe*, Histoire de l'art contemporain, Paris, 1935.

R. *Escholier*, La peinture française. XXe siècle, Paris, 1937.

C. *Zervos*, Histoire de l'art contemporain, Paris, 1938.

R. *Huyghe*, Les Contemporains, 1939, 2a ed., 1949; Eng. trans., New York, 1939.

G. *Lemaître*, From Cubism to Surrealism in French Literature, Cambridge, Mass., 1941.

B. *Dorival*, Les étapes de la peinture française contemporaine, 3 vols., Paris, 1943-46.

R. *Huyghe*, La peinture actuelle, Paris, 1945.

L. *Mumford*, Art and Technics, New York, 1952.

H. *Read*, The Philosophy of Modern Art, London, 1952.

University of Padua, La mia prosppettiva estetica, Brescia, 1953 (Lectures by G. A. Borgese, G. Capone Braga, C. Carbonara, J. Choix-Ruy, F. Flora, M. Fubini, C. Mazzantini, F. Messina, E. Paci, L. Pareyson, N. Petruzzellis, U. Spirito, B. Tecchi, G. Toffahin, F. Torre-franca, L. Venturi).

W. *Haftmann*, Malerei im 20. Jahrhundert, Munich, 1954; Eng. trans., New York, 1961.

C. *Giedion-Welcker*, Plastik des 20. Jahrhunderts. Volumen und Raumgestaltung, Stuttgart, 1955; Eng. trans., rev. and enlarged ed., New York, 1960 (extensive bibl).

H. *Sedlmayr*, Die Revolution der modernen Kunst, Hamburg, 1955.

B. *Dorival*, Les peintres du vingtième siècle, 2 vols., Paris, 1957; Eng. trans. New York, 1958 (bibl.).

G. *Dorfles*, Le oscillazioni del gusto e l'arte moderna, 1958; Il divenire delle arti, Turin, 1959.

R. *Assunto*, Teoremi e problemi di estetica contemporanea, Milan, 1960.

G. *Morpurgo-Tagliabue*, L'esthétique contemporaine, Milan, 1960.

G. *Dorfles*, Simbolo Comunicazione Consumo, Turin, 1962.

Art theories in England and the United States: —

R. *Fry*, Vision and Design, London, 1920; Transformations: Critical and Speculative Essays on Art, London, 1926, new ed., Garden City, 1956; Cézanne, a study of his development, London, 1927, ed. 1952; Reflections on British Painting, London, 1934.

G. *Price-Jones*, Le condizioni attuali della critica d'arte in Inghilterra. Roger Fry e la critica inglese contemporanea, L'Arte, XXXVIII (1935), pp. 480-490.

V. *Woolf*, Roger Fry: a Biography, London, New York, 1940.

H. *Hannay*, Roger Fry and Other Essays, London, 1937.

H. *Read*, Art Now: An Introduction to the Theory of Modern Painting and Sculpture, London, 1933; rev. ed., 1948, 1954.

J. *Dewey*, Art as Experience, New York, 1934.

J. T. *Soby*, After Picasso, New York, 1935; The Early Chirico, New York, 1941.

W. R. *Valentiner*, Origins of Modern Sculpture, New York, 1946.

S. C. *Pepper*, The Basis of Criticism in the Arts, Cambridge, Mass., 1946; Principles of Art Appreciation, New York, 1949.

T. *Munro*, The Arts and Their Interrelations, New York, 1949.

On Cubism: —

A. *Gleizes* and J. *Metzinger*, Du cubisme, Paris, 1912; Eng. trans., London, 1913.

A. *Salmon*, La jeune peinture française, Paris, 1912.

G. *Apollinaire*, Les peintres cubistes: Meditations esthetiques, Paris, 1913; Eng. trans., New York, 1944, 1949.

BIBLIOGRAPHY

A. Ozenfant and *C. E. Jeanneret*, Après le cubisme, Paris, 1918.

A. Salmon, La jeune sculpture française, Paris, 1919.

A. Gleizes, Du cubisme et de moyen de la comprendre, Paris, 1920; La mission créatrice de l'homme dans le domaine plastique, Paris, 1922; Traditions et cubisme, Paris, 1927; Vers un conscience plastique, Paris, 1932; La signification humaine du cubisme, Paris, 1938.

W. Uhde, Picasso et la tradition française, Paris, 1928; Eng. trans., New York, 1929.

G. Janneau, L'art cubiste, Paris, 1929.

J. W. Power, Eléments de la construction picturale, Paris, 1932.

C. Zervos, Pablo Picasso (catalogue raisonné), 11 vols., Paris, 1932-60.

P. Eluard, A Pablo Picasso, Geneva-Paris, 1944.

A. H. Barr, Jr., Picasso. Fifty Years of His Art (extensive annotated bibl.), New York, 1946.

A. Vallentin, Pablo Picasso, Paris, 1957 (with bibl.).

A. Lothe, La peinture, le coeur et l'esprit, Paris, 1933.

F. Olivier, Picasso et ses amis, Paris, 1933.

G. Stein, Pablo Picasso, Paris, 1938; The Autobiography of Alice B. Toklas, New York, 1933.

A. H. Barr, Jr., Cubism and Abstract Art, New York, 1936.

D. H. Kahnweiler, Juan Gris, sa vie, son oeuvre, ses écrits, Paris, 1946; Eng. trans., New York, 1947.

G. Braque, Cahier de Georges Braque: 1917-1947, New York, 1948.

G. C. Argan, Il Cubismo, 1948.

C. Gray, Cubist Aesthetic Theories, Baltimore, 1953 (bibl.).

R. Delaunay, Du cubisme à l'art abstract, ed. P. Francastel, Paris, 1957 (documents and bibl.).

J. Romero Brest and *E. Crispolti*, "Cubism and Futurism," Encyclopedia of World Art, IV, New York, 1959.

BIBLIOGRAPHY

J. *Golding*, Cubism: A History and an Analysis 1907-1914, London and New York, 1959 (extensive annotated bibl.).
R. *Rosenblum*, Cubism and Twentieth Century Art, New York, 1961.

Futurism: general, political, and artistic manifestoes, letters, and other documents: —
M. *Drudi Gambillo* e T. *Fiori*, Archivi del Futurismo, 2 vols., Rome, 1958, 1962 (extensive bibl.).

Sources: —
F. T. *Marinetti*, Le futurisme, théories et mouvement, Paris, 1911.
A. *Soffici*, Primi principî di un'estetica futurista, re-issued, Florence, 1920.
L. *Fillia*, Pittura futurista: Realizzazioni, affermazioni, polemiche, Turin, 1919; Il futurismo, Milan, 1928; Pittura futurista, Milan, 1929; La nuova architettura, Florence, 1931.
G. *Severini*, Du cubisme au classicisme, Paris, 1921; Ragionamenti sulle arti figurative, Milan, 1936; Tutta la vita di un pittore, Milan, 1946.
U. *Boccioni*, Opera completa, Foligno, 1927.
F. *Cangiullo*, Le serate futuriste, Naples, 1930.
A. *Soffici*, Ricordi di vita artistica e letteraria, Florence, 1931 (2nd enlarged ed., 1942).
J. *Romero Brest* and E. *Crispolti*, "Cubism and Futurism," Encyclopedia of World Art, New York, 1959.
J. C. *Taylor*, Futurism, New York, 1961.

Expressionism: —
H. *Bahr*, Expressionismus, Munich, 1919; Eng. trans., London, 1925.

379

U. Apollonio, Die Brücke e la cultura dell'espressionismo, Venice, 1952 (bibl.); "Expressionism," Encyclopedia of World Art, Vol. V, 1959.

B. S. Myers, The German Expressionists, New York, 1957 (bibl.).

Surrealism, Dadaism, etc.: —

A. Breton, Manifeste du Surréalisme, Paris, 1924; 2nd ed., Paris, 1930; Le Surréalisme et la peinture, Paris, 1928, New York, 1945; Qu-est-que ce le Surréalisme, Brussels, 1934, Eng. trans., London, 1936.

J. Cocteau, Le Mystère Laïc, Paris, 1928; Essai de critique indirecte, Paris, 1932.

L. Aragon, La peinture au defi, Paris, 1930.

A. H. Barr, Jr., Fantastic Art, Dada, Surrealism, New York, 1936 (bibl.), 3rd ed., 1947.

H. Read, Surrealism, London, 1937.

M. Nadeau, Documents surréalistes, Paris, 1948.

D. Wyss, Der Surrealismus, Einfuhrung und Deutung, Heidelberg, 1950.

M. Jean, Historie de la peinture surréaliste, Paris, 1959.

A. Breton e *J. L. Bedouin*, Storia del Surrealismo, 2 vols., Milan, 1960.

W. Verkauf (ed.), Dada. Monograph of a Movement, Teufen, Switzerland, 1957 (bibl.).

Abstract art. Sources and general works: —

W. Kandinsky, Ueber das Geistige in der Kunst, Munchen, 1911, Eng. trans., Concerning the Spiritual in Art, New York, 1947; Punkt und Linie zu Fläche. Beitrag zur Analyse der malerschen Elemente, Munich, 1926, Eng. trans., Point and

Line to Plane: Contribution to the Analysis of the Pictorial Elements, New York, 1947.

F. Klee (ed.), Tagebücher von Paul Klee, 1898-1918, Cologne, 1957.

P. Klee, "Schöpferische Konfession," Tribüne der Kunst und Zeit, XIII (1920); Pädagogisches Skizzenbuch (Bauhausbücher n. 2), München, 1925, Eng. trans., New York, 1944; Das bildnerische Denken, Basel and Stuttgart, 1956, Eng. trans., The Thinking Eye, New York, 1961.

P. Mondrian, La néo-plasticisme, Paris, 1920. Per gli articoli su De STIJL e altra bibliogr. cfr.

H. L. C. Jaffe, De Stijl 1917-1931, Amsterdam, 1956 (extensive bibl.).

M. Larionou, Luczim (Il raggismo), Moskva, 1913.

Th. van Doesburg, De nieuwe beweging in de schilderkunst, Delft, 1917; Classique, baroque, moderne, Paris, 1921; Grundbegriffe der neuen gestaltenden Kunst (Bauhausbücher), 1924; L'architecture vivant, Paris, 1924.

G. Vantongerloo, L'art et son avenir, Antwerp, 1924.

A. Kemeny, "Die abstrakte Gestaltung von Suprematismus bis Heute," Das Kunstblatt, VII, 1924.

E. Kallai, "Konstruktivismus," Jahrbuch der Jugendkunst, 1924, 374-386.

K. Malevich, Die gegenstandlose welt (Bauhausbücher, 11), 1927.

L. Moholy-Nagy, The New Vision, New York, 1947.

A. Herbin, L'art non figuratif non objectif, Paris, 1949.

G. Nicco Fasola, Ragione dell'arte astratta, Milan, 1951.

L. Dègand, Témoignage pour l'art abstrait, Paris, 1952.

C. Estienne, L'art abstrait est-il un accademisme?, Paris, 1950.

M. Seuphor, L'art abstrait, Paris, 1950.

M. Tapiè, Un art autre, Paris, 1952.

L. Venturi, Arte figurativa e arte astratta, Florence, 1955.

P. Dorazio, La fantasia dell'arte nella vita moderna, Rome, 1955.

M. Seuphor, Dictionary of Abstract Painting, New York, 1957.

G. Poensgen-L. Zahn, Abstrakte Kunst, eine Weltsprache, Baden Baden, 1958.

M. Seuphor, The Sculpture of This Century, New York, 1960.

N. Ponente, Peinture Moderne, Tendance Contemporaines, Lausanne, 1960; "Non-objective Art," Encyclopedia of World Art, Vol. X, New York, 196?, (bibl.).

Architecture: —

A. Sant'Elia, Manifesto dell' Architettura Futurista, Lacreba, 10 ag. 1914; reprinted in Archivi del Futurismo, cit. I, 1958, pp. 81 ff.

G. C. Argan, "Il pensiero critico di A. Sant'Elia," l'Arte, XXVIII (1930), pp. 491-498.

B. Zevi, "Poetica di Sant'Elia e ideologia futurista," L'Architettura, II (1956), pp. 476-477.

Le Corbusier, Vers une architecture, Paris, 1923, Eng. trans., London, New York, 1927; Urbanisme, Paris 1925; Une Maison —un Palais, Paris, 1928; Précisions sur un état présent de l'architecture et l'urbanisme, Paris, 1930; Croisade, ou le crépuscule des académies, Paris, 1933; Quand les Cathédrales etaient blanches, Paris, 1937, Eng. trans., New York, 1940.

Le Corbusier e P. Jeanneret, Oeuvre complète 1910-1957, 5 vols., Zurich, 1937-57.

Le Corbusier, Le Modulor, Paris, 1950, Eng. trans., London, 1954; Modulor 2, Boulogne (Seine), 1955; Entretien avec less étudiants des écoles d'architecture, Paris, 1957, Eng. trans., New York, 1961; Le poème électronique, Paris, 1958; L'urbanisme des trois établissements humains, Paris, 1959.

F. Choay, Le Corbusier, New York, 1960.

L. H. Sullivan, The Autobiography of an Idea, New York, 1922.

W. Gropius, The New Architecture and the Bauhaus, London, 1935.

G. C. Argan, Walter Gropius e la Bauhaus, Turin, 1951.

H. Bayer, W. Gropius, I. Gropius (ed.), Bauhaus 1919-1928, New York, 1938; 2nd ed., 1952.

S. Giedion, Walter Gropius, Milan, 1954.

B. Taut, Die Neue Baukunstin Europa und America, Stuttgart, 1929; Eng. trans., Modern Architecture, London, 1930.

F. L. Wright, Modern Architecture, Princeton, 1931; An Autobiography, New York, 1932, London, 1946; Architecture and Modern Life, New York, 1937; On Architecture, New York, 1941.

N. Pevsner, Pioneers of the Modern Movement, London, 1936; new ed., Pioneers of Modern Design, New York, 1949; An Outline of European Architecture, Harmondsworth, 1957.

C. Bauer, Modern Housing, Boston and New York, 1934.

L. Mumford, The Culture of Cities, New York, 1938; London, 1944.

S. Giedion, Space, Time and Architecture, Cambridge, Mass., 1941.

P. L. Nervi, Scienza o arte del costruire, Rome, 1944.

B. Zevi, Architettura organica, Rome, 1944; Poetica dell'architettura neoplastica, Milan, 1953; Saper vedere l'architettura, Turin, 1956; Architettura in nuce, Florence, 1960; Storia dell'architettura moderna, Turin, 1961.

CHAPTER XIII

Consult the bibliography of the preceding chapters.

INDEX

INDEX